PENGUIN BOOKS

MUSES, MADMEN, AND PROPHETS

Daniel B. Smith is a New York–based journalist and author. His work has appeared in *The New York Times Magazine*, *The Atlantic Monthly*, *Granta*, and *n+1*.

MUSES, MADMEN, AND PROPHETS

HEARING VOICES
AND THE BORDERS
OF SANITY

DANIEL B. SMITH

PENGUIN BOOKS

PENGUIN BOOKS

Published by the Penguin Group

Penguin Group (USA) Inc., 375 Hudson Street, New York, New York 10014, U.S.A.

Penguin Group (Canada), 90 Eglinton Avenue East, Suite 700, Toronto,
Ontario, Canada M4P 2Y3 (a division of Pearson Penguin Canada Inc.)

Penguin Books Ltd, 80 Strand, London WC2R 0RL, England

Penguin Ireland, 25 St Stephen's Green, Dublin 2, Ireland (a division of Penguin Books Ltd)

Penguin Group (Australia), 250 Camberwell Road, Camberwell,
Victoria 3124, Australia (a division of Pearson Australia Group Pty Ltd)

Penguin Books India Pvt Ltd, 11 Community Centre, Panchsheel Park, New Delhi – 110 017, India

Penguin Group (NZ), 67 Apollo Drive, Rosedale, North Shore 0632, New Zealand (a division of Pearson New Zealand Ltd)

Penguin Books (South Africa) (Pty) Ltd, 24 Sturdee Avenue, Rosebank, Johannesburg 2196, South Africa

Penguin Books Ltd, Registered Offices:
80 Strand, London WC2R 0RL, England

First published in the United States of America by The Penguin Press,
a member of Penguin Group (USA) Inc. 2007
Published in Penguin Books 2008

1   3   5   7   9   10   8   6   4   2

Grateful acknowledgment is made for permission to reprint the following copyrighted works:

"Floating" and excerpt from "Denmark" from *Visits from the Seventh: Poems* by Sarah Arvio. Copyright © 2002 by Sarah Arvio. Used by permission of Alfred A. Knopf, a division of Random House, Inc.

Excerpt from "An Interview with John Berryman," *The Harvard Advocate*, October 27, 1968. By permission of the publisher.

Excerpt from "It's the End of the World According to Carp" by Edward Helmore, *The Observer* (London). By permission of the author.

Excerpt from *The Works and Days, Theogony, The Shield of Herakles* by Hesiod, translated by Richmond Lattimore (Ann Arbor: The University of Michigan Press). Copyright © 1959 by the University of Michigan, renewed 1987 by Alice Lattimore. By permission of the publisher.

Excerpt from *The Iliad of Homer*, translated by Richmond Lattimore. By permission of The University of Chicago Press.

Excerpt from *Men and Ideas: History, the Middle Ages, the Renaissance* by Johan Huizinga, translated by James S. Holmes and Hans van Marle. Copyright © 1959 by Meridian Books and The Free Press. Reprinted by permission of Princeton University Press.

Excerpt from "Four for Sir John Davies" from *The Collected Poems of Theodore Roethke*. Copyright 1953 by Theodore Roethke. Used by permission of Doubleday, a division of Random House, Inc.

THE LIBRARY OF CONGRESS HAS CATALOGED THE HARDCOVER EDITION AS FOLLOWS:

Smith, Daniel B., 1977–

Muses, madmen, and prophets : rethinking the history, science, and meaning of auditory hallucination / by Daniel B. Smith.

p.   cm.

Includes bibliographical references and index.

ISBN 978-1-59420-110-3 (hc.)

ISBN 978-0-14-311315-7 (pbk.)

1. Auditory hallucinations.   I. Title.

RC553.A84S65   2007

616.89—dc22   2006050653

Printed in the United States of America
Designed by Stephanie Huntwork

TO THE MEMORY OF

LEONARD JAY SMITH

(1945–1998)

There are two voices, and the first voice says, "Write!" And the second voice says, "For whom?" . . . And the first voice says, "For the dead whom thou didst love."

—JOHN BERRYMAN, quoting Kierkegaard,

who is in turn quoting Hamann

· CONTENTS ·

Hearing voices when no source can be found or when no one else does is an ancient, multifaceted experience. It reaches back into the prehistoric archeological record and stretches forward to the present day. It appears in timeless religious texts that we read again and again, and in newspaper articles that we read once and then discard. It evokes insanity (to most people), but it also evokes poetry and God and the physics of sound. It occurs in cultures in all regions of the Earth and is an appropriate topic of study for an array of disciplines, including psychiatry, psychology, neurology, philosophy, anthropology, theology, and linguistics.

Muses, Madmen, and Prophets takes many of these aspects of the experience into account. This was not something that I had originally planned. When I first began to read and think about voice-hearing—the convenient name that I will frequently use for the phenomenon throughout this book—all I knew was that it was a symptom of psychiatric illness. I soon learned that this was a simplistic understanding. Just below the popular interpretation there was a sea of voices clamoring for a hearing. The intention of this book is to provide one.

The book won't do so thoroughly. It can't. The experience is quite simply too diverse to cover in a single work, particularly one of modest length. The reader should therefore be aware that I have been selective. The most important cut I've made in the material is cultural. There is a fascinating anthropological literature on voice-hearing in

African, Asian, and Native American societies, but I have limited myself to voices as they exist in the history of the West: North America and Western Europe. The only exceptions to this rule are those cases in which a cultural comparison or outside fact is useful in making a specific point or where the history of the West can be located only outside its geographical boundaries—as in the birth and growth of the world's major monotheistic religions in the Near East.

I hope readers will enjoy discovering what I've chosen to include—inevitably a more fraught set of judgments—as they proceed, just as I have been cheered by the heterogeneity of the subject. Before they do so, however, it will be helpful for readers to know that this book itself is written in three different "voices." This aspect of *Muses, Madmen, and Prophets* is due to what I perceived early on to be three different demands made upon me by the material.

The first demand was intellectual. The vast majority of the literature on voice-hearing is academic in tone. Voice-hearing is an unusual and mysterious experience: Why do people hear voices? What does it mean? Where does it come from? For centuries, these questions have led authors to dissect, probe, and categorize the experience in the hope of better understanding it. In order to synthesize and present this material to the reader, I've had to take something of a similar approach in several chapters.

The second demand was emotional. Much more than a "phenomenon," voice-hearing is, as I've already referred to it, an experience. It accompanies people as they go about their everyday lives. It is woven into their sense of self, whether they want it to be or not. A full account of voice-hearing must pay its respects to this fact. Yet I do not hear voices and never have. In light of this problem, I decided early on to do what I could to gain a closer, more personal understanding of what it is like to hear voices. The chapters marked by the heading "Interlude" are narratives of my attempts. They are written in a much more casual mode than what surrounds them.

The third demand was moral. Voice-hearing is an experience of which society has always taken notice and offered interpretations. People who have had the experience live within a context that influences them and with which they have idiosyncratic relationships. To fully explore this aspect of the experience, this book concludes with three case studies. I chose the subjects of these chapters—Socrates, Joan of Arc, and the German psychiatric patient Daniel Paul Schreber—because the documentation on their lives was particularly rich and because they are all figures who came into stark, tragic conflict with the culture of their times. I hope that these conflicts will yield some insights into the interplay of personal and public meaning that inevitably defines unusual experiences in human life.

MUSES, MADMEN, AND PROPHETS

PRELUDE

THE PATHOLOGICAL
ASSUMPTION

*Indeed, if every inspiration that comes to one with such
commanding urgency that it is heard as a voice is to be condemned out of hand by the learned qualification of a morbid
symptom . . . who would not rather stand with Joan of Arc
and Socrates on the side of the mad than with the faculty of
the Sorbonne on that of the sane?*

—JOHAN HUIZINGA, "Bernard Shaw's Saint"

In the summer of 1995, when I was seventeen years old, my oldest brother and I self-published a memoir that my grandfather
had written over the course of his retirement in West Palm Beach.
The job wasn't supposed to be ours. My father had promised to type
up and edit the manuscript himself, but for some reason it had sat on
his desk for months, untouched. Then June brought him cheap, convenient labor. He delegated the task, we agreed, and for a week of
afternoons my brother manned the computer in my father's small
home office as I sat on the carpet and dictated from a thin stack of
loose-leaf paper, scrawled over with barely legible script and topped
by a cover page that read: *The Smith Family Chronicles.*

The title was misleading. My grandfather's book was neither
chronological nor particularly familial. Rather, it was a loosely packed

grab bag of memories, anecdotes, poems, complaints, and prayers, set down with little concern for artfulness, context, or even grammar. Most of the material wasn't even fresh, in fact, but consisted of chestnuts that my grandfather had fed his children and grandchildren for years and that he had now reheated for the purpose of posterity or vanity or both. Veterans of these tales, my brother and I therefore performed our duties in a state of skeptical admiration. We were exasperated by my grandfather's literary effort, but we were charmed by it as well.

My father had a less charitable reaction to the *Chronicles*. He did not read the book until a week later, when we presented him with the first copy—a slim volume, velo-bound, that we printed at a copy shop where my brother worked that summer and routinely stole products and services—and when he did he encountered a chapter that, although we had not noted its importance, struck him with the force of a deep and disturbing revelation. As a rule, my father was not quick to show emotion, but this chapter caused him to balloon with rage. He railed at a great injustice that had been done to him. He fumed and festered over time wasted and anguish unnecessarily endured. Finally, he flew to Florida and demanded an explanation.

No one knows precisely what was said at that meeting. Both of the participants are dead, and in life neither talked about it. But we do have the chapter that sparked the discussion. It is a modest section in a modest book—330 words long, rambling, and betraying not the slightest hint of its own importance. Its title is "Voices."

Voices

I have always heard them, but it took some time for me to recognize that they had a significance. Mostly they appeared when there was a decision-making problem. You had to listen very carefully or you missed it. More often than not you did miss it. When after a decision was made, incorrectly, I would think back in retrospect and recall that a voice in my head told me the proper thing to do. Misinterpretation is the key word. Listening to the voice and interpreting the correct choice in what you're thinking becomes a habit and in time, your awareness can almost always help you decide an issue. This is not tried and true.

With exams, true or false, multiple choice questions, I was 80% correct. I became good at this. Even when choosing wrong, I know it was my fault for not listening carefully. In my business ventures, if there was a problem, or a decision to be made, I almost always listened carefully and decided correctly.

I tried this with betting at the racetrack. It didn't work. My mind got clouded with voices telling me that this horse could win or maybe this one is ready to win. In the end, I lost more times than I won. Do you think a higher power was trying to tell me something?

Mother and I have a regular gin game with friends from the mountains who now live here in Century Village. We take turns on alternate Fridays playing in one another's homes. I point out this phenomenon. When it is my turn to discard a card from my hand, invariably, an inner voice will tell me that he needs the card. I have proven this, time and time again, by holding back the voice card discard, but later throwing it, he always picks up and needs this card. I have almost lost all of this awareness. Patience and fortitude are not attributes of the elderly (I am not!!).

The ordinary reader of this chapter likely wouldn't think much more than that my grandfather was describing an unusually strong sense of intuition. My father, however, wasn't an ordinary reader. At the time he read the *Chronicles*, he was forty-nine years old, and for more than three decades he had heard unseen voices telling him what to do. These voices weren't elaborate, and they weren't disturbing in content. They issued simple commands. They instructed him, for instance, to move a glass from one side of the table to the other or to use a specific token in a specific subway turnstile. Yet in listening to them and obeying them, his interior life had early become, by all reports, unendurable. The voices had first begun to make their demands when he was thirteen, and since that time he had attended to them in anguish.

He had also attended to them in silence. For twenty-five years my father told no one about his voices, not even his wife, with whom he had three children. He feared that if they were exposed, he would be deemed insane. In the end, this silence undid itself. In 1983, overstrained by his voices and overtaxed by the effort required to conceal them, my father succumbed to a nervous breakdown. Frightened and tired, he at last revealed his voices to my mother and checked himself into the psychiatric ward of a nearby university hospital, where he was diagnosed with "major depression with psychotic features"—a sort of catchall, able to contain both his despair and the experiences that, to my mind, caused it. He stayed for two weeks and returned home to a family that was on the brink of dissolution and a career that seemed over; in his absence, his law firm had dismissed him on the grounds of mental unfitness.

In the years that followed, my father's fears did not come true. My mother didn't leave him, his mental stability quickly returned, and in time he regained his professional footing. But the *Chronicles* made him feel that his long struggle might have been avoided. This is not hard to understand. For years he had writhed in shame. He had been terrorized by the thought of what might happen if he revealed his voices and, perhaps, by the knowledge of what might happen if he did not. And for all that time my grandfather had not only been hearing voices as well, he had been doing so without angst or confusion, using them for, of all things, picking horses at the track and beating retirees at gin rummy. My father felt that he had been denied his salvation.

Fifteen years on, it's hard to say whether my father was right, whether he might have lived a less tortured life had he known about my grandfather's voices earlier. All that can be said for sure is that, without knowing about them, my father experienced his voices as a malignant force. Though they weren't cruel, they caused him profound distress. Though they didn't try to harm him or others, he thought of them as dangerous, insidious enemies. Though they don't seem to have been harsh, he considered them pathological: undesirable, unnatural, injurious. My father assumed from the start that his voices were the sign of illness, and he wanted them as much as one might want a tumor in the brain.

Or less so, since a tumor can be excised. My father's voices could not. Though he learned to live his life well enough in their presence, they never stopped talking. And he never truly began. When someone mentioned his voices, he would grow embarrassed, dismissive, or irate. It was obvious to those of us in the know—a club containing only the immediate members of his family—that his shame was complete and impenetrable. So we learned not to ask. Until his death of cancer, in 1998, we allowed my father's voices to remain in the one place where he felt they were safe: the silent, hidden recesses of his mind.

In April 2002, on the front page of its Metro section, the *Boston Globe* published a photograph of a police officer standing in court holding an AK-47 assault rifle with a wooden handle, a banana clip, and an evidence tag dangling from its trigger guard. The gun had been used two years earlier by a man named Michael McDermott to kill seven people at a technology consulting firm in Wakefield, Massachusetts. McDermott, a diagnosed schizophrenic, claimed he had committed the crime under the orders of Saint Michael the Archangel, who had descended from heaven and ordered him to assassinate Hitler and six of his generals. A smaller photograph, printed below the article, showed McDermott entering the courtroom in prison blues. He looks intimidating and wild. His hair shoots out from his head like a lion's mane. His face is obscured by a thick, matted beard. Addressing the jury, his lawyer explained, "He has his hair like that because it keeps the voices down."[1]

When people are asked for their first impression of the words *hearing voices,* this is typically the kind of story that comes to mind. It is the kind of story that displays with memorable force the heights to which madness can ascend, the kind of story that shows what can happen when a human being becomes unmoored from reality and the ability to reason. In McDermott's world, nothing seems to be stable—not time, not thought, not emotion, not perception. He appears almost as the embodiment of madness. And because we cannot hear them or know their intentions, because we don't know what they are telling him, his voices seem to be madness's most frightening representatives.

This impression is extreme, but it's not completely incorrect. Hearing voices—what the clinical literature refers to as "auditory hallucinations," or, more precisely, "verbal auditory hallucinations"— is indeed one of the prototypical symptoms of schizophrenia, and schizophrenia is the gravest mental illness in the psychiatric pantheon. According to experts, as many as 75 percent of people with schizophrenia hear voices.[2] It is a myth that these individuals pose an inherent threat to others; researchers have found no direct link between auditory hallucinations per se and physical aggression, though people who hear voices that order them to commit acts of violence (a relatively minuscule group) do on occasion obey.[3] It is not a myth, however, that voices pose a threat to the hearer. The overwhelming majority of schizophrenics who hear voices describe the experience as being always or almost always negative. For quite a few patients, voices are the very worst of the disease's symptoms—what one woman has described as a "constant state of mental rape."[4] Schizophrenic voices can take any number of horrible forms. They can issue commands, echo the patient's thoughts, provide a running commentary on everyday actions, or berate, curse, and insult the hearer. Often they chatter all day, making it impossible for a person to think or work or carry on a conversation. The experience can be so unremitting and demoralizing that patients are frequently driven to acts of desperation. As many as one-third of people with schizophrenia attempt suicide. As many as one-fifth hear voices that command them to do so.[5]

Yet what is rarely realized or openly expressed is that voices are not exclusive to schizophrenia. Obscured by the dramatic stories that make it into the news, and by our own concern about the horrors of psychosis, is the fact that auditory hallucinations are able to take a number of different forms and are associated with a number of different conditions. Even within psychiatry this is true. Approximately 20 percent of patients suffering from mania and 10 percent of patients suffering from depression hear voices.[6] Psychological trauma is also closely related to the phenomenon. Combat veterans diagnosed with post-traumatic stress disorder report high rates of voice-hearing. So do women who have been sexually abused—more than 40 percent, according to one study.[7] Voices can even come in the very throes of trauma. The civil rights activist James Cameron, the only one of three men to survive a 1930 lynch mob, heard a voice as he was about to be hanged. "Take this boy back," the voice said to Cameron, who had been falsely charged with killing a white man and raping the man's girlfriend. "He doesn't have anything to do with any shooting or raping."[8] No one else heard it.

Auditory hallucinations are also known to occur as the result of nonpsychiatric, "organic" conditions. Doctors in Hawaii recently treated a man who began to suffer from voices soon after he had surgery to remove a blood clot from his brain. One day while his wife was driving him in her car, he heard a "deep male voice" telling him to grab the steering wheel and crash the car. Later, he heard vampires telling him to bite her. ("Cover your neck!" he warned.)[9] Voices can be a symptom of brain tumor, Parkinson's disease, migraine headaches, hyperthyroidism, temporal lobe epilepsy, Alzheimer's disease, and various types of delirium. Recreational drugs such as LSD, psychedelic mushrooms, ecstasy, and cocaine sometimes cause voices, but the phenomenon is more commonly associated with alcohol. Either during or after a binge, chronic alcoholics can experience auditory hallucinations that closely mirror schizophrenic voices; for years clinicians have had trouble telling the two apart.[10]

What is even less commonly realized is that auditory hallucinations extend to people who are not suffering from any pathology at all—that is, people hear voices without any distress or impairment in functioning. Sometimes people even enjoy the experience. One of the most widely cited examples of this was reported in 1971 by a Welsh doctor named Dewi Rees. Rees questioned three hundred patients who had recently lost a spouse and found that 13 percent had heard the voice of their dead husband or wife, and 10 percent had actually held a conversation with the deceased. Of this group of "grief hallucinators," as they are sometimes called, the vast majority, 80 percent, reported that they had found the experience pleasurable. Apparently the hallucination helped smooth the process of mourning.[11]

The idea that auditory hallucinations can occur in people who are free of mental and physical illness is not a new one. For decades researchers have conducted large-scale epidemiological surveys into the matter, though intermittently. One of the more famous efforts of this kind was conducted in the late nineteenth century by the Society for Psychical Research, a British organization that investigates

paranormal phenomena such as clairvoyance and out-of-body experiences. Under the direction of the philosopher Henry Sidgwick,
the society questioned 17,000 adult men and women as to whether
they had ever heard a voice when no one was around to speak. (The
American psychologist and philosopher William James was one of
the interviewers.) Excluding those respondents who seemed either
physically or mentally unstable, the researchers concluded that 3.3
percent of the population had experienced a vivid auditory hallucination at one time or another in their lives. A small but not insignif-
icant number, 159, heard voices on multiple occasions.[12]

The society's findings are not the most reliable according to
today's scientific standards: The researchers had an obvious stake in
proving the veracity of unusual experiences, the interview data wasn't
carefully verified, and the sample collected didn't reflect the makeup
of the general population. In light of these facts, Allen Tien, a psychiatrist at Johns Hopkins University, reproduced the study in 1991.
Analyzing data gathered from more than 18,500 people as part of a
landmark effort by the National Institute of Mental Health, Tien
drew several notable conclusions. First, the overall incidence of auditory hallucinations had remained remarkably stable over the course
of almost a century. The demographics, however, had shifted somewhat. In Sidgwick's day, the people most likely to hear voices were
in their twenties; in Tien's, voice-hearing spiked in the middle-aged
and the elderly. Finally, and most notable, two-thirds of those who
reported hearing voices today felt no distress as a result of the experience and had no plans to seek professional help.[13]

Tien's work has been hailed as the most comprehensive survey of
hallucinations in the general population conducted so far. But in light
of a smaller-scale study published eight years earlier by the psychologists Thomas Posey and Mary Losch, of Murray State University in
Kentucky, his findings weren't particularly surprising. Intrigued by the
idea that, as they put it, "normals hear voices," Posey and Losch de-

vised a list of fourteen quotations illustrating a broad range of examples of auditory hallucinations, some of which were particularly characteristic of schizophrenia, and asked 375 healthy volunteers to state whether they had ever experienced something similar. (The psychologists were careful to emphasize that what they were studying was not voices heard in the head, like thoughts, but heard aloud, "as if someone had spoken.") The results of Posey and Losch's study have been widely reported in the scientific literature. Fifty-seven percent of the sample answered yes to "Sometimes I have thought I heard people say my name . . . like in a store when you walk past someone you don't know"; 39 percent to "I hear my thoughts aloud"; 11 percent to "When I am driving in my car . . . I hear my own voice from the backseat"; and 5 percent to "Almost every morning while I do my housework, I have a pleasant conversation with my dead grandmother."[14]

What are all these surveys telling us? They could be telling us, of course, that the researchers didn't adequately determine the mental status of their respondents. Perhaps those who stated that they heard voices were in fact mentally ill and were living undetected in the community. Not everyone who suffers from a psychiatric condition is under psychiatric care, after all. But given the diligence of most of the researchers involved, the scientific safeguards through which much of the data passed, and the relatively high numbers that were uncovered, this seems unlikely. The surveys seem to be telling us, rather, that auditory hallucinations are not limited to the mentally ill. They seem to be telling us that for many years we have been paying attention only to the harshest voices that make their way to our ears, and forgetting the softer ones that lie underneath.

In 1961, the novelist and essayist Aldous Huxley—a man well known in his day as a champion of unusual experiences—made the following remarks to an international gathering of psychologists:

[We] now live in a period when people don't like to talk about these experiences. If you have these experiences, you keep your mouth shut for fear of being told to go to a psychoanalyst. In the past, when [they] were regarded as creditable, people talked about them. They did run, of course, a considerable risk because most [of these experiences] in the past were regarded as being inspired by the devil, but if you had the luck to convince your fellows that [your experiences] were divine, then you achieved a great deal of credit. But now . . . the case has altered and people don't like talking about these things.[15]

The subject of Huxley's speech, obscured here in brackets, was "visionary experiences"—those mysterious apprehensions of a "luminous other world" beyond our own that mystics and saints have been striving to attain and explain for centuries. But with the exception of the reference to psychoanalysis, which has since fallen out of favor in therapeutic circles, his summary applies perfectly to the history of voice-hearing as well. For hundreds of years, hearing a voice that no one else did was regarded as a creditable phenomenon. As the distinguished medical historian German Berrios has put it, "Experiences redolent of hallucinations . . . were in earlier times culturally integrated and semantically pregnant, i.e., their content was believed to carry a message for the individual or the world."[16]

Today, this quality of meaningfulness is conspicuously absent from our understanding of voice-hearing. The experience now draws its meaning from medical psychiatry, the discipline that conducts the lion's share of the research into the phenomenon, and to medical psychiatry voice-hearing technically has no meaning. What matters most to the contemporary clinician is the experience's form—what grammatical tense and "person" it speaks in, whether it seems to occur in external or psychological space, whether it speaks continuously or intermittently. This information is the key to making a correct diagnosis, and to prescribing the most effective treatment.

Discussions of meaning are commonly thought to distract from this work.

To be sure, psychiatry's attitude toward voice-hearing saves lives: The vast majority of patients who take psychiatric medications for auditory hallucinations experience a reduction in the symptom, and sometimes the drugs silence the voices altogether.[17] The problem is that psychiatry's attitude resonates far beyond the clinic. Tanya Luhrmann, an anthropologist at the University of Chicago, has put this problem poetically. "Psychiatric knowledge," she writes, "seeps into popular culture like the dye from a red shirt in hot water."[18] In regard to voices, the knowledge that has seeped into the culture the deepest is the perspective that they are by definition incapable of carrying a meaning that is useful to the hearer. In traditional psychiatry, voice-hearing is little more than a neurochemical glitch, to which the only proper response is medical, pharmaceutical treatment.

Historically, this viewpoint is quite new and represents a profound interpretive shift. The written record of Western history stretches back more than 2,500 years, and from the beginning voice-hearing was plainly apparent and positively valued. Indeed, the phenomenon is associated with some of the fundamental texts and figures of Western culture. For instance, the ancient Greek epic the *Iliad*—composed around 750 BCE and one of the oldest examples of European literature—is rife with voices. The characters who inhabit the tale, the legendary heroes of the Trojan War, are constantly being spoken to by the gods of the Greek pantheon, who urge them into battle, devise their strategies, and cause them to quarrel. In ancient Greece, voice-hearing is also central to the workings of the oracles emanating from shrines, those holy sites that dotted the mainland and that drew individuals and states in search of counsel from the gods. Even the great philosopher Socrates heard a *daimonion*, or "divine thing." Like my grandfather's voice, Socrates' voice offered him simple guidance in regard to everyday tasks.

In the history of monotheistic religion, voice-hearing is even more formative than it was in ancient Greece—literally so. The god of the ancient Hebrews is a god who speaks almost without pause. The book of Genesis proclaims, "In the beginning . . . God said, 'Let there be light,'" and from that moment forward Yahweh's voice becomes the motive force behind the history of the Jews. It is the divine voice that sets monotheism on its way when it orders Abraham to leave his home and make a "great nation." It is the divine voice that orders Abraham to sacrifice his son Isaac and then stays his hand before committing the crime, that repeats the blessing of fruitfulness and renown to Isaac and to Jacob, and that leads Moses through the desert and delivers to him the laws of Israel. And it is the divine voice that speaks to all the biblical prophets—from Isaiah to Malachi—and compels them, not without trouble, to carry the divine message to their countrymen.

The divine voice speaks less forcefully but more profoundly in the history of Christianity. John the Baptist receives a heavenly call in the Gospels in the same way as his prophetic predecessors. But in Christian theology, Jesus Christ doesn't hear the word of God—he *is* the word of God. In this paradoxical way, voice-hearing was made talismanic to Christianity. "Faith cometh by hearing," Saint Paul declared, and ever since, the devout have obeyed in droves. The Church fathers Saint Augustine and Saint Thomas Aquinas both heard voices. So did the mystics Hildegard of Bingen and Teresa of Ávila, the schismatic Martin Luther, the Quaker George Fox, the preacher and author John Bunyan, and the poets John Milton and William Blake. The divine voice runs like a steady trail through Christian history.

And then, it seems, the trail runs cold. Sometime late in human history, after centuries of chattering, the unseen voice seems to have stopped speaking in its old ways. Precisely why this happened is a matter of some complexity. Psychiatry did not rise up one day and slay the ancient voice like a mythical dragon. Rationality did not up and murder irrationality. But somewhere around the eighteenth century, the culture's way of thinking and talking about unusual experiences altered markedly. What was once revelation and inspiration became symptom and pathology. What was piety and poetry became science and sanity. In public discourse, voice-hearing became a force of harm and an experience to eradicate.

This alteration was hardly an unmitigated success. Traditions as ancient and foundational as the unseen voice are impossible to extinguish. Our religious and literary heritage perennially validates them. What is more, the sheer multiplicity of human life acts as a natural barrier against the dominance of any single interpretation of human experience. The old meanings persist. But they are harder to hear. In many cases, they have quieted or disguised their voices or retreated to more distant precincts. To find them and listen to what they have to say, you have to clear your ears of the new assumptions.

2

THE HOUSE OF MIRRORS

The brain might be said to be in touch more
with itself than with anything else.

—GERALD EDELMAN, *Bright Air, Brilliant Fire*

When Benjamin Rush—physician, father of American psychiatry, and signer of the Declaration of Independence—attempted to explain voice-hearing in 1812, he wasn't sure where exactly the source of the experience could be found. He was positive the experience pointed to an underlying disease. He wrote in *Medical Inquiries and Observations, upon the Diseases of the Mind,* one of the earliest psychiatric texts, that there were many people who "fancy they hear voices" as the result of "a morbid affection." But he hedged his bets as to the disease's location. Voice-hearing was caused, he wrote, by "a change in the natural actions of the brain, or of the organs of hearing." The brain or the ear: Rush wasn't committing.[1]

Nearly two hundred years later, scientists aren't so circumspect. The brain is now the undisputed center of inquiry into the mystery of voice-hearing. Open a recent scientific text on hallucinations and you will be met with such esoteric terms as "axonal conduction time," "increased density of GABA(A) receptors in the superior temporal gyrus," and "cortico-(thalamo)-cortical interactions." Yet the brain is not where a scientific inquiry into voice-hearing properly begins. In order to understand what causes voices to be conceived immaculately, the first thing one has to do is understand what causes voices according to the normal rules of the world. The path to voice-hearing begins with the human voice.

imagine a husband and wife seated across from each other in a living room. The wife wants to say something to her husband. When she finds the words, the first step she takes is to release her breath from the inflated lobes of her lungs into the branched tubing of her respiratory system. The main channel in this system is the trachea. It is approximately eight inches long, rigid, and segmented like the hose of a shower nozzle. Its purpose, in this case, is to serve as the conduit for the breath toward the first obstacle necessary for the production of speech: the vocal cords.

Vocal cords are not really cords; they don't work in the manner of guitar strings. Rather, they are thin, muscular flaps, reminiscent of labia, that block the top of the trachea like the lid of a truck's horn. When one wants to breathe, these flaps are loose. When one wants to speak, they form a barrier by pressing together, sealing off the throat from the breath. Its progression stanched, the breath accumulates behind the vocal cords. The pressure builds. Before long, the pressure becomes so great that the vocal cords can no longer maintain their seal, and they release—not all at once but fluidly, periodically, the way the length of an earthworm ripples as it moves across the soil. With speech this event never occurs in isolation. As the breath makes its dash upward, the pressure below the vocal cords decreases rapidly, and the cords, their strength regained, seal together again. More breath creates more pressure, which again builds. Another breaking point is reached, the cords again release, the pressure drops, the cords seal, and so on in a rapid, alternating dance of advance and retreat.

By this process between flesh and breath is created the basic mechanical component of sound: the movement of an object. All sound—a voice, a G-minor chord on a banjo, the hum of a refrigerator—is made because of the movement of an object. When an object moves, it causes an alteration in air pressure, a pulsing of molecules. A sound that exists because of a uniform and constant alteration in air pressure, as in the ringing produced by a tuning fork, is called a pure tone. With the complicated apparatus of the human vocal system, such a pure sound is impossible to create; it would elude even the practiced control of a trained singer. Speech, however, does not require purity; speech requires variety capable of expressing content, and therefore, in addition to the vocal cords, the respiratory system is outfitted with a series of muscles with Latinate names—the depressor anguli oris, the posterior cricoarytenoid, the sternocleidomastoid—whose purpose in speech production is to manipulate the flow of breath as it passes through the body.

After the wife's breath passes the vocal cords, it makes its way through this muscular assembly line, all the while being shaped into the words she has decided to speak. After passing her lips— the last of the muscles—it shoots into the room like steam from a teakettle. Breath collides with air, completing the first of two alchemic steps on the way to speech: the transformation of breath into molecular movement. The air molecules in front of her mouth compress and open in pulses tuned to her words. These pulses travel forward and outward like an inflating balloon, moving toward their target.

At this point in the process, the voice becomes hard to define. Is the converted breath, hovering in the air between speaker and listener, yet a voice? Is it audible? It is enough to state that at this point the voice has taken leave of the wife's possession. She is no longer its owner or master. She has pushed it out into the world. It is independent.

At last, the husband receives the voice. He has had little choice

in the matter. The pinna—the part of the ear, made of folds of car-
tilage, that juts out from the head—is intended to help voices in
their search for a destination. Try to stop yourself from hearing a
voice once it is spoken. You won't be able to run fast enough. The
human voice is adept at finding its entrance, and once it breaches
the barrier of the ear, all is lost. The barbarians have entered
the castle.

Paradoxically, the only way to describe the voice now is as the
province not of the wife's body but of the husband's. Having made
its way into his ear and into the thin tube of the auditory canal, it re-
sponds to the confinement as water does in a hose: with speed. It
races headlong, until it crashes into the taut sheath of flesh known
as the tympanic membrane. In response, that membrane booms like
the instrument from which it takes its name. It vibrates and echoes,
mimicking the complex vibrations of the air.

Beyond the tympanic membrane lie three minuscule bones that
rest lightly against one another so that the movement of one causes
a movement in the next. It is a Rube Goldberg–ish setup, the single
purpose of which is the second alchemic step necessary for communication: the transformation of molecular movement into an electrical
impulse. Why evolution has fitted human beings with so jerry-rigged
a system for hearing is anyone's guess, but it is a strangely efficient
system. The hammer strikes the anvil, which strikes the stirrup,
which strikes a tiny organ like a pin striking a bell. Very little energy
is lost.

The bell that is struck is the cochlea, a snail-shaped, hair-lined,
fluid-filled device and one of the triumphs of evolution. The cochlea
is so ornately constructed that despite two thousand years of direct
observation, biologists have been able to discern only a minute fraction of what it does. What is well known is that in the cochlea, molecular movement is converted to electricity. The movement of the

fluid within the shell of the cochlea causes the hairs along its twist-
ing length to vibrate. This vibration in turn stimulates the slender
cells of the auditory nerve.

The auditory nerve is the final pathway to the brain. It transports
the electrical signal of speech across the axons of its component neurons and into an upper section of the brain known as the primary auditory cortex, which processes sound and also is involved in the
production and comprehension of language. This lump of inert matter absorbs the incoming electrical impulses, which are transmitted
along the neurons in linear fashion and then branch out in a complex network, and somehow converts them into the comprehension
of a voice. The hearer hears.

The wife has said, "I want a divorce."

This single sentence completed the journey from first breath to
comprehension in approximately one second. It was a deft manipulation of physics and biology, traversing space and time and several
hundred body structures. But the long path of the voice was only pro-
logue. A voice does not begin its true existence until after the brain
of the hearer has absorbed and converted the electrical signals of the
neurons. The voice then spreads, via the brain's complex neural network, into wider and deeper areas of the brain. The brain copies the
external voice, discards the original, and then remakes the copy in
its own image based on the meaning the voice might have for the
brain and its owner. The brain molds the voice over and over again
like a child playing with a lump of clay. The voice both deviates
from the original that produced it and becomes inseparable from
what it is stimulating.[2]

It is easier to see how the brain digests and incorporates a stimulus in a symptom that is halfway between normal speech and voice-
hearing. Tinnitus is the perception of buzzing, ringing, hissing, or
other simple sounds in the absence of external sounds. In the majority

of tinnitus cases, a source of the buzzing can be found in some damage to the microscopic hairs in the cochlea. An "external"—meaning
outside the central nervous system—defect is the cause of tinnitus.
There is a source for the disorder, and thus the noise can be turned
off—theoretically, at least.

But the brain quickly wrests control of the stimulus. The noise
produced by a faulty cochlea is processed by the brain like a voice,
and as usual the brain has much to say. The mere damage of cilia in
the inner ear in short order implicates a wide range of areas in the
central nervous system, even areas as far from the ear as the frontal
lobes. It is as if the original stimulus were a burglar ducking into a
house of mirrors to elude capture. Several tinnitus studies have shown
that the more a sufferer tries and fails to find a cure for the noises in
his head, going from doctor to doctor for advice, the louder and
more persistent the noises become. The sense of frustration becomes
inexorably linked to its cause, feeding it. Researchers call this the
"headless chicken" phenomenon.[3]

The pathetic futility of this cycle is heightened by the fact that
the stimulus itself, even before it reaches the brain, is a chimera. A
voice that is heard is never the same as the voice that is spoken. As
a sound wave travels, it weakens. It comes across obstacles and is reflected, refracted, and modified. What is more, the pinna—the external flap of the ear—further alters the sound entering the auditory
canal.[4] In the end, there is no such thing as a true sound or a
true voice.

How can one examine such an elusive shape-shifter? In his philosophical treatise *On Being Blue*, William Gass (paraphrasing the poet
Rainer Maria Rilke) explains the difficulty inherent in examining an
object of desire: "Love requires a progressive shortening of the senses:
I can see you for miles; I can hear you for blocks; I can smell you,
maybe, for a few feet, but I can only touch on contact, taste as I de-

vour. And as we blend, sight . . . blurs."[5] A similar blurring occurs as we follow a voice into the brain. The quality of our understanding of a voice moving toward the brain decreases asymptotically, until the lines of sense and experience appear as one even if they are not. The voice becomes inscrutable, describable only in the language of metaphor.

And when a voice is emotive, it also becomes intractable. For our jilted husband, only time, perhaps, will dull the influence of the voice he heard, turning it into a brittle husk, like the shell of a cicada on a tree. Until then, however, the presence of the voice—what psychologists refer to as an "auditory image"—will continue to make itself known whenever it so chooses: while he is walking down the street, while he is driving to work, while he is lying in bed. Until such time as it decides otherwise, he will be subservient to the internal life of his wife's words, and within his skull the setting will forever be the living room in which they were first spoken.

If normal voice-hearing leads to the point that all experience is internal, hallucinated voice-hearing begins there. Hallucinated voice-hearing conflates source and destination. All preliminary steps are bypassed. There is no breath, no manipulation of air, no movement of bones or cochlea, not even a stimulation of the auditory nerve. With voice-hearing the brain, working alone in its watery chamber, creates a voice out of nothing but its own duplicitous silence. And it does so with such reality and finesse that the individual whose brain is engaging in such operations experiences the voice as if it were external.

How is this possible ? How can the brain create a voice in the absence of an external stimulus? How can the brain bypass the structures of the auditory system so successfully that it can produce not just sound but a voice, complete with modulation in pitch, tone, and volume, and with emotional tenacity? How can the brain transcend the external world?

These questions have puzzled observers for thousands of years. The most common solution to them has of course been religious. The Greek historian Plutarch, for example, wrote of Socrates that his voices were a privilege granted because of his spiritual superiority: "Now the voice that Socrates heard was not, I think, of the sort that is made when air is struck; rather it revealed to his soul, which was, by reason of his great purity, unpolluted and therefore more perceptive, the presence and society of his familiar deity, since only pure may meet and mingle with the pure."[6]

The spiritual interpretation of what causes voice-hearing has been even more popular in its negative form. Heinrich Krämer and Jakob Sprenger's *Malleus Maleficarum*, a guide to witchcraft and sorcery first published in 1487, took great pains to describe the vocal capabilities of demons:

> Devils have no lungs or tongue, though they can show the latter, as well as teeth and lips, artificially made according to the condition of their body; therefore they cannot truly and properly speak. But since they have understanding, and when they wish to express their meaning, then, by some disturbance of the air included in their assumed body, not of air breathed in and out as in the case of men, they produce, not voices, but sounds which have some likeness to voices, and send them articulately through the outside air to the ears of the hearer.[7]

Since the medicalization of mental experience, the demonic taint associated with voice-hearing has largely faded away, but the spiritual view has not. Many voice-hearers today explain their experiences in terms of some mystical communion with another person, usually dead. This type of explanation predominates when a voice occurs only once. For example, Kim Callahan Hedden, a Washington, D.C.–based writer, heard a voice when she was thirty-eight years old and waiting for laboratory results that would tell her whether she had cancer. One day at work Hedden went to the bathroom and, while washing her hands, heard a "flat, woman's voice . . . as though she were tired and old," say, "You will be OK." After she heard the voice, her fears about her health disappeared, and she soon learned that her lab results were negative. The voice, Hedden thinks, was that of the murdered daughter of a retired senator who had his office directly across the hall from her own. "I believe very strongly that certain spaces can be inhabited by voices," she told me.

In a discussion of the history of voice-hearing, the reason for much of the experience's content, and the reactions of hearers, the belief that voices have a spiritual source external to the self is central. When discussing the science of voice-hearing, however, the spiritual view is, by definition, moot. We now live at a time when we have the tools and the knowledge, paltry though they still are, to confirm a suspicion that goes back to ancient Greece: that the brain is the source of all cognitive processes and thus the source of all its offshoots, that nothing—no movement, no thought, no belief, no idea, no feeling of love or hate or desire or fear—can exist without the brain. No matter our religious beliefs, the unassailable physical fact is that the phenomenon must have a neurological correlate that, in theory, we can explain, chart, and describe. Any scientific exploration of voice-hearing is bound by what the neuropsychologist Christopher Frith and his colleagues have called "a fundamental assumption": "[F]or every mental state . . . there is an associated neural state."[8]

Unfortunately, accepting the brain's centrality in causing voices has not helped solve the mystery of how—or why, if such a question can be asked—it does so. There are two main obstacles blocking an answer to the question "What causes voice-hearing?" The first is the

complexity and elusiveness of the brain. The second is the extraordinary complexity of voice-hearing itself, which not only manifests
itself in an array of forms but implicates an array of psychological
and, thus, neurological faculties.

First, the brain. The cerebral cortex—the eighth-of-an-inch-thick
sheath of topographically erratic tissue that deals with "higher" brain
functions such as speech and thought—contains approximately ten
billion individual neurons interwoven with one another in a three-
dimensional network and in constant communication by way of
chemical transfers across microscopic gaps called synapses. In the
cerebral cortex, which makes up a minute fraction of the brain's matter, there are approximately one million billion connections between
neurons. The possible combinations of connections within the cerebral cortex approach incalculability. And the brain is not a static
organ. It is alterable, dynamic, less a computer, to which it is too
often compared, than an entire atmosphere, with innumerable molecules rocking and sparking and calming with unpredictable constancy. A further obstacle is that the brain is largely self-referential.
It is constructed in such a way that the majority of its matter only
receives input from and gives output to other parts of the brain. This
brain matter neither directly influences nor is directly influenced by
the outside world. In other words, much of the brain speaks to itself alone.[9]

The secrecy of the brain's activity has led some scientists to seek
a less internal solution to voice-hearing. These scientists suggest
that rather than the brain creating something out of nothing, voice-
hearers must be misinterpreting information, something we all do
from time to time. They cite evidence that voice-hearers subvocal-
ize—that they subtly and unconsciously move their vocal apparatus when they think, which would suggest that their voices are in
fact produced by their own quiet whispering. Some researchers
would seem to have proven the so-called whisper hypothesis, as the

philosophers G. Lynn Stephens and George Graham have dubbed it, quite dramatically.[10] In 1949, Louis Gould, a psychiatrist, published a report in which a patient's subvocalizations neatly matched his hallucinations. Gould wrote:

> The subvocal speech continued, "She knows. She's the most wicked thing in the whole, wide world. She knows everything. She knows all about aviation." At this point [the patient] stated audibly: "I heard them say that I have a knowledge of aviation."[11]

In 1981, two psychiatrists were even able to coax a patient into gradually increasing the volume of his whispering until he was having a conversation with his voice at a normal volume.[12]

Might subconscious whispering be the cause of voice-hearing? It would certainly make things simpler if it were. To eliminate voices, one would merely have to instruct a voice-hearer to block his own ability to whisper and thus dam the river feeding the hallucinations. Indeed, this is what some clinicians have done, with positive effect. They have told patients to open their mouths wide, thus otherwise engaging their vocal cords, or to hum to themselves. And yet there is convincing evidence that the whisper hypothesis cannot provide an overarching explanation for voice-hearing. Many voice-hearers, for example, hear their voices coming from distant parts of the room and not from their bodies. Furthermore, the whisper hypothesis does not explain auditory hallucinations that are *not* made of voices. One voice-hearer I interviewed, a sports journalist based in Chicago, sometimes hears not just voices but full orchestras in his head. Certainly this man, whose voices are the result of a seizure disorder incurred after a fall down a flight of stairs in childhood, is not capable of playing full symphonies under his breath. Finally, in 1981, neurologist Edmund Critchley reported on congenitally deaf psychiatric patients who insisted, through sign language, that they heard audible voices in their head. These men and women had never heard speech before and therefore could not possibly hear their own whispers.[13] It seems that although subvocalization is *often* the case, it does not provide a satisfactory framework to think about voice-hearing in general. The answer has to lie inside the brain.

Can we determine how the brain causes voices? We have some promising tools for the task in neuroimaging technologies, most notably positron emission tomography (PET) and functional magnetic resonance imaging (fMRI). These technologies allow researchers to observe the brain in vivo—the former by measuring the brain's metabolization of glucose, the latter by measuring blood flow. Since their development in the 1980s and 1990s, they have helped map the neural bases of thought and have proven to be the strongest forces in the advancement of the brain sciences. The neuroimaging revolution has even led some to pronounce the imminent solution of the mind-body problem. In 1996, Tom Wolfe predicted that the field of neuroscience "is on the threshold of a unified theory that will have an impact as powerful as that of Darwinism a hundred years ago."[14] Some have responded to such vigorous optimism by pointing out that an overreliance on imaging can make us into modern-day phrenologists and that in regard to complex cognitive phenomena, all imaging can do is provide us with a tool to confirm psychological theories. Some have gone even further and argued that no matter how logical a materialist view of the mind is, that view can never be proven with technology or any other scientific advancement, so ineffable is the activity of the mind.

Whether this argument reflects wisdom or defeatism or some combination of the two, the blunt fact is that neuroimaging has not significantly deciphered the physiology of voice-hearing. In 1999, the journal *Psychiatry Research Neuroimaging* published a review of the neuroimaging of hallucination that began by citing an observation made by Jean-Etienne-Dominique Esquirol, a nineteenth-century French asylum director who, responding to the work of Benjamin Rush and others, introduced an exclusively brain-based model of hallucination. "The site of hallucination," Esquirol wrote in 1838, "is not in the peripheral organ of sensation, but in the central organ of sensitivity itself; in fact, the symptom cannot be conceived but as a result of something setting the brain in motion." As Esquirol wrote elsewhere: "In hallucinations everything goes on in the brain." The authors of the review responded gloomily to this early scientific pronouncement. "More than 150 years since Esquirol's death," they wrote, "the exact location of this aberrant functioning remains unclear."[15]

The science of voice-hearing has remained static in large part because of the complexity of the phenomenon itself. Hallucinations may simply be too diverse a phenomenon to be pinpointed in the brain. Voice-hearing comes in a range of intensities, from single words to lengthy speeches; it can be the result of an organic or psychiatric disorder, or of no underlying problem at all. By asking, "What causes voice-hearing?" then, we are asking too broad a question. What is more, voice-hearing necessarily implicates a vast system of psychological functions, including perception, emotion, cognition, memory, consciousness, and attention. Unsurprisingly, studies on voice-hearing have exhibited the prominent involvement of diverse sections of the brain: Wernicke's area, which makes spoken language comprehensible; Broca's area, which generates speech; Heschl's area, which aids in hearing; the left parahippocampal region, which is associated with the perception of unexpected stimuli; the thalamus, which relays information for processing in other parts of the brain; the hippocampus, which helps lay down long-term memory; the frontal lobes, which are involved in emotional responses; and so on. There appears to be an extensive network of brain areas associated with voice-hearing. And that network undoubtedly is not uniform from voice-hearer to voice-hearer. In the end, how the brain treats a voice may depend the most on the hearer's experience of that voice.[16]

Hearing voices is considered to be one of the strangest of human experiences. Is it? Neuroscience does not allow us to gain an adequate understanding of how voice-hearing works, but by giving us an idea of how the brain operates in general, it does allow us to assess the phenomenon's strangeness.

Consider, for instance, that you are chopping an onion for an omelet, and you accidentally cut your finger. Your finger hurts. Where is the pain, in the finger or in the brain? In his book *Complications*, the physician Atul Gawande writes of a patient who began to suffer from chronic back pain after a fall at a construction site. Men and women with such pain are common. Chronic back pain, Gawande reminds us, is near epidemic in the United States, "second only to the common cold as a cause of lost work time." But test after test showed no physical defect in the man's back. His muscles, spine, disks, nerves—all were in check, all were whole and healthy. His physicians scratched their beards, double-checked their films, consulted one another. The man's pain was so strong that it caused him to vomit and to defecate in his pants. Was he lying? Did he *want* to feel pain? Such men and women are also common. Even the man himself suspected impure motives. He felt shame.[17]

The man's pain had no "source": no wound, no burn, no buildup of lactic acid in the muscles. But what we call source is no more than a signal. The pain, if we choose to name the sensation as an entity in and of itself, is always in the brain. That is where the neurons fire and where the information is assembled, no matter the location at which we experience the pain. If it helps, consider the signal a staff member and the brain the president. The information is hurried through the chamber and handed quickly to the president, who announces the fiat: Pain! Sometimes the president gets power-hungry and begins dispatching troops without permission. And why not? Why does the brain need permission when it has power? Exercises in executive prerogative pour forth: itches, hunger, tingles, sweat, erections. And all of it comes from the brain. Need we be concerned with what exists outside?

In 1866, the neurologist Silas Weir Mitchell published an early report of the phenomenon known as "phantom limb" syndrome, disguised as a short story. At a key moment in the story, George Dedlow, a Union soldier, wakes up after having been wounded in battle:

> I got hold of my own identity in a moment or two, and was suddenly aware of a sharp cramp in my left leg. I tried to get at it to rub it with my . . . arm, but, finding myself too weak, hailed an attendant. "Just rub my left calf," said I, "if you please."
>
> "Calf?" said he, "you ain't none, pardner. It's took off."
>
> "I know better," said I. "I have pain in both legs."
>
> "Wall, I never!" said he. "You ain't got nary leg."
>
> As I did not believe him, he threw off the covers, and, to my horror, showed me that I had suffered amputation of both thighs, very high up.
>
> "That will do," said I, faintly.[18]

Approximately 80 percent of amputees experience sensation in a limb after it has been severed from the body. They feel the limb in specific positions. They feel pain. One man feels his amputated arm jutting out from his body as if it were the arm of a weather vane; he walks through doors sideways in order to fit through. Others try to walk on a nonexistent leg that absolutely feels as if it is there, and fall.

The first rule of sound is that its production relies on the movement of an object. And what is the brain? It is an organ in constant movement. Its molecules are objects; its current flows. From this movement springs dreams alive with imagery. One psychiatrist has written: "The dream meets the definition of hallucination in every respect and most of us, according to a large body of physiological data, spend from one to two hours dreaming every night."[19] Dreams and dreamlike states—vivid imagery popping into one's mind—occur so frequently, this psychiatrist writes, that perhaps the question we should ask is not "Why do hallucinations occur?" but "Why don't they occur more often?"

Voice-hearing is strange, but by degree, not by kind. No mental phenomenon, no matter how strange, is unfamiliar by kind. We are all floating on the careless, rocking sea of the brain. The biologist Gerald Edelman has used a different metaphor for the brain; he likens it to a jungle, a comparison I find apt not just for the intended suggestion of complexity but for the suggestion of competitive balance. The brain is an unstable ecosystem. Feral cats devour reptiles that support the insects that in turn increase the number of reptiles, which in turn increases the number of cats. Canopy trees suffocate smaller flora, and the canopy trees, in competing with one another, allow light to shine through and bring the flora back to life. And so on. Burdened with a like neural environment, we expect minor brutalities to happen—the cresting and dipping sine curve of unwanted thoughts, temporary melancholies, fits of uncontrollable lust, aberrant desires, forgotten memories, hateful fears, intractable longings. Dreams and images. It is only when the brain's brutalities refuse to abate or are spectacular in appearance that we take note of the unstable complexity that has been there all the time and question the soundness of the system.

And then we question our sanity and are driven by the shame of subservience into silence—or we are further driven to understand. When the latter occurs, where can we turn if the brain refuses to give up its secrets? One of the most sensible criticisms of neuroimaging studies has been that they often scrutinize the brain at the expense of the patient's experience. The critics of neuroimaging offer technophobes a comforting thought. If you want to understand voice-hearing or any complex psychological phenomenon, you must ultimately, no matter where else you choose to look, make the long pilgrimage to the oracle: the voice-hearer himself.

3

NOBLE AUTOMATONS

O, what a world of unseen visions and heard silences, this insubstantial country of the mind! What ineffable essences, these touchless rememberings and unshowable reveries! And the privacy of it all! A secret theater of speechless monologue and prevenient counsel, an invisible mansion of all moods, musings, and mysteries, an infinite resort of disappointments and discoveries.

—JULIAN JAYNES, *The Origin of Consciousness in the Breakdown of the Bicameral Mind*

Early in the *Iliad*, in the tenth year of the Trojan War, Agamemnon—the leader of the expedition to Troy and the most powerful and prideful of Greek chieftains—announces to Achilles that he plans to rob him of his bride in retribution for supporting the return of a woman Agamemnon had taken from a local priest. Enraged, Achilles sets out to do what he would normally do in such situations: slaughter his challenger and everyone in his path. Just as Achilles is pulling his sword from his scabbard, however, the goddess Athena, protectress of the Greeks, descends from the heavens to placate his wrath and coax him onto a more prudent path:

The goddess standing behind Peleus' son caught him by the fair hair, appearing to him only, for no man of the others saw her. . . .

"I have come down to stay your anger—but will you obey me?—
from the sky; and the goddess of the white arms Hera sent me,
who loves both of you equally in her heart and cares for you.
Come then, do not take your sword in hand, keep clear of fighting."[1]

Achilles, uncharacteristically but wisely, takes Athena's advice; he
does not seek his revenge.

Critics have interpreted the role of the gods in the Homeric
epics in various ways. Some have considered them a metaphor for
the internal turmoil of the characters, some as a narrative device,
some as reflective of an ancient pagan belief system. But only Julian
Jaynes, a professor of psychology at Princeton, considered the intrusion of the gods in the Homeric epics literally. In his only book,
The Origin of Consciousness in the Breakdown of the Bicameral Mind, a cult
favorite first published in 1976, Jaynes put forth his view that the
ancient Greeks depicted in the *Iliad* actually *heard* the voices of the
gods instructing them. His interpretation of the *Iliad* was evidence
in support of a greater theory: that man was once guided not by a
unified consciousness but by verbal hallucinations—instructions
spoken from within one's own brain. Ancient voice-hearing, according to Jaynes, was caused by a physical split between the right
and left hemispheres of the brain that only "mended" itself three
thousand years ago in response to cataclysmic cultural changes,
leading to the consciousness we possess today. Before that, everyone was a voice-hearer:

Who then were these gods that pushed men about like robots and
sang epics through their lips? They were voices whose speech and
directions could be as distinctly heard by the Iliadic heroes as voices
are heard by certain epileptic and schizophrenic patients, or just as
Joan of Arc heard her voices. . . . The Trojan War was directed by

hallucinations. And the soldiers who were so directed were not at all like us. They were noble automatons who knew not what they did.[2]

Anyone who now considers the problem of how voices are possible must contend with the theories—not to mention the enthusiasm, the ecstatic prose, and the polymathic erudition—of Julian Jaynes. He has his admirers, including the novelist John Updike and the philosopher Daniel Dennett, and he has his detractors. ("How many students of cognitive science," one reviewer has written, "have read this deeply unfashionable book under, as it were, the bed-covers?")[3] But his theories have been undeniably influential.

I cite Jaynes's theory that we were all once floridly hallucinatory not because I believe it is true—perhaps the only thing that his boosters and critics agree upon is that it can't be proved—but to introduce the idea that the problem of voice-hearing is in large part indistinguishable from the problem of consciousness, and that the relationship between the two has been fruitful in determining the attributes of each. This is because voice-hearing provides a vivid thought experiment in regard to one of the great problems of science: how the matter of the brain creates the feeling of the mind. With voice-hearing, the brain pops its head, like the Loch Ness monster, above the surface. For an instant one can actually "see" or, rather, "hear" the brain. Some thinkers believe that if we could catch that instant, we might have an opportunity to peer into the biology of consciousness.

Jaynes's speculative theory also provides one of the finest descriptions available of the single most important phenomenological attribute of voice-hearing, an attribute that is also linked inextricably to the study of consciousness: lack of control over our thoughts. When an individual hears a voice, he is at that moment not the agent of his own thoughts but the vessel for them. He becomes, at the moment of voice-hearing, separate from himself, without control over his own mind—in effect, one of Jaynes's noble automatons. The sense of ownership of one's thoughts that is a hallmark of our conscious lives—the "I-ness" of consciousness—is dissolved, disintegrated. The voice-hearer becomes flooded with the awareness of the confident man caught in the earthquake—that the ground's solidity has all along been nothing but a well-maintained illusion.

To Jaynes this perilous sensation did not register among ancient man. For Achilles and Agamemnon, the lack of conscious control went unnoticed because it was neurologically determined, and it was neurologically determined because it was culturally necessary: Without a reliable political structure, unseen verbal commands kept the social order intact. Voice-hearing was a form of disembodied political rule. To modern man, by contrast, the lack of conscious control over one's thoughts almost always registers acutely. The abrogation of the conscious will is among our greatest fears, associated with madness and the dissolution of identity. For the voice-hearer, saddled with a brain that produces sensation unilaterally, he is forced to be an automaton but robbed of any sense of nobility.

In 1908, a German neurologist named Kurt Goldstein examined a fifty-seven-year-old woman who was exhibiting an odd symptom. One of her hands would not follow her commands. It tried to pull off her bed covers, to spill her drink, to choke her. The woman could control the hand only by forcefully moving it with the other. "I hit it and say: 'Behave yourself, hand,' " the woman told Goldstein. "I suppose there must be an evil spirit in it."[4]

The phenomenon introduced by Goldstein is known as alien-hand syndrome—or, more colorfully, the Dr. Strangelove effect—and it has been documented extensively ever since. It is typically caused by damage to or a severing of the corpus callosum, a tight bundle of nerve fibers that allows the two hemispheres of the brain to communicate with one another. Patients who have had their corpus callosum damaged or destroyed are called split-brain patients. They have a "bicameral mind," as Jaynes would say, and their behavior and experiences have been an invaluable source of information about how the hemispheres interact and how the brain creates the feeling of an integrated selfhood. The patients also serve as an invaluable resource when exploring how we should interpret occasions on which the brain bypasses the conscious will.

Consider another example from the annals of alien hand. In 2000, Benson Hai and Ib Odderson, physicians in Port Jefferson, New York, and Seattle, respectively, published a case study with the wonderful title "Involuntary Masturbation as a Manifestation of Stroke-Related Alien Hand Syndrome." The paper told the story of a seventy-three-year-old man whose left hand began pleasuring him against his will shortly after he suffered from a stroke. After going to the hospital with complaints of weakness on his left side, the man was transferred to a rehabilitation facility, where his more bizarre troubles began:

> The patient's wife . . . expressed deep concern when her husband's left hand would publicly expose his genitals and begin masturbating. This occurred on many occasions when the patient was conversing with his caregivers and was confirmed by the authors on their daily rounds. The behavior was never seen to occur through the action of the right hand.[5]

If an observer did not have recourse to the knowledge of the physical damage to this patient's brain, he could perhaps be excused if he interpreted the man's actions in psychological terms—as the intrusion, perhaps, of the id into the ego. Certainly part of the man wished to masturbate in public; he simply must examine the part of him that did and figure out why it wanted to do so. With our knowledge of the man's neurological injury, however, comes a responsibility to confront different questions. We are able to "see" an injury prior to which the man did not engage in such strange, albeit enjoyable, behavior. Some part of the man's right brain, which controls the left side of the body, would seem to be acting in such a way as to create a purposeful action in his left hand. In the search for the cause of his behavior, we have no need to confront obscure motives. It is the man's brain, not his subconscious, that is at fault. The questions then are: Are his actions still his own? Is he responsible for actions he has not *experienced* as his own?

Questions of responsibility become more complicated when we consider an individual whose brain is apparently whole and yet the individual still claims an inability to control his own actions. Examples for this are not hard to find. The dissolution of conscious control is the distinguishing characteristic of most mental illnesses. One man whom I have written about suffers from an especially severe case of obsessive-compulsive disorder. He spends hours each day on his hands and knees picking leaves from his front yard or scrubbing the bathroom and kitchen floors, polishing tiles, dusting, scouring— all against his will. He says he feels as though he is under the control of some external force. He still has a conscious will, of course; he is not a puppet. He can cause himself to move and to think certain thoughts. He pays his bills and sees his family and goes to church every day. But when he attempts to apply his will to prevent himself from performing certain actions, he finds that he can't. He is competing with another will that seems beyond him.

Inevitably, the battle between two wills—one experienced as self-generated and another experienced as external to the self—that is the hallmark of OCD leads to great self-recrimination, the result not only of having one's self co-opted but of a real cultural stigma. Many people of this man's acquaintance, for example, cannot understand why he simply does not stop cleaning. He seems to them, and to himself, unforgivably flawed. He has had two wives, both of whom have divorced him. The only solution he has found to this kind of judgment, aside from suicide, is stealth. Deeply ashamed, he spends a great deal of energy trying to hide his illness from others.[6]

The example isn't arbitrary. Though it is rarely acknowledged to be the case, voice-hearing has a great deal in common with obsessive-compulsive disorder. Like OCD, voice-hearing often manifests itself in the form of direct commands that the hearer feels compelled to obey. Also like OCD, voice-hearing occurs in such a way as to make the experience akin to a painful cleaving of the will. It is difficult enough to ignore voices that come from the outside. To ignore voices that come from within takes a heroic effort that is made more difficult by the knowledge that one's assailant is one's self. The experiences of OCD and voice-hearing—voice-hearing that at least is not accompanied by a complete lack of what psychiatrists call "insight"— are both marked by an awareness that the conscious will is secondary in power and importance to the unconscious will.

"one of the most extraordinary facts of our life," wrote William James, "is that, although we are besieged at every moment by impressions from our whole sensory surface, we notice so very small a part of them. The sum total of our impressions never enters into our *experience*, consciously so called, which runs through this sum total like a tiny rill through a broad flowery mead."[7]

James placed great emphasis on attention and effort, on the ability of the conscious will to decide where that tiny rill—the "stream of consciousness," as he more famously put it—will go and what it will carry. But what happens after that effort is made? I may steer my thoughts in the direction of voice-hearing, as I do every morning when I sit down to write, but offense invariably gives way to defense. I am besieged—an apt word—by memories and images and associations that I must work strenuously to ward off. I remember a movie I saw the night before; I think of what a friend said to me about her romantic problems; I take note of a chore I've promised to complete. I can, by an effort of the will, brush these thoughts aside, distract myself retroactively, call up other thoughts. But I am powerless to prevent the initial cognitive assault from occurring. Simply put, thoughts often just occur. One cannot control their entry into consciousness.

The matter of how much control we have over which thoughts appear in consciousness can be demonstrated by way of a well-worn but instructive thought experiment. The experiment goes like this: Do not think of a fish. If the person who reads this statement knows what the word *fish* means, he will inevitably think of one. It will be beyond his conscious control. Perhaps one person will think of a carp, another of a flounder, another of a shark, but some representation of a fish—verbal, visual, olfactory, etc.—will enter into his or her consciousness. The thinking will be automatic.

There is a long-standing and heated debate over how much of our mental activities are automatic, over to what extent we are merely, as T. H. Huxley famously put it, "conscious automata." Regardless of quantity, however, there is undoubtedly a quality of automaticity to our everyday lives. The lack of willful control that is so clear in alien-hand syndrome and so psychologically destructive in obsessive-compulsive disorder and other mental disorders and symptoms is in fact the definitive aspect of what we like to think of as "normal" mental life as well.

In a brilliant article on the cognitive basis of voice-hearing published in 1986, the psychiatrist Ralph Hoffman, whose work focuses on the treatment of hallucinations, illustrated automaticity of action with the simple example of driving to work:

It so happens that I can, if I wish, consciously access a set of goals and subgoals (wish to drive car, wish to be transported to work, wish to be on time for work, etc.), certain beliefs (my car will start, my work place is accessible by certain roads, etc.), and the rudiments of a behavioral plan (walk to car, open door, turn ignition key, etc.). Though I generally get myself to work without being explicitly conscious of any such plan and its relationship to goals and beliefs, it is almost impossible to imagine how such . . . behavior could occur without representations such as these in a psychologically real sense.[8]

The key word in this passage is *representations*. Certain thoughts can be said to exist in our mind but not in our consciousness. We are unaware of them; we are limited by what James called the "narrowness of consciousness." The brain engages in vast operations into which we have a severely restricted view, as if we were looking from a small, attic-size window.

What would happen if we did not have the ability to act on "autopilot," so to speak? For one, we would likely be frozen by the myriad claims to our attention, like a mother overwhelmed by the onslaught of demands from too many children. If I were consciously aware of all I was engaged in while writing, for example, I would have no time to think of what I wanted to say. I would be much too busy directing the movement of my fingers on the keyboard, my posture in the chair, or the placement of a capital letter at the start of each sentence. "Writing" would become impossible. It is the automaticity of action that permits me to decide "I will write" and then, when engaged in writing, to concentrate only on higher functions such as argument and sentence structure.

Unconscious actions that follow from decisions of the "I will . . ." variety have been called conscious automaticity. There is *unconscious* automaticity as well, and it accounts for a large proportion of our everyday behavior. These behaviors do not require any conscious decision to call them into action. They are automatic reactions to the external world. The conscious will comes into play mainly on a macroscopic level, on what direction we guide that stream in or what rocks and branches we throw into it. On the microscopic level, the brain's activity takes over. The benefit of the brain's complexity is that it has evolved toward apparent top-down efficiency, leaving the conscious will to be the issuer of executive decisions. Automaticity allows us to act quickly—to respond to our name without thought when it is called out or to jump out of the way of a falling brick.

But our automatic thoughts are not just of this reflexive variety. We are also able to recall spatial and temporal information very well without any conscious attention, and we even react emotionally, without any conscious awareness, to facial expressions, physical gestures, and even hints about a person's character. In a 1996 study, for example, a group of subjects was asked to order scrambled sentences that happened to contain words which are commonly associated with old age, such as *Florida, wrinkled, gray,* and *retired.* Another group was asked to order scrambled sentences that did not contain such words. Both groups were then timed without their knowledge as they left the experiment and walked down the hall. The subjects that had read sentences containing the old-age words walked significantly slower, as if they were acting out what those words signified. Later questioning revealed that they had no conscious awareness that the sentences they read contained the words in question, let alone that they had reacted to it. They had been moved by forces of which they had no conscious awareness.[9]

Where does this leave the conscious will? Much in our daily lives is driven by operations of the brain outside our control, but we obviously don't experience the world in this way. We go through each day quite satisfied with the fact that we are not automatons, that we have willed our actions and our thoughts, and that we are in control of our lives. When we drive to work, to use Hoffman's example, we do not experience as unintended our subtle manipulations of the gas and break pedals, our shifting of the gears, and our glancing in the side-view mirror. And while it is true that perhaps we don't think about them as intended, either—we don't think about them at all— if asked whether we chose to engage in those actions, we would *feel* as though we had willed them into being.

This feeling of conscious will in the absence of any real conscious control has been examined extensively by Daniel Wegner, a Harvard psychologist. In his book *The Illusion of Conscious Will*, Wegner develops the thesis that the brain creates the experience of willful action even when, as decades of psychological research have illustrated, an action is reflexive or illusory. The brain does this in order to provide the individual with a sense of control over his actions and thoughts, and a pragmatic belief that others are in control of their actions and thoughts, so that he might be able to distinguish sentient beings from inert objects. The experience of will, Wegner concludes, is just "a feeling that occurs to a person." It is an illusion— a necessary one that allows us to act morally and responsibly, but an illusion nonetheless.[10]

The cause of the illusion of conscious will, according to Wegner, is the very fact that we are privy only to a very small portion of our mental activity. Imagine, Wegner writes, that by some magical power you have the ability to know exactly how and when a tree branch will move in the wind, and that the same magical power will make certain you will be thinking about the branch prior to each of its movements. It would probably seem to you that you were the agent of the branch's movement, that you had caused it to move. Despite the fact that it was the wind that caused the branch's movement, the knowledge you possessed would make it *seem* that you had power over the branch. "People experience conscious will," Wegner writes, "when they interpret their own thought as the cause of their action."[11]

People are often wrong. Many studies of stimulus reaction time
have showed that the experience one has of consciously willing an
action often follows that action by a mathematically significant
amount of time. One of the most famous experiments regarding this
phenomenon was conducted by the physiologist Benjamin Libet in
the early 1980s. Libet asked a group of subjects to move a finger at
will while they wore electrodes on their scalp that would measure
electrical potentials prior and up to the action itself. "Let the urge to
act appear on its own any time without any preplanning or concentration on when to act," Libet told his subjects. The subjects were also
asked to report, based on the movements of a specialized, refined
clock known as an oscilloscope, precisely when they experienced a
"conscious awareness of 'wanting' " to move their finger. What Libet
found was that the brain geared up for the movement prior to the
subjects' being consciously aware that they intended to move. Furthermore, the subjects were aware of their finger moving *before* the
finger actually moved. Will, Libet concluded, is an add-on that is
often inconsequential to the action itself.[12]

If you accept the validity of Libet's study—and by no means does
everyone—then you might concede that the lack of conscious control over normal mental operations is similar to the lack of control
that occurs in voice-hearing. The difference is that voice-hearers *experience* their lack of control quite dramatically. They are phenome-
nologically different from the rest of us. Unintendedness is the norm,
but so is the experience of the will. When he hears a voice, the voice-
hearer possesses one but not the other, and he is rightly troubled by
this split in his conscious world. But it is worthwhile to consider that
when the illusion of control is lost—when the brain whirrs in such
a way that it seems as though someone who is not there has spoken
aloud, when it seems that there is no will in our thoughts or our experiences or our perceptions—perhaps it is not the encroachment of
unreality that we are witnessing but the arrival of reality, of the hor-

rible truth: the absence of true will. This is not to say we should glorify the voice-hearer. To do so would be to glorify what is often a disturbing aberration in consciousness. Those voice-hearers who jealously uphold their originality and their insight are to be envied by those voice-hearers who don't, but they are not in the majority. The majority are the sufferers, the men and women who have had their tail fins bumped unceremoniously by their own thoughts and gone wildly, frighteningly spinning groundward.

· 4 ·

INTERLUDE

LISTENING

If a man is mad, he shall not be at large in the city,
but his family shall keep him in any way they can.

—PLATO

If you dig even a little into the literature of voice-hearing, you will quickly come across a range of psychological treatments—cognitive therapy, self-monitoring, desensitization, counterstimulation (distracting oneself by humming, gargling, or singing), aversion therapy (administering shocks and other punishments), earplugs, first-person singular therapy (a sort of existential bolstering of responsibility), thought stopping (yelling back at the voices). These treatments have different levels of efficacy depending on the hearer and the type of voice heard, but some have been able not only to mitigate the experience but to suppress it altogether.[1]

My father sought no treatment. His reaction to the phenomenon was passive: He listened. He asked of his voices, "What shall I do?" and when told, he obeyed. To treat his depression, he did knock on the doors of psychiatry and psychology. He swallowed Prozac and Luvox and Effexor in great, muscular quantities. He saw a psychiatrist to prescribe and monitor his pills and, every so often, to discuss his problems. He even bought a large lamp to simulate the summer sun in the winter months.* But for his voices he did nothing. Under their weight he simply sagged and then fell. It was a defensive response to a brutal assault, a reflex that Philip Roth has described well in reference to a 1959 conference at which he was mercilessly criticized for his representation of Jews in *Goodbye, Columbus*. Confronted with such a forceful frontal attack, Roth writes, "I had actually to suppress a desire to close my eyes and . . . drift into unconsciousness."[2] This reactive narcolepsy was in spirit something like my father's response to his voices.

It was also, it has long seemed to me, an emblematic response. I first learned about my father's voices when I was sixteen years old. He told me because he feared that I might inherit his affliction. (None of his children did, though a year later my grandfather's memoirs confirmed that the experience can be inherited.) I was never able to decide, in those early years after I was let in on my father's secret, whether it was the relentless attack of his voices that had weakened his resolve or whether it was an innately weak resolve that prevented him from seeking treatment. The truth seemed to lie somewhere in between, in an inscrutable symbiosis of stimulus and response. Whatever the proportions, the result was a man who appeared to his youngest son as inert and defeated, a man whose continuing silence loudly broadcast a failure of nerve.

This teenage judgment now embarrasses me, not only because my father was no doubt doing a fine job judging himself, but also because, since that time, I've responded to adversity often enough with

---

*I can still summon the virulent buzz of that bulb, sounding like a swarm of bees, the scalding heat that I always imagined was about to ignite the *New York Times* my father read beneath it during his early-morning treatments, and the dizzying white solar glow of the dining room lit up by the lamp. It was too bright to face; one had to look away or flee to another room.

the same open-armed invitation to defeat: Let me sleep! It embarrasses me also because I don't have a precise idea of what my father's response was to. His petty, commanding voices, so resonant as an idea, are, as an experience, as confoundingly mute as he was about them. It's a problem that time and learning alone are unable to solve.

A few years ago I learned of an organization called the National Empowerment Center, based in northern Massachusetts. The stated mission of the NEC is "to carry a message of recovery, empowerment, hope and healing to people who have been diagnosed with mental illness." One of the ways it tries to do this is through the Hearing Voices Curriculum, a program that teaches social workers, psychiatric nurses, day care workers, police officers, and other interested parties what it is like to hear voices. The centerpiece of the program is an audiotape titled "Training and Simulated Experience of Hearing Voices That Are Distressing." I thought that if I could listen to this tape, I might gain a better understanding of what my father faced every day. And so, in the summer of 2002, I called Patricia Deegan, a cofounder of the NEC and the curriculum's author, and asked her to send me a copy of the tape. I received it in the mail the following week.[3]

Deegan told me over the phone that if I wanted to get the most out of the tape, I should go out in the world and experience the daily struggles of the voice-hearer. I should try to navigate my way through normal activities while the voices chattered away. I took her advice and chose to listen to the tape on the streets of Manhattan, where I was then living. I chose as my point of departure my brother David's apartment on West Fourth Street, in Greenwich Village. At noon on a Saturday in late August, I placed the headphones over my ears, said good-bye to my brother, and rode the rickety elevator down to the street. Once outside I pressed *play* and walked east toward Washington Square Park, where, in the southwest corner, the real voice-hearers often assemble to play chess and argue.

The tape began with Patricia Deegan's voice. "It is our belief," she said, "that just as rehabilitation students can gain insight into the experience of *physical* disability by using wheelchairs, so, too, can mental health professionals and students experience a simulation of some of the challenges facing people with psychiatric disabilities." Deegan offered disclaimers: "Do not listen to this tape while driving a car, operating machinery, or in a context other than the training experience. . . . If for any reason this tape causes you distress, feel free to turn the tape off. . . . Remember, this is not a marathon. Turn the tape off if you feel you want to."

The beginning of the simulation itself was not unlike the beginning of an avant-garde rock song or the soundtrack of a horror movie. There was static and light murmuring and a slow crescendo of electric noise, and then a heartbeat and what sounded like heavy breathing and demonic mumbling. Also, there was some coughing. Nothing so disturbing or so distressing as to force me to throw off my headphones, but annoying. What was more annoying was that, because of a combination of the cheap Walkman I had bought at an electronics store that morning and the torrents of electromagnetism feeding the innumerable cell phones, radios, and televisions in the neighborhood, a constant white noise masked much of the hallucinatory orchestra on the tape. Sitting in the park, watching two men fight over whether one of them had touched a rook, it became clear that if I was to take the experiment any further, I would have to retreat indoors, away from any interference. I made my way to a twenty-four-hour diner on Waverly and Sixth Avenue.

I felt rude walking into the restaurant with my headphones blaring what could have been, for all the blond, middle-aged waitress standing by the entrance knew, two-chord thrash punk. But the experiment demanded constancy, so I left the headphones on and took a seat at the counter, near the cash register. I ordered a chicken salad sandwich on toasted rye and a Diet Coke with lemon (a meal my father would have ordered). Delivering this simple request to the waiter behind the counter was not so simple; it took persistent effort to peer, as it were, through the curtain of voices and noise that had now begun to assault me with more force. To the staccato pulsing of whispers and grunts had been added a woman's voice, which soon grew into full counterpoint and then dominant melody. It was a soft voice, gentle but insistent. "It's you," the voice said. "You are the one. It's you. It's you I came for. It's you. It's you. It's you and you with the way. . . . You know you have the way. You are the one. It's you. It's you who has the way. . . . You know you are the one. The one with the way. It's you. It will be okay." *At last,* I thought as I waited for my sandwich to arrive. *Some content.* The quasi-religious nature of the voices was familiar. It was like Joan of Arc's voices: prophetic, revelatory, annunciating.

Also familiar was the Gertrude Stein–ish nature of the voice: Jumbled repetitive language, often based on random connections, is common of the speech of people with schizophrenia. In 1913, Eugen Bleuler, the Swiss psychiatrist who coined the term *schizophrenia,* published the following example:

> Then, I have always liked geography. My last teacher in the subject was Professor August A. He was a man with black eyes. I also like black eyes. There are also blue and gray eyes and other sorts, too. I have heard it said that snakes have green eyes. All people have eyes. There are some, too, who are blind. These blind people are led by a boy. It must be terrible not to be able to see. There are people who can't see and, in addition, can't hear. I know some who hear too much. There are many sick people in Burgholzli; they are called patients.[4]

Researchers have tried with some success to establish a link between the streaming diction of patients and their hallucinated voices, searching for an umbrella cognitive dysfunction under which to place the variant schizophrenic symptoms.

But my father was not schizophrenic; at least, he did not exhibit what are typically considered the characteristic symptoms of schizophrenia: abnormal and disordered thoughts, a deterioration in social functioning, and bizarre delusions. He experienced only the hallucinations, which were much more mundane than this supplicant chanting in my ears. He was a lawyer from Long Island, not a grandiose madman.

The woman's supplicating voice soon faded, making way for a more forceful masculine voice. What this voice had to tell me prohibited much musing. "Hey!" the voice shouted. "You smell like shit. You smell. You are disgusting. They're looking at you and seeing you and they see everything you do and you are dis-*gus*-ting. Hey, stop it! Stop it, now! Don't touch that. Don't touch it. . . . You smell like shit. You . . . smell . . . like . . . shit. Like swine. Everyone smells you. Shut up!"

This voice I recognized as well. It was the voice of persecution that schizophrenics often hear. I had recently read a memoir by a mental health advocate named Ken Steele that featured such taunting voices. Steele, who died in 2000, had begun to hear horrific suicidal voices when he was fourteen. *"You're worthless, no good,"* his voices would yell at him. *"Look how ugly you are. . . . You're a fucking pig. . . . Kill yourself. . . . Set yourself afire."*[5] As far as I know, my father's voices were never persecutory in content, but I was fairly certain that their relentlessness had made my father feel persecuted. So I resolved to get into character as best I could, to imagine myself actually at the mercy of such terrible statements.

My imagination was more or less paralyzed, however, by an image that I could not seem to push out of my head—that of a grown man in a padded recording studio getting paid $15 an hour to set his jaw and say things like "You smell like shit, you're a pig!" into a microphone. I pictured this man and sat there and ate my sandwich, and the desire for greater empathy lost more ground to an additional problem: The commands narrated by my angry actor were not in synch with reality. Steele's voices had gained their force by having knowledge of his external reality, by commenting on objective fact. Steele would run into the woods, and his voices would give him specific instructions on which tree to hang himself from. Even my father's voices, according to his medical records, were responses to external fact. There is by definition a fundamental synchronicity between the two consciousnesses, so to speak, that is the core of voice-hearing. This is what makes voices so convincing. They are possessed with a mystical passkey into both internal and external reality.

I was therefore somewhat dissuaded from becoming one with my taped voice by the fact that his instructions—"Take your hands out of your pockets!" "Go inside!"—were at odds with external fact. My hands were wrapped around a sandwich, not in my pockets. I was already inside. At only one admittedly creepy point did the voice's directives and external fact coalesce. I was sitting and digesting, trying alternately to attend to and to ignore the voices, when I turned around to look at the other diners. As I turned, I saw a handsome young man with frighteningly bright blue eyes. He was staring at me. Just then the voice said to me, "They're all watching you. They all see you."

I came *close* to shivering. I looked around to see if, in fact, they all were watching me. To my left, sitting alone at the counter, was a fat, balding man wearing a white dress shirt unbuttoned to his stomach, exposing two saucer-size pink nipples. He was reading legal documents intently and eating a cheeseburger. He, at least, wasn't the slightest bit interested in me. Nor was the waitress passing by or the line cook behind the counter or the kid who came in and ordered a take-out meal, the contents of which I couldn't hear. (Another problem: The foam and plastic of the headphones muffled all outside noise. A real voice-hearer would have had to contend with his in-

ternal voices *and* external noise; because of my headphones, my
reality was skewed toward the voices.)

Exasperated, full, and nearing the end of the tape, I left the diner
and went to buy a newspaper. The newsstand on Sixth Avenue was
closed, however, and the deli next door didn't sell papers. Since I was
growing tired—not of the voices but of the distractions and inade-
quacies of the street—I headed back to my brother's apartment.

My brother was lying on the couch, watching *Some Like It Hot*
on DVD.

"How's it going?" he asked me.

"A voice is telling me I smell like shit," I told him.

"You do smell like shit," he said. On the TV screen, Tony Curtis
was wearing a dress and playing the saxophone.

I retreated into my brother's bedroom, where I found a copy of the
New York Times. When I had spoken to Patricia Deegan on the phone,
she told me that as part of the experiment I should also try to read
or write as I listened to the tape, since that is how I spend most of
my time. With the voices still chattering away, I read an article in the
Metro section about an ex–New York City cop who was thrown off
the force for cocaine use. His wife subsequently threw him out of
their apartment for losing his job. The man reacted to his loss of job
and family by using his newly rented studio in Queens as a sniper's
nest, shooting at passersby from his window with a rifle in an attempt, I suppose, to expend his rage. He hit an elementary-school-
teacher in the shoulder. I got through the article at a slower pace than
usual, but I was able to read. Eventually, the tape clicked off.

I was once asked, in the only sociology class I ever took in col-
lege, to "experience powerlessness" for a day, to "become" a black man
or a woman or a homosexual. It was an assignment that managed
both to oversimplify the subtle dynamics of power and to make a

mockery of the task of increasing one's compassion. But I was being graded, so I decided that on a trip home to New York I would "become" homeless for a day. I would put on soiled jeans and my father's old army jacket and beg for change at the entrance to the 116th Street subway. Once back in New York, however, I became distracted by other matters. There was holiday shopping to be done; my brothers and I went out to dinner; I saw some friends. So on the Sunday night that I returned to school, I sat down at my desk and made the thing up. I wrote about clothes that were too well laundered to pass as the rags of an indigent; of having rich Barnard coeds rebuff my requests for change and of that not mattering anyhow because I had $40 in my pocket and so didn't need any change; and of the ultimate "lesson"—that "experiencing powerlessness" is a futile exercise, that if one is in a position of power, one can hardly approach the knowledge of powerlessness, let alone experience it.

I got an A. It was my first success as a creative writer. And although in one sense the paper was just a deception driven by anger and laziness, there was an honesty in its theme, which was, to wit, that there is an intractable futility in any attempt to "understand" the experience of any human being other than yourself. That the truth of individual experience is safely guarded behind the wall of the cranium and the knowledge of innumerable facts and feelings that are impossible to share. The eminent neurologist Walter J. Freeman has outlined this infuriating problem, pointing out that what goes on in any individual's brain depends on past experiences that are too complex to enumerate. "The only knowledge each of us has," Freeman writes, "is what we have constructed within our own brains."[6]

Freeman also makes the point, however, that there is great value in the quixotic attempt to get at that knowledge, no matter how impossible. If one is to live honestly, one must denounce defeatism and take up arms against the impossible. Can I get at the truth of my father's voices? Probably not. But the search is all I have.

5

THE TYRANNY OF MEANING

One must be so careful with names. . . .
—RAINER MARIA RILKE, *Letters to a Young Poet*

In 1972, David Rosenhan, a professor of psychology and law at Stanford University, organized and directed the secret admission of eight men and women—a graduate student, three psychologists, a pediatrician, a psychiatrist, a painter, and a housewife—into the psychiatric wards of several American hospitals. Rosenhan's purpose was to measure the extent to which psychiatric authorities could distinguish the mentally ill from the mentally healthy. To make his experiment as fair and accurate as possible, he stripped it of all but an elementary dishonesty. Rosenhan instructed his volunteers, whom he termed "pseudopatients," to present themselves in hospital admissions offices complaining that they were hearing voices that said the words *empty, hollow,* and *thud.* Beyond that, they were to stop feigning the experience as soon as they were admitted, to act in the hospital precisely as they would in normal life, and to answer all questions truthfully except for those that might lead to their being discovered.

The results of the study were stark. Not one of the volunteers was detected. All were admitted to the hospital, diagnosed with severe mental illness—seven of the eight with schizophrenia—and prescribed potent antipsychotic medications. Furthermore, all reported that upon being admitted they were treated by the hospital staff as if they were like any other psychiatric inpatient at the time—which is to say, they were ignored, to the point where some were able to take copious notes in open view without drawing attention to themselves. Only the legitimate patients suspected the illegitimate ones. "You're not crazy," one patient insisted. "You're a journalist, or a professor. You're checking up on the hospital."[1]

Rosenhan's study, published the following year in the prestigious journal *Science* under the title "On Being Sane in Insane Places," caused a furor. Psychiatry's many critics, flourishing in the wake of a series of damaging books—Thomas Szasz's *The Myth of Mental Illness*, Ronald Laing's *The Divided Self*, Michel Foucault's *Madness and Civilization*, Ken Kesey's *One Flew Over the Cuckoo's Nest*—gloated over what appeared to be a decisive victory for the madman-as-social-victim school of thought. The article seemed proof that mental illness was at best a fluid concept and at worst a projection of the observer's beliefs. The profession's practitioners, meanwhile, were put even more firmly on the defensive than they had been before. Robert Spitzer, a doyen of the psychiatric establishment, published a lengthy critique in the *Journal of Abnormal Psychology* in which he pointed out that all branches of medicine rely on the honest reporting of experience:

> If I were to drink a quart of blood and, concealing what I had done, come to the emergency room of any hospital vomiting blood, the behaviour of the staff would be quite predictable. If they labelled and treated me as having a peptic ulcer, I doubt I could argue convincingly that medical science does not know how to diagnose that condition.[2]

Rosenhan's study still has the power to cause controversy. In 2004, the psychologist and author Lauren Slater reported that she had attempted to replicate the experiment. For days she let her personal hygiene lapse and then presented herself at nine psychiatric emergency rooms with the complaint that she was hearing a voice saying the word *thud*. Universally denied admission, she was nevertheless prescribed antipsychotic medication on several occasions. Spitzer responded with a second lengthy critique, this time in the *Journal of Nervous and Mental Disease*.[3]

This is how "On Being Sane" is usually discussed: as a central document in the ongoing debate over the validity of psychiatric classifications. Yet it is also a piece of literature that more than any other encapsulates the status of voice-hearing in the modern West. This is unspoken in the original article. Rosenhan offers two reasons for choosing a voice that said *empty, hollow,* and *thud* as the phenomenon with which he would breach the ramparts of institutional psychiatry. First, the experience had never before appeared in the clinical literature and therefore would not corrupt the experiment with precedent. Second, it had "an apparent similarity to existential symptoms"—in other words, *empty, hollow,* and *thud* suggested despair. But the tacit, predominant reason Rosenhan chose the phenomenon was that of all the experiences he might have used—suicidal thoughts, paranoia, obsessions, compulsions, phobias, panic attacks—auditory hallucination was the most patently, the most unequivocally, the most definitively indicative of mental illness. Nothing quite suggested pathology like hearing a voice.

How did an experience of such great antiquity and cultural import come to be considered not only pathological but definitively so—the pinnacle of mental disturbance? The most obvious answer is that voice-hearing draws its status from the status of the illness with which it is most commonly associated. Schizophrenia is the clinical centerpiece of psychiatry. It accounts for half of all admissions to psychiatric hospitals, costs $40 billion a year to treat in the United States, and is one of the top ten causes of disability worldwide.[4] According to the National Institute of Mental Health, schizophrenia is "a devastating brain disorder—the most chronic and disabling of the severe mental illnesses."[5] And hearing voices is one of its prototypical symptoms.

Voices and schizophrenia have not always been so closely related, however. In the late nineteenth century, when the concept of schizophrenia was first developed by the German psychiatrist Emil Kraepelin, it was called "dementia praecox." The term means "senility of the young," and it was meant to reflect the typical onset of the illness in late childhood or early adulthood. Kraepelin considered the all but inevitable outcome of the disorder to be a sort of catatonic recoiling into the self. He didn't ignore the existence of auditory hallucinations; they were, he wrote, "peculiarly characteristic" of dementia praecox, and he provided many examples in his work. But he didn't see the experience as the disorder's primary feature. What distinguished a patient with dementia praecox, Kraepelin argued, was that he became slowly and irreversibly mentally disabled.

Eugen Bleuler, the Swiss psychiatrist who rechristened the disorder "schizophrenia" in 1908, deemphasized auditory hallucinations to an even greater extent. Kraepelin believed voices were connected biologically to an underlying disease; Bleuler believed they were psychological reactions. The true symptoms of schizophrenia, Bleuler wrote, had to do with thought and emotion. Schizophrenics had trouble making clear associations between ideas; they held conflicting attitudes about other people; they displayed inappropriate emotions; they withdrew into an inner world of imagination. By the word schizophrenia, Bleuler meant to imply not a split personality, as is often thought, but a disconnect among psychological functions such as thinking, memory, and perception.

This dynamic model of schizophrenia held for decades, until it became clear that it wasn't much of a help to psychiatrists in the field, who needed a good way to determine who was sick and who was not.

Kurt Schneider, a psychiatrist who was hired to rebuild the University of Heidelberg's medical school after the fall of Nazi Germany, answered this call with a simple checklist of "first-rank" symptoms of schizophrenia. Schneider agreed with Kraepelin and Bleuler that voices weren't fundamental to schizophrenia. They were undeniably easy to recognize, however, and so when he wrote up his list, he placed them at the top. The primary symptoms of schizophrenia, Schneider wrote, were "audible thoughts," "voices heard arguing," and "voices heard commenting on one's actions."[6]

Schneider's system took some years to catch on, but when it did, it dramatically altered the way psychiatrists thought about schizophrenia. The British psychologist Richard Bentall has noted that when Schneider's list was first translated into English, in the late 1950s, many researchers in the United States and England assumed he had found "a more precise way of identifying 'real cases' of schizophrenia."[7] His model began to appear with increasing frequency in academic journals and was incorporated into structured clinical interviews. Then the architects of psychiatry's influential diagnostic manuals caught on. The World Health Organization's *International Classification of Disease*, used by psychiatrists to diagnose patients throughout Europe, relies heavily on Schneider's list. So has every edition of the American Psychiatric Association's *Diagnostic and Statistical Manual of Mental Disorders* since 1980.[8]

The placement of voice-hearing at the center of the idea of schizophrenia didn't make diagnosis a foregone conclusion. Just as the average neurologist encountering a headache does not reflexively diagnose brain cancer, the average psychiatrist encountering voices does not reflexively diagnose schizophrenia. Still, the close relationship between symptom and syndrome has deeply colored the experience. The public's understanding of unusual experiences follows psychiatric thought closely, and the vast majority of academic research on voice-hearing examines the phenomenon not in its own right but through the lens of psychosis—as "schizophrenic" voices. In public, psychiatrists are usually careful to note that voice-hearing is not exclusive to schizophrenia or, for that matter, to mental illness. But some, through a zeal to provide a safe medical haven for potential sufferers, incautiously conflate the two. In his best-selling *Surviving Schizophrenia*, the psychiatrist E. Fuller Torrey writes that voices "are so characteristic of the disease that a person with true auditory hallucinations should be assumed to have schizophrenia until proven otherwise."[9]

And yet, the relationship between voice-hearing and schizophrenia is not what caused the experience to take on such a patently pathological feel. For one, the concept of schizophrenia appeared too late in history to be the main culprit. It ramped up the pathological profile of voice-hearing, but it didn't create that profile. What it did is more elemental and was well illuminated by a debate that occurred a few years ago in the pages of the British journal *The Psychologist* between Anthony David, a psychiatrist at London's Institute of Psychiatry, and Ivan Leudar, a psychologist at the University of Manchester. The subject of the debate was the question "Is hearing voices a sign of mental illness?" David argued in the affirmative, Leudar in the negative.

The debate was strained from the start. David and Leudar had no trouble agreeing that voice-hearing is not in and of itself an indication of mental illness. But beyond that basic point they were unable to settle on what criteria they should use to answer the question. Should they examine the content of voices? The level of distress caused? The grammatical form the voices take? If the first, what would this do to the reliability of psychiatric taxonomy, which traditionally focuses on form? And what if the "pathological" content did not cause any distress? If the second, what if the distress was caused by something other than voices? If the third, on what authority were they to pass judgment on the madness of grammatical tenses? The debate did more to reveal the philosophical muddle into which discussions of psychopathology inevitably devolve than to answer the question that sparked it.

But like all useful philosophical discussions, the debate helped highlight the linguistic difficulties at the core of the subject. The pitfall of language tripped up the clinicians from the beginning, when Leudar proposed terms for the debate. "I do not accept that auditory and verbal hallucinations must be studied only as hallucinations," he wrote. "The term 'hallucination' implies an intrinsic confusion— something subjective is wrongly experienced as 'real.' . . . Even before we investigate the experience, the term tinges it with a logically intrinsic pathology where there may be none." The initial bracketing of hallucination in quotation marks hovered over the remainder of the debate, clearly distinguishing the two men. Whereas Leudar used the word only once after his opening salvo, and then in explicit criticism of orthodox psychiatry, David used it frequently and without compunction.[10]

The difference isn't negligible. In the history of voice-hearing, no event has been as consequential in creating the modern meaning of the phenomenon as the introduction of that simple word *hallucination*.

The spanish nun, mystic, and reformer Teresa of Ávila composed *The Interior Castle*, her classic work of mystical theology, over the course of six months in 1577. Intended as a spiritual map for the nuns under her direction, *The Interior Castle* imagines the human soul as a seven-chambered castle "made entirely from a diamond or very transparent crystal." Teresa's purpose in writing the book was to lead her nuns toward the innermost seventh chamber, where they would receive an understanding of the Holy Trinity and become married for eternity to Jesus Christ. She was, apparently, a well-qualified guide.

At sixty-two she was known throughout Spain for her spiritual purity, and, as numerous self-abasements throughout the book make clear, she knew what could threaten the apprehension of God's glory. One of the dangers she was concerned about pertained to sensory visitations from God. The reader, Teresa argued, was likely to receive divine favors, but she had to be certain that they were in fact divine and not the result of, for example, melancholy or a hyperactive imagination. For in these latter instances a person could not be considered visionary at all. Instead, she had to be considered *"como enferma"*: "as if sick."

Como enferma. In an influential 1967 article, the American psychologists Theodore Sarbin and Joseph Juhasz claimed for this phrase an illustrious place in the history of the senses. It was, they argued, a deliberate attempt by Teresa to protect her nuns from the Spanish Inquisition. For years Teresa had been on the brink of persecution because of her flamboyant raptures, which often overcame her in public. She did not want her students to run the same risk, so she proposed that voices and visions could be caused by mental illness as well as by divine or demonic influence. By doing so, Sarbin and Juhasz wrote, Teresa set into action a momentous passing of social control over unusual sensory experiences from the confessional to the doctor's office:

> By declaring those nuns who were visionaries *enferma* (sick) Teresa could prevent the Inquisition from acting against them. Infirmity (sickness) is not something that one does, but rather something that happens to one, and therefore, one cannot be blamed (or praised) for it. This humane act was one of a series by religious and lay authorities aimed at removing the Inquisition from a position of control over reported imaginings.[11]

It is a matter of conjecture whether Teresa's book had as formative an impact on history as Sarbin and Juhasz maintained. It is also a matter of conjecture whether her use of the word *enferma* was a savvy political decision or whether it was, as theologians might have it, an honest description of a physical pitfall along the metaphysical path. Likely it was both: Teresa was at once pragmatic and spiritually scrupulous. But whatever the historical and religious particulars, the example serves as an important reminder of the complexity inherent in the pathologization of voice-hearing. Between the beginning of the Reformation in the early sixteenth century and the rise of psychiatry in the late eighteenth, there rests a 250-year blooming of a new empirical frame of mind, a "scientific revolution" that mitigated the centuries-old authority of the Church and instituted the Enlightenment ideals of rationality and skeptical inquiry. That revolution is what made the transformation of voice-hearing from a religious to a pathological experience possible.

Teresa's use of the word *enferma* also serves as a reminder of the singular importance of language in the weakening of religion's authority over experience. Theological reformation, political instability, technological innovation, scientific advancement—all contributed to the alteration in human consciousness that we now refer to as the rise of modernity. But the way that those contributions registered themselves in the human mind, the mechanism by which they took root and spread, and often even the way that they began was through language. The alteration of words served as the vehicle for the alteration in understanding that has led us to our present point of view.

For psychiatry this is particularly true. The profession arose as an organized discipline in the late eighteenth century, when physicians embraced the notion that institutionalization, previously thought of in terms of warehousing, could be curative. But its growth as a cultural force—the triumph of its interpretation of human experience—began in the nineteenth century, when psychiatrists made an energetic attempt to devise and propagate new medical names for age-old experiences. Like the early theorists of

Christianity, these early psychiatrists embraced an intellectual mission: They systematized what had hitherto been a trend of thought. They codified a mood.

With hindsight, it is clear that the psychiatric codifiers were responding to the achievements of their predecessors. From about 1750 to 1800 the work of proto-psychiatrists was characterized by a revolutionary fervor. (The term *psychiatry* was not coined until 1808.) With a sense of the inevitability of progress that defined the Enlightenment, men such as William Battie (1704–1776) in London, Vincenzo Chiarugi (1759–1820) in Florence, and Philippe Pinel (1745–1826) in Paris preached the therapeutic gospel of compassion and seclusion from society. Their efforts were an unmitigated success. There occurred an increase not only in a commitment to hospital medicine but in the number of patients actually committed to asylums. Yet the most lasting effect of the reforms instituted by the first psychiatrists was arguably the boon it offered to the scientific minded. Given more patients, subsequent doctors could establish a clearer picture of insanity.

Of the second wave of psychiatrists, one benefited directly from the initial reforms. Jean-Etienne-Dominique Esquirol (1772–1840) was Pinel's favorite student, the anointed disciple of the most influential psychiatrist in Europe. He eagerly took up the causes of his mentor, lecturing extensively on the need to treat the insane with kindness and fighting to imbue the discipline with a sense of scientific legitimacy. In 1817, Esquirol introduced the first formal course of clinical instruction in France. What is more, throughout the early decades of the nineteenth century he almost single-handedly poured the diagnostic foundation of the profession by transforming, in a series of landmark papers, the raw data of the crowded asylums into specific classifications of mental disorders, identifiable by way of their symptoms. He collected and revised these papers into his 1838 book *Des Maladies Mentales*, which the historian Roy Porter has called "the outstanding psychiatric text of his age."[12] And the most outstanding and influential paper was one in which Esquirol for the first time in history identified, labeled, and offered a strict medical definition of unshared sensory experiences. He termed these experiences "hallucinations."

When Esquirol introduced the word *hallucination* into the medical lexicon, it had only a modest etymological pedigree. Its roots are the Latin verb *alucinor*, meaning "to wander in the mind" or "to ramble on," and the related noun *allucinatio*. Both seldom appear in classical Roman texts. (*"Sic vestras halucinationes fero quemadmodum Iuppiter . . . ineptias poetarum,"* Seneca wrote in *De Vita Beata*: "I shall put up with your ramblings as Jupiter puts up with the nonsense of poets.")[13] *Hallucination* appeared just as seldom in the modern European languages. Its first appearance in English was in a 1572 translation of a monograph by the Swiss cleric Ludwig Lavater (the title, beginning "Of ghostes and spirites walking by nyght, and of strange noyses, crackes, and sundry forewarnynges," runs for nearly a full page). It was used there as it was used elsewhere—to describe not only perceptions for which there was no external evidence but also for misperceptions for which there was external evidence.[14] In this sense the word *hallucination* had something in common with other sensory terms in circulation in early modern Europe. It was just another way to point to unusual experiences. Most of these terms were religious, such as *locution*, *apparition*, *possession*, *revelation*, and *inspiration*.

The first generation of psychiatrists had not noted this lexical confusion so much as they had sidestepped it. They simply resolved to call all unshared sensory experiences "visions," no matter the sense to which they applied. It was a state of descriptive affairs that plainly offended Esquirol's notion of order. In his 1838 book, the pertinent section of which was a modest revision of a paper that had appeared in an 1817 medical dictionary, he laid out the problem with obvious irritation. "Who would dare say visions of hearing, visions of taste, visions of smell?" he asked. "And yet the images, *ideas* and *notions,* which seem to belong to the functional alteration of these three senses, present to the mind the same characters, have the same seat, that is to say, the brain, and are produced by the same causes." He concluded that something needed to be done:

> A generic term is wanting. I have proposed the word *hallucination,* as having no determinate signification, and as adapted consequently, to all the varieties of delirium which suppose the presence of an object proper to excite one of the senses, although these objects may be beyond their reach.[15]

Esquirol had two goals in mind in introducing the term *hallucination.* First, he wanted to bring under a single medical canopy all the previous existing names used to describe sensory experiences for which there was no external basis. This would allow doctors everywhere to speak in a common scientific language, with a common scientific reference point. To accomplish this goal, Esquirol not only named the experiences, but offered them their first explicitly clinical definition. His formulation bespoke an awareness of the cultural transformation taking place. "A man . . . who has the inward conviction of a presently perceived sensation at a moment when no external object capable of arousing this sensation is within the field of his senses, is in a state of hallucination," Esquirol wrote. *"He is a visionary."*[16]

Second, Esquirol wanted to institute a clear theoretical demarcation between the concept of hallucinations and what he now called, again offering the first explicitly clinical definition, "illusions." For Esquirol, hallucinations had a centralized cause. They occurred as a result of the brain creating sensory impressions out of whole cloth. Illusions were "sensory errors." They required a combination of the external world and the invention of the brain. Again he was insistent about the need for linguistic clarity:

> The ancients did not distinguish *visions* from illusions of the senses. Some moderns adopting the term which I proposed as a substitute for visions have confounded hallucinations with illusions; dividing them, indeed, into mental hallucinations (*visions*), and sensorial hallucinations (*illusions of the senses*). Their authors have not distinguished with sufficient clearness the essential difference which exists between these two orders of phenomena. In hallucinations everything goes on in the brain. Visionaries, and those in a state of ecstasy, are hallucinated. They are in a reverie, though quite awake. . . . In illusions, on the contrary, the sensibility of the nervous extremities is altered: it is exalted, enfeebled, or perverted. The senses are active, and the actual impressions solicit the reaction of the brain.[17]

Esquirol's innovations did not meet with immediate success. As the British historian Tony James has discovered, the word *hallucination* appeared seldom in medical texts prior to 1830. After that date, the innovations gained pace and were soon adopted by the medical establishment. This slow growth in momentum is not particularly surprising. Esquirol was the primary psychiatric educator of his time, and his students did not come of intellectual age until the 1830s. What is surprising is the peculiar and forceful mechanism by which Esquirol's terminology drove a new logic of pathology. Esquirolian terminology was not accepted without discussion by the psychiatrists of the nineteenth century. Those who followed him recognized the perils of pathologizing voices and visions. Indeed, the most vigorous debate that took place in French psychiatry into the mid-century regarded the question of whether hallucinations were inherently pathological. But the overwhelming sense that one gets from those debates is of their futility. By the time psychiatrists were arguing over the extent to which medicine should claim ownership over unshared sensory experiences, they had already adopted Esquirol's strictly medical terminology. The inevitable result was that even those who had misgivings about psychiatry's land grabs could not avoid tilling the soil.

Naturally, there were those who did not have misgivings and who made the job of dissent that much more difficult. Like many of history's great medical theorists, Esquirol was diligent in outlining the limits of his theories. Though hallucinations were "most frequently the lot of feeble minds," he allowed, they could also occur in "men the most remarkable for their strength of understanding, the depth of their reason, and their vigor of thought."[18] But he had students whose apostolic zeal led them to abandon moderation. Notable among these was François Leuret (1797–1851), whose main contribution to the success of the concept of hallucination, an 1834 book titled *Psychological Fragments on Insanity*, took up Esquirol's arguments with great rigidity. Contradicting his teacher, Leuret presented hallucinations as indisputably pathological, and he made this point in a way that was sure to gain attention and that set off a trend that has been termed "retrospective medicine": he diagnosed the heroes of the past. Evaluating such famous instances of mystical experience as Moses' vision of God, Ezekiel's vision of the wheel, and Teresa of Ávila's ecstasies, Leuret concluded that their subjects could only have been insane. "Seeing such obvious cases of madness, considered by theologians as evidence of sainthood," he wrote, "the reader will doubtless absolve me from the reproach which he might have felt entitled to make, that I have so frequently appeared to exceed the bounds of the psychology of the insane."[19]

Louis François Lélut (1804–1877), who was not a student of Esquirol's, was more circumspect. In the same year that *Psychological Fragments* appeared, Lélut published *In Search of Analogies Between Mad-*

ness and Reason. This essay had a plainly humanistic purpose. Lélut's project was to show that there was no strict dividing line between madness and sanity. To accomplish this he compared various manifestations of insanity with the mundane psychological extremes of rage, fear, despair, and love. Hallucinations gave him more trouble than other aspects of madness—he strained to find contemporary analogies—but unlike Leuret he did not conclude from this that hallucinations were inherently pathological. Rather, he argued that the dearth of everyday hallucinations was a reflection of cultural and historical forces at work. There were no hallucinators outside of the asylums in nineteenth-century France because "that is all that may happen for our modern times, in which, because of the risk of being taken for a hallucinated madman, one can no longer claim to be in communication with the divinity or with any supernatural agents whatever." This had not always been the case. Throughout history, men and women of genius—he named Socrates, Muhammad, Joan of Arc, Martin Luther, and Ignatius Loyola—had proudly claimed to hear voices and to see visions. Framing the debate in the clearest terms yet, Lélut positioned himself with those who did not want hallucinations conceived of as a singularly medical phenomenon:

> Can there exist more or less continual, chronic hallucinations, considered by the hallucinator as real sensations, which are nevertheless compatible with an apparently whole state of reason, and which allow the individual who suffers them, not only to continue to live with his fellow men, but even to bring to his conduct and the management of his interests all the soundness of judgment which is desirable? One would be inclined to reply in the negative, yet observation shows that this would be wrong.[20]

But Lélut was not uniform in his stance. As Tony James has shown, his essay was marked by conflicting tendencies: If he mainly attempted to prevent psychiatry's sole ownership of hallucinations, he at times seemed to advocate the universality of its theories. It was a paradox that was contained in his frequent use of the word *hallucination*, and he could not ward off the inevitable resolution. A mere two years later Lélut swung toward Leuret with the publication of his famous *Du Démon de Socrate* (*On Socrates' Personal Deity*). In that book, to which he strangely appended his earlier essay, Lélut proved himself a staunch defender of medicine as an interpreter of human experience. Utilizing all the clinical resources at his disposal and applying them methodically to ancient Greek sources, Lélut came to the conclusion that Socrates was in reality no different from the patients housed in Parisian asylums. James has summarized his thesis as follows: "Unless we are to believe that the ancients misinterpreted Socrates' own words about the nature of his inspirations, or that these words were a form of hoax, we must conclude that Socrates suffered from auditory—and perhaps an occasional visual—hallucinations. Since only mad people so suffer, Socrates, in spite of all other virtues he may have possessed, must have been mad."[21]

The sheer audacity of this argument was a challenge not only to philosophers, who received the book warily, but to rearguard orthodox thinkers, for whom it was a terrifying precedent. Whom, they wondered, would Lélut diagnose next: Jesus? The first to accept the challenge was the Roman Catholic doctor Alexandre Brierre de Boismont (1798–1881). In his 1845 book *On Hallucinations*, Brierre mounted a direct protest against Leuret and Lélut. Yet while he embraced the historical relativism that the latter had displayed in *In Search of Analogies*, he refused to get bogged down in clinical discussion. The subject, he wrote with a flair for polemic, was much broader and much more grave. He was defending nothing less than Europe's cultural inheritance: "If all hallucinations had to be placed amongst the products of a delirious imagination, then sacred works would no longer be anything but a mistake; Christianity, that pow-

erful motivating force for social and individual movement, a mistake; our fathers' beliefs, our own, our children's, mistakes."[22]

On Hallucinations was what today would be called a crossover hit.
It went into three editions and was read and discussed by a number
of leading writers of the time, including Alphonse de Lamartine,
George Sand, and Baudelaire. But as one of its reviewers made
painfully apparent, Brierre's arguments were ultimately stymied by the
same paradox that had forced Lélut's hand. Writing in the prestigious, newly established journal *Annales Medico-Psychologiques*, Alfred
Maury decimated Brierre's book. It was, he wrote, a simple matter
of logic:

> For we shall say to our author: you recognize that these great char-
> acters whom you are honourably defending may have had halluci-
> nations; you recognize, and history records, that they took these
> illusions for celestial or diabolical apparitions, for real facts; there-
> fore you admit that they were hallucinators, that they were insane;
> for what are the latter, if not minds who believe in their hallucina-
> tions as if they were serious facts? In addition you put forward the
> view . . . that for these characters these hallucinations were motives
> for action, determining causes, giving rise to great projects. Thus the
> illustrious characters in question had hallucinations like today's hal-
> lucinators; like them they gave them credence; like them they acted
> in consequence of the imaginary sensations they experienced. What
> difference does M. Brierre persist in recognizing between these char-
> acters and those who are before our eyes?[23]

The trap, then, was inescapable. The mere adoption of the word
hallucination meant the adoption of its definition, and that definition
left no room in which to maneuver. And though the discussion did
not end there—from February 1855 to April 1856 the Paris-based So-
ciété Médico-Psychologique held a series of wide-ranging debates on

hallucinations that again found Brierre, the organization's secretary, on the defensive—in a sense nothing more needed to be said. The language packed its own internal logic, and that logic could not be breached. With one linguistic swoop, Esquirol had diagnosed not only his patients but the entirety of Western culture.

The effects of that act can still be felt. Esquirol's definition of hallucination as "the inward conviction of a presently perceived sensation at a moment when no external object capable of arousing this sensation is within the field of [the] senses" is nearly identical to the definition currently on offer by the American Psychiatric Association, the publisher of the *Diagnostic and Statistical Manual*. A hallucination, that book's editors write, is "a sensory perception that has the compelling sense of reality of a true perception but that occurs without external stimulation of the relevant sensory organ."[24] More important, the word *hallucination* continues to project a kind of syllogistic radiance. Used universally as a description for sensory experiences for which there are no external stimuli, and associated with a profession the express purpose of which is to treat mental illness, it bathes all such experiences in the glow of pathology.

In the mid-1980s, Marius Romme, a professor of social psychiatry at the University of Limburg, in the Netherlands, began to worry about the fate of one of his patients. Patsy Hage, thirty years old, heard voices telling her what and what not to do. She had been hospitalized several times, diagnosed as schizophrenic, and prescribed antipsychotic medication. The drugs lessened the anxiety that Hage's voices caused, but they failed to quiet the voices themselves and had the unfortunate side effect of making her thinking foggy and dull. Therefore, she frequently didn't take them, and the voices had begun to take over her daily life. She fell into a depression that Romme felt powerless to pull her out of. She talked more and more about suicide.

The only aspect of their meetings that seemed positive to Romme was that Hage had recently read the work of Julian Jaynes, the psychologist who suggested that voice-hearing was universal in ancient times; she took comfort in the theory. Desperate and with no other leads, Romme began to wonder whether she might benefit from communicating what she had read with other voice-hearers and finding others who would accept it.

With this in mind, Romme arranged to appear with Hage on a popular Dutch talk show on which they invited people who heard voices to contact them. The strength of the response surprised him: 450 people called in. Even more surprising, one-third of the respondents claimed that they were able to live alongside their voices without great difficulty. It immediately struck him that this smaller group, whose members interpreted their voices in a variety of ways, would serve as a valuable therapeutic resource for those who had a harder time coping with their voices. He identified twenty men and women who were able to speak articulately about how they had learned to manage their voices and asked them to serve as the speakers at a conference for voice-hearers. The governing principle of the meeting, which was held in October 1987 in a labor union hall in Utrecht, was that all interpretations of voice-hearing, no matter how unusual, would be accepted. Clinicians would be in attendance, but only as guides and observers. John Strauss, an eminent Yale psychiatrist who was there as a guest, later described the mood:

> The general atmosphere of the entire congress was of a meeting of a group of people with common interests and experiences. Although medical aspects of these experiences were discussed, there was no sense that this was a medical meeting or a meeting of medical patients. The participants freely shared their experiences, their many interpretations of these experiences including religious views or a range of other human reactions, and their approaches to coping.

Some people were obviously troubled by their voices and saw them as part of a mental illness, but many had very different ways of understanding these experiences and appeared to be competent, not disabled, and depending on one's view of the nature of voices, not in any way "ill."[25]

The meeting was a success. Its inclusive stance struck a chord among the participants. A self-help organization, Foundation Resonance, grew out of the conference and quickly began to gain notice elsewhere. Grassroots voice-hearing organizations began to pop up in Denmark, Finland, Italy, Portugal, Sweden, Germany, Japan, Australia, Malaysia, and England. Before long a full-fledged "Hearing Voices Movement" had formed, motivated by a therapeutic philosophy that Romme developed with his partner and colleague, a journalist named Sandra Escher. They called this philosophy "An Emancipatory Approach." It was clear what the emancipation was meant to be from. In lectures, journal articles, and books, Romme and Escher argued that referring to voices as auditory hallucinations was not only technically incorrect—many people heard voices that were not signs of mental illness—but stigmatizing and harmful. The orthodox psychiatric model was to eradicate or mitigate voices. According to Romme, this failed to take into account the ineradicable importance that the phenomenon played in people's lives. The insistence that the experience was pathological, he and Escher argued, was maladaptive. The people who coped best were those who found ways to bring their voices in line with their experiences. Those who tried to escape suffered the most.

Not surprisingly, Romme and Escher's work met with criticism. In 1993, they published *Accepting Voices*, the core of which was the stories of thirteen voice-hearers who had learned to interpret their experiences in a positive way. Reviewing the book in the *British Medical Journal*, Raymond Cochrane, a British psychologist, called it "ill advised" and "potentially dangerous." "Anything that may encourage people to accept the reality of delusional belief, and even to attribute to these beliefs some mystical supernatural power," he wrote, "can only prolong the existence of these beliefs and make recovery from schizophrenia more protracted and more uncertain."[26] But not everyone was pessimistic. Indeed, many were enthusiastic. Romme and Escher's initial report on the Utrecht conference, published in the journal *Schizophrenia Bulletin*, was cited widely in academic journals, and their conclusion that "the real problem is not so much the hearing of . . . voices, but rather the inability to cope with them" has helped spawn a new "cognitive" approach to hallucinations. In 1994, the psychologists Max Birchwood, of the University of Birmingham, and Paul Chadwick, of the Royal South Hampshire Hospital in Southampton, published a landmark study in which they proposed that the anguish experienced by voice-hearers is directly related to a belief in the experience's malevolence and power.[27] (Romme and Escher's work has been embraced most enthusiastically in England, which has always been less conservative in clinical matters than the United States.) The psychologist Anthony Morrison, of the University of Manchester, similarly found that negative beliefs about voices increase both the incidence and the distress of the experience, and further observed that these negative beliefs are sometimes linked to the cultural dominance of the pathological interpretation of voice-hearing. Interpretations of loss of control, Morrison has written, "largely concern impending madness, and as such, may be related to patients' negative appraisals of their psychosis, which are often reinforced by both [psychiatric] services and the media."[28]

But the greatest enthusiasm has come from voice-hearers themselves, who have responded as much to Romme and Escher's often electrifying rhetoric as to their theoretical innovations. (Hallucinators, Romme has said, "are like homosexuals in the 1950s—in need of liberation, not cure.")[29] These voice-hearers have coalesced into groups of increasing vocality and influence in psychiatric circles. Arguably the most vocal and influential has been a British self-help organization that was formed in 1988 on the model of the original Dutch voice-hearing organization. The Hearing Voices Network, based in Manchester, describes itself as "a network of people who hear voices, relatives, carers and workers who work toward gaining a better understanding of the experience of hearing voices and seeing visions and reducing ignorance and anxiety about these issues." It has dozens of affiliated groups throughout the United Kingdom, and each summer it holds its annual gathering in a large Methodist hall in downtown Manchester. In 2003, I attended.

Like the first Utrecht meeting, HVN's annual gathering attracts a wide array of voice-hearers, both those who are visibly troubled by their experiences and those who glory in them. (Ron Coleman, a prominent member, has declared himself "psychotic and proud," and wants to work toward a day when he can "walk the streets talking to his voices and not be denied his freedom.")[30] It also attracts mental health workers who attend for moral support and, frequently, because they consider HVN to be a paradigm of consumer-driven psychiatric reform. One clinician, to whom both reasons apply, chaired the gathering. Philip Thomas, a robust man with short gray hair and a thin white beard, is a psychiatrist affiliated with the University of Bradford and the coauthor, with Ivan Leudar, of *Voices of Reason, Voices of Insanity*, an iconoclastic study of verbal hallucinations. At the morning session, held in a sweltering auditorium, he announced from the stage that HVN's main achievement was in "creating a space for people to experience their voices outside of the influence of psychiatry and psychology." Sitting next to him at a long folding table was Peter Bullimore, a cochair of the organization. Bullimore, a voice-hearer, former psychiatric patient, and longtime critic of traditional medical interventions for psychosis, announced to loud applause the advances that HVN had made in the previous year: a new, confidential helpline; growth to more than 1,200 members; and nearly 150 regional self-help groups across Great Britain.

The juxtaposition of psychiatrist and antipsychiatric activist sitting next to each other on stage and working toward the same goal was jarring, and over lunch, served buffet-style in a narrow vestibule outside the auditorium, I asked Thomas about the potential irony of a psychiatrist working to diminish the influence of his own profession. Thomas has been criticized by colleagues for his active role in the consumer survivor movement, but he told me that he found no contradiction in his participation. "My role as a clinician is to help people reduce their suffering," he said. "In many cases, I'm not convinced medical psychiatry is well equipped to accomplish that."

In fact, Thomas resists not only the pathological interpretation of voice-hearing but all interpretations that claim to be authoritative. In *Voices of Reason*, he and Leudar argue that even to ask what causes voice-hearing "impoverishes" the phenomenon, robbing it of its true existence as an experience driven by a number of psychological and cultural factors, and that in our time psychiatry has done this by locating the origins of distress exclusively within the individual. "This serves two functions that are important politically," Thomas and Leudar write. "First, it plays down the importance of social, cultural, economic and political factors in understanding human distress. Second, because the distress is constructed in terms of disordered brain function, it means that both the person and the social contexts in which the person exists have no control or influence on what happens."[31]

This emphasis on lack of control is what has driven HVN's success. The organization's appeal is that it offers its members a level of ownership over their experiences that many feel psychiatry has stripped them of. This feeling is not always theoretical. Several people at the conference told me stories of having been institutionalized, or "sectioned," against their will, and many more complained about the deadening effects of antipsychotic medication. Some of these complaints were couched in tones of underdoggish irreverence. Carol Batton, a diminutive, hyperkinetic woman referred to in the organization's literature as the "HVN poet," recited antipsychiatric doggerel at steady intervals throughout the day. ("Paranoid doctors, / Scared you might kill— / Kill you by medicating / Over the hill. / They do it to anyone, / moderately ill.") Others were grave. In an HVN newsletter distributed at the conference, Bullimore wrote of being diagnosed as schizophrenic and placed on tranquilizers. "After a few weeks," he wrote, "I became a walking zombie living in a drug induced world not knowing one day from another wondering if life was worth living. I stayed in this surreal existence for ten years losing my family and my business."[32] But all made the very serious claim that a frightful experience was being made even more frightful by the practical implications of the psychiatric model.

A story told to me by Jacqui Dillon, a member of HVN's management committee and a mental health activist, whom I met at the conference, vividly illustrates HVN's animating complaint. Dillon, a mother of two with bright eyes and a broad smile, first began to hear voices after being subjected to sexual and physical abuse as a child. Her voices were a source of both solace and discomfort; they eased her loneliness, but they also sometimes told her to harm herself. When Dillon decided to tell a psychiatrist about her experiences, however, she found that her doctor was prepared to interpret her voices only as a symptom of psychosis. "I explained to her that my voices were parts of me and that I just wanted support in being able to listen to them," she later wrote to me in an e-mail.

She looked confused. For her, the fact that I listened to my voices was evidence of my illness, and wanting to keep them in order to un-

derstand more about myself was seen as me being resistant to treatment. I believed that she was only focusing on the negative aspects
of my voices . . . but she didn't stop to consider that this might be
because of the desperation I sometimes felt. Or to consider the ways
that my voices helped me—how only they could soothe me at 3
o'clock in the morning when everybody else was asleep, or the voices
that helped me work things out, with their insightful, and often witty
comments. All the psychiatrists that I tried to tell either feared me,
denied my experience or told me that I would never, ever recover
from what had happened. They told me that I had an illness. I was
mentally ill.

Dillon's story is emblematic of the quarrel that HVN and its sister organizations have with psychiatry. According to traditional psychiatric manuals, voice-hearing is not an inherently pathological
phenomenon. The controversy lies in how this diagnostic neutrality
plays out in real life. The accusation that HVN makes is that no
matter how noncommittal it is in its theoretical understanding of
hearing voices, in practice psychiatry interprets the experience in a
manner that leaves little room for the hearer. If you go to a psychiatrist and announce that you are hearing voices, you will likely be diagnosed with a mental illness and asked to consider your experiences
within a biomedical framework. Your subjective experience of your
voices will be downplayed so that the voices can be treated as the
physician has been trained to treat them—which is to say, in objective, pathological terms. You will be asked to remove your experience
from yourself. In a 2000 speech to HVN, Romme claimed that an individual who goes to a psychiatrist complaining of voice-hearing has
an 80 percent chance of being diagnosed with schizophrenia.[33]
It is partly to HVN's credit that this portrait of psychiatric intervention is slowly growing outdated. In the United Kingdom and
increasingly in the United States, a less stringently biomedical ap-

proach to voice-hearing has steadily been encroaching upon the traditional one. Whereas the latter emphasizes syndromes and pharmacological compliance, the former emphasizes symptoms and an engagement with the patient's personal beliefs and experiences. As an article in the *American Journal of Psychiatry* recently explained, this model does not require that a patient accept a diagnostic label: "The goal . . . is not to try to persuade or force the patient to agree that he or she has symptoms of a mental illness. Rather, the goal is to reduce the severity of, or distress from, the symptom regardless of whether the patient accepts a diagnostic label." If a patient chooses to view his voices in terms of the biomedical model, fine. But it is destructive, this model states, to foist that interpretation on him. Instead, the clinician should work to find an explanation of voice-hearing that is acceptable to the patient. The approach is "designed to work directly on understanding and coping with the positive symptoms of psychosis rather than 'containing' them."[34]

This new therapeutic philosophy, which hopes to extend the success of cognitive-behavioral therapy in treating depression and anxiety to experiences typically deemed redolent of schizophrenia, seems perfectly suited to the concerns of HVN. It is pragmatic and oriented toward recovery rather than pathology. It even adopts some of HVN's characteristic language: The word *coping* is a hallmark of Romme's work. And yet, in a sense, even this approach does not go far enough. HVN is greatly concerned with the therapeutic stance that psychiatry takes toward voice-hearing. But it is perhaps even more concerned with the cultural meaning that is ascribed to the phenomenon and therefore to its members. The cognitive-behavioral therapist who encounters a voice-hearing patient will by definition be open to any interpretation of the experience that works, be it religious, paranormal, or biomedical. But among themselves, and by extension in the realm of public discourse, they will invariably speak of them as "hallucinations," which, in tacit criticism of its power, HVN always places in quotation marks.

Can the word *hallucination* really be destructive? The suggestion contradicts much recent psychopathological theory that has found medicalization to be healthful. Psychoeducation, the process of getting patients to accept the pathology of their experiences, is the psychological intervention for psychosis that has the greatest empirical support. And yet, there have always been those even within psychiatry who have noted the harmful reach of pathological terminology. Eugen Bleuler, the early theorist of schizophrenia, recognized the paradox into which a discipline that seeks to name and treat pathologies of the mind can lead its intended subjects. Often, he wrote, people "will admit that they are afraid to reveal their experiences because they will be considered pathological, and they themselves 'crazy.' "[35] In 1983, the American psychiatrist Ian Stevenson addressed the effects of "hallucination" directly in an article in the *American Journal of Psychiatry*. Outlining the word's psychiatric etymology and its varied manifestations, he suggested finding a nonpathological alternative:

> Most persons who have unusual sensory experiences tell few people, or no one, about them. They rarely know that many other people have had similar experiences and have also remained silent about them for fear of being considered abnormal or worse. They have heard that hallucinations are symptoms of insanity, and they have no way of knowing that such experiences are not necessarily indicators of mental illness, either present or to come.[36]

The problem that Stevenson raises is not the stigma associated with mental illness. Nor is it the malevolence of psychiatry. It is, rather, the practical and often immeasurable effects of language: the soft tyranny of offering a single pathological term for an experience that, both historically and in the present, reaches into more varied and more exalted forms of human consciousness than is typically assumed.

6

THE SOFT-SPOKEN GOD

Ye heard the voice of the words, but saw no similitude,
only ye heard a voice.   —DEUTERONOMY 4:12

I n the winter of 2002, in response to a flyer that the administration of a New York psychiatric hospital had agreed to post on its
walls, I received a phone call from a man named Richard K.[1] A
Queens native in his late thirties, Richard was an outpatient at the
hospital, where he was receiving treatment for schizoaffective disorder, a subset of schizophrenia that takes into account a pattern of
depression or manic depression. He was calling, he said, to tell me
about his voices. He had heard them for nearly twenty years.

Richard first began to hear voices when he was fourteen years old
and in junior high school. He was sitting at a desk toward the front
of his class when he heard laughter and mumbling coming from
somewhere behind and to the left of him. Richard, who was by nature a shy, awkward boy and accustomed to being made fun of,
turned around to confront what he presumed was a bully. All he
found, however, were the silent, bewildered faces of his classmates.
It was, he recalls, a terrifying episode, and one that began to repeat
itself with unnerving frequency both inside and outside of school.
Walking home in the afternoons, Richard would hear someone calling his name from across the street. Invariably, the voice had a tinny
quality, as if someone were speaking through an old microphone.

He worried that he was going insane. Richard knew that voices were a symptom of insanity, and to learn what he should do, he confided in his older brother, the only person in the world whom he thought he could trust. His brother assured him that he was not crazy, but he advised Richard not to tell anyone else about his voice. "If you do," his brother warned, "they'll pump you full of Thorazine and lock you away forever." In the late 1970s, this was still a possibility, and Richard remained silent. But the voice continued to speak, and it proved to be both a distraction and a liability. The following year Richard entered a public high school, and in the harsh social atmosphere he was teased mercilessly for his odd, detached demeanor, the result of his attendance to the voice. The cruel treatment only increased his sense of paranoia and isolation. "High school," Richard told me, "messed up my voices bad."

High school also caused Richard's voice to multiply. When he was in the tenth grade, the teasing became so painful that a second voice emerged to help him cope. This voice was different in quality from the first. For one thing, it was internal. Richard could hear it vividly, but only within the confines of his own skull. For another, in contrast to the metallic anonymity of the first voice, this new voice spoke in a tone so specific that Richard could easily visualize its source. It was, he was sure, a tall man in a dark suit and tie, with a shiny ring on his finger. He gave the voice a name to match its image. It was "the Executive," and its purpose was to order the disorder inside Richard's head—to counsel him when he needed advice and to soothe him when he became overwrought.

The Executive gave Richard a much-needed sense of psychological security. For the first time he felt he had some guidance on how to think and behave. But at the same time that comfort came at a price, for true to the Executive's title, he soon began to attract an administration. Before long there emerged a complex political structure inside Richard's head. First, there was the Troika, a three-member cabinet that advised the Executive on the daily strategy of conducting Richard's life. Next there was the Full-Movement Council, a legislative body comprised of several hundred members that was called to order whenever an important life decision needed to be made.[2] Finally, there was the Anti-Executive, an opposition leader who sought to undermine the beneficent work of his counterpart. Though these voices had begun as a way to structure Richard's thoughts and emotions, they soon became even more of a distraction to Richard than his first voice had been. When they all spoke at once, he said, it was as if a "symphony of untuned instruments was playing very loudly inside my head."

Richard's voices persisted after he graduated from high school, and they continued to play a destructive role in his life. They contributed to the breakup of his marriage (he had not told his wife about them, and she became terrified when he heard voices coming from a radio that was not on) and to a psychotic breakdown, for which he was admitted to the hospital at which he is still being treated, both with psychotherapy and with antipsychotic medication. Richard's treatment, he told me, has made his voices less frequent, and he is now able to function well. For the past eight years he has worked as a case worker for a city welfare agency, a job of unusually high stress. Yet the treatment has not erased the voices altogether. He still hears them, and he still communicates with them when he is alone.

In at least one case, Richard is grateful that the success of his treatment has been limited. Several years ago he began to hear a voice that he finds neither troubling nor distracting, and he wishes to maintain it at all costs. This voice is distinct from its predecessors, he says, both in origin and in kind. It is so distinct, in fact, that despite his experience with the phenomenon, he is unable to explain what it is like to hear it. When pressed, he resorts to metaphor: "It is like a sign. It is like an impression in my soul. I listen to the impression and I give words to it. I verbalize the impression." As opposed to his previous voices, this voice does not make Richard feel tainted with madness. On the contrary, it makes him feel gifted. "It is not easy to hear the voice," he told me. "The universe that we live in screens it out, like a prism refracts light. And so what I hear is almost like prophecy itself."

This voice, Richard said, is the voice of God.

For the past two hundred years, religion has often felt threatened by medical science in regard to how to interpret religious experiences. This conflict is somewhat different from what is sometimes said to exist between religion and science in general. Those two monolithic forces, with all they include, are often pitted against each other, but in the final analysis their problems can be resolved by banishing religion to its own camp. By all definitions, the domain of science is physical; it searches for empirical facts. The domain of religion, by contrast, is metaphysical; it reaches for causes and ultimate meanings. The skirmishes that characterize the contemporary struggle between science and religion—evolution versus creation, Africa versus Eden, and so on—are therefore best thought of as instances of religion breaching its proper borders. Held to the transcendental, religion is not threatened by science.

With religious experience, however, it is not so easy to draw a neat division of interests. Phenomena such as trances, ecstasies, visions, and voices can be considered to have a metaphysical claim—that they come from God—but they manifest themselves in the physical world, in the realms of biology, chemistry, neurology, and genetics. Even as they gesture toward the heavens, religious experiences stand rooted in the world of science, which can touch them, feel them, examine them, and attempt to explain them. The threat that the religious sometimes feel comes not so much from the success of these

investigations as it does from their inevitable effect. In the estimation of religion itself, religious experiences are exceptional and unusual. When passed through the lens of science, these qualities often
become pathology. From the perspective of the believer, the result
is the degradation of a divine entity.

In most cases this couldn't be further from the point of medical
science's interest in religious experiences, which is clinical. In *The
Varieties of Religious Experience*, William James observed that many of the
notable men and women in history who have heard religious voices
and seen religious visions have also been prone to fits of depression,
anxiety, obsessions, and compulsions. They have been the reclusive,
the anguished, the neurotic, and the maladjusted among us, people
who today would likely attract a psychiatric diagnosis. What is more,
religious experiences have often been the direct cause of mental
pathology. Direct contact with God, if there is such a thing, appears
to be one of the more painful experiences known to humankind.[3]

No figure offers a better example of this than Muhammad, who
Islamic tradition states received his revelation from Allah atop Mount
Hira in 610 CE. According to Muslim belief, Muhammad climbed
Hira to partake in a series of spiritual exercises, and on the seventeenth night of Ramadan he was visited in a cave by the Archangel
Gabriel, who descended from heaven and ordered Muhammad with
a single word: "Recite!" As a rule, prophets are initially resistant to
their calling. Muhammad didn't flout this tradition. "I am not a re-
citer!" he protested. Like all prophets, however, he was ultimately
overwhelmed by the divine presence. Against his will he found himself speaking what was to become the ninety-sixth sura, or chapter,
of the Holy Quran:

Recite in the name of the Lord who created!
He createth man from a clot of blood.

Recite: and thy Lord is the Most Bountiful
He who hath taught by the pen,
taught man what he knew not.

Muhammad reportedly received and spoke these words in a
trance, and when he came to, he was in a state of utter turmoil.
Hearing the divine voice had been so wrenching, so out of the realm
of ordinary experience, that it drove him to despair. He couldn't be
a prophet, he thought. He must be possessed or a madman—or,
worse, a poet. Hysterical, he ran to his wife for protection, cower-
ing in fear. In a panic he nearly threw himself from the mountain to
his death. In time, the early Islamic historians wrote, his anguish
lessened, but it never fully disappeared. Each time he was visited by
Gabriel—and he was for a period of several years, as the text of the
Quran accumulated—Muhammad was also visited by an all but in-
tolerable psychological pain. "Never once did I receive a revelation," he reportedly said, "without thinking that my soul had been
torn away from me."[4]

Stripped of their religious elements, Muhammad's experiences are
strikingly similar to those of many voice-hearers today who are under
psychiatric care. Marius Romme and Sandra Escher, the psychologists whose research inspired the formation of the Hearing Voices
Network, have described three phases that characterize a typical
course of voice-hearing: the "startling phase," in which the sudden
onset of voices causes anxiety, confusion, and fear; the "phase of organization," in which the hearer struggles to find a way to cope with
his experience; and "the phase of stabilization," in which the hearer
develops a more consistent way of living alongside his voices.[5] In the
way that it caused what a psychiatrist today might call panic attacks,
suicidal ideation, and mood lability, leading to a partial recovery,
Muhammad's revelation fits neatly into this scheme.

And yet an appropriate reply to this kind of medical interpretation is that an experience such as Muhammad's cannot be stripped of its religious elements without, so to speak, losing its soul. Divine voice-hearing and other religious experiences are able to withstand physiological analyses. They would even be able to withstand the elucidation of their causes, if science could find them. What they can't withstand is the popular assumption that in being investigated and described by science, as they have been for several centuries now, religious experiences have lost their claims to spiritual veracity. The imposition of science's interest in pathology onto religion's interest in value and meaning does a sort of annihilative violence. It kills the very thing it wishes to understand.

This, at any rate, has been a frequent refrain of modern religious writers for whom scientific thought has been interpreted as a thick barrier against belief. For instance, in 1995 the religious philosopher Nicholas Wolterstorff published a book-length study of divine speech based on the assumption that since the eighteenth century the claim that God speaks has become disreputable among civilized people. "What we want to know," he explained, "is whether we—intelligent, educated, citizens of the modern West—are ever entitled to believe that God speaks." Wolterstorff is solidly on the side of divine voice-hearing, but that he believes his is the minority position is clear from how mightily he labors. Under the forbidding gaze of Enlightenment philosophy, particularly the work of John Locke ("Reason must be our last judge and guide in everything"), Wolterstorff consumes nearly three hundred pages mounting a vigorous defense, marshaling a torrent of complex linguistic theory to the task. After much difficulty he finally decides that, yes, we moderns are "entitled" to believe that God speaks.[6]

For other writers the "voice of reason" has posed less of a philosophical than a spiritual problem. In his book Hearing Things, about "spiritual arts of listening" during the American Enlightenment, the historian Leigh Eric Schmidt traces this current of emotion through the work of late-twentieth-century intellectuals. What he illuminates is a deep sense among many that we are living through a period of spiritual "hearing loss"—"a predicament of listening, a fracturing of words and revealer, a loss of God's living voice." This sense of loss, which is often visceral and anguished, is in Schmidt's estimation tied up with a popular narrative that pits religious faith against all the currents of "modernization." In the words of the Jesuit historian Michel de Certeau, whom Schmidt quotes, the West has suffered irreparable spiritual damage at the hands of industrialization and commercialization and overpopulation and secularization. "Progress" has muzzled God:

> Before the "modern" period, that is, until the sixteenth or seventeenth century, [Holy Scripture] speaks. The sacred text is a voice. . . . The modern age is formed by discovering little by little that this Spoken Word is no longer heard, that it has been altered by textual corruptions and the avatars of history. One can no longer hear it. . . . The voice that today we consider altered or extinguished is above all that great cosmological Spoken Word that we notice no longer reaches us: it does not cross the centuries separating us from it. There is a disappearance of the places established by a spoken word, a loss of identities that people believed they received from a spoken word. A work of mourning.[7]

This sense of nostalgia for a time in which the heavenly sounds— the "music of the spheres"—could be more easily heard is not difficult to identify in popular culture as well. Its notes can be heard in the backlash against pervasive advertising, in the popularity of contemplative havens such as meditation classes and yoga studios, and even in the phrase *noise pollution*. And by the strange physics of sentiment, it is real because it feels real. Modernity has achieved a measure of victory because many perceive that it has. As Richard K. said to me, it is difficult today to hear the voice of God. The universe that we live in screens it out.

But as Schmidt correctly points out, when looked at from a different vantage point, this mournfulness can seem misplaced. Not everyone, it seems, has been playing by the rules of the Enlightenment. Richard is a case in point. Though raised as a Jew, when he first heard the voice of God, he converted to Christianity and began to attend a Lutheran congregation on the western end of Long Island. The congregation he joined was charismatic; it emphasized the importance of direct religious experiences such as prophesying, faith healing, and a second baptism in the Holy Spirit. Charismatic churches grew out of an even more ecstatic strain of evangelical Christianity known as Pentecostalism. It is a form of worship that adds speaking in tongues to the spiritual mix and, in little more than a hundred years of existence, has become one of the most robust faiths in the country. There are now an estimated twenty million self-described Pentecostals in the United States. Globally, the faith's rise has been even more remarkable. It has been projected that there will be more than one billion Pentecostals by 2050. "For better or worse," the historian Philip Jenkins has written, "the dominant churches of the future could have much in common with those of medieval or early modern European times."[8]

Even those Western churches that discourage charismatic religious experiences tend in practice to encourage it. Most mainstream evangelical congregations, whose members make up a significant proportion of the American population, are overtly hostile to religious enthusiasm, feeling that it distracts from the spiritual authority of Scripture. But as the anthropologist Tanya Luhrmann has recently shown, by placing an emphasis on the spiritual resonance of the Bible these congregations foster the very experiences they seem to reject. In a study of a typical evangelical church in southern California, Luhrmann found that nearly half of the congregants reported some type of sensory hallucination. These experiences were produced, she argues, through the simple act of prayer, which when pursued in an intensive enough manner can lead to a psychological state perfectly suited to unusual sensory experiences. Like Schmidt, Luhrmann concludes that the modern world is not quite so modern after all. In mainstream American churches, she writes, prayer "becomes the conduit of anomalous psychological experience it was for the early 19th century reformers, the medieval ecstatics, and the early pastoralists who sought to be still and hear the voice of God."[9]

Even further, prayer becomes the conduit for an anomalous experience that, in historical terms, is not anomalous at all. To be sure, a glance back at the history of Western religion reveals a buzzing hive of religious experiences: visions, ecstasies, trances, tongues, faith healing—and that's just in the Bible. But the voice of God has always had pride of place as the most constant and common of religious experiences. Some of this can be explained in terms of imitation, of course— that is, because prophets and saints described their religious experiences as the voice of God, others do as well. But this explanation has an inadmissible circularity: What about those whom William James called the "pattern-setters" of religious experience? Why did those original prophets and saints hear or claim to hear the voice of God? Why, since the age of the pagan Greeks, has divine voice-hearing been so intimately intertwined with the dedicated religious life? Why has it been the emblem of a personal communion with God?

john bunyan, the preacher and author, first heard the voice of God in the early 1650s while he was gambling on the village green in Elstow, a small town in the south of England. He was playing a game called cat, in which an oval piece of wood is struck with a bat on one end, made to spin into the air, and then struck again. He had just made his first hit when, as the cat rose, he heard a voice "dart from heaven into [his] soul." He tells the story in *Grace Abounding to the Chief of Sinners*, his spiritual autobiography. *"Wilt thou leave thy sins, and go to heaven?"* the voice asked. *"Or have thy sins, and go to hell?"* Reviewing the cost of the many sins he had committed thus far—fornication, inebriation, blasphemy—Bunyan concluded that leaving them now couldn't possibly save his soul. He stayed in the game. But the voice wouldn't relent. In the days and weeks that followed, it continued to harangue him:

Now about a week or fortnight after this, I was much followed by this scripture, *Simon, Simon, behold, Satan hath desired to have you . . .* and sometimes it would sound so loud within me, yea, and as it were call so strongly after me, that once above all the rest, I turned my head over my shoulder, thinking verily that some man had behind me called to me, being at a great distance methought he called so loud.

. . . Suddenly there was, as if there had rushed in at the window, the noise of wind upon me, but very pleasant, and as if I heard a voice speaking, *Didst ever refuse to be justified by the blood of Christ?*

Then breaking out in the bitterness of my soul, I said to myself, with a grievous sigh, *How can God comfort such a wretch as I?* I had no sooner said it, but this returned upon me, as an echo doth answer a voice, *This sin is not unto death.*

. . . Those words did sound suddenly within me, *He is able:* but methought the word *able* was spoke so loud unto me, it showed such a *great* word, it seemed to be writ in *great* letters, and gave such a jostle to my fear and doubt (I mean for the time it tarried with me, which was about a day) as I never had from that, all my life either before or after that.[10]

The history of Western religion as we know it today is about three thousand years old. It stretches from biblical Judaism, which considered Yahweh to be a sort of muscular tribal god, better and stronger than that of its enemies, to the myriad spiritual innovations of the modern world. Throughout this history, God has been purported to speak to man in a dizzying array of forms. Reluctant Moses heard God in a bush and immediately tried to squirm out of his prophetic mission. Samuel, during a time when "it was rare for Yahweh to speak," heard God calling his name as he lay in bed; it took him three times to realize that it was not his boss calling him. Augustine heard a child's singsong voice leading him toward Scripture as he paced nervously in his garden. *"Tolle lege!"* it cried. "Take it and read!" Joseph Smith, the founder of Mormonism, claimed to have been visited by an angel named Moroni, who directed him toward a record, inscribed on golden plates, of God's presence in America. But for all the ways in which God's voice has purportedly spoken, it is striking how consistently, across broad theological and ecclesiastical divides, the experience has been described in indirect and even downright paradoxical terms. Again and again, people who claim to hear the voice of God bracket the experience in quotation marks, as though the experience is real but not in the way we might imagine, as though it is forceful but not quite a normal perception.

John Bunyan's experience exemplifies this descriptive obliqueness. In the many instances of divine voice-hearing that he recounts in his autobiography, he never quite hears something. It is always "as if" he hears something. He does not hear God; he "thinks" he hears God. The voice does not come to his ear or to his mind; it comes to his "soul." Each time Bunyan describes the heavenly voice, he removes it from the physical world by deliberate qualification.

In this careful linguistic maneuvering, Bunyan has illustrious companions. Those who directly equate divine voice-hearing with the human senses are outliers in the history of religion. The majority have taken a detached, metaphysical approach. Sometimes, as in the case of Antoinette Bourignon, a seventeenth-century Flemish mystic, the gulf between God's voice and the human sense of sound is expressed with a Bunyanesque "as if." One passage in her autobiography reads:

> She spent whole nights in prayer, oft repeating: *Lord, what wilt thou have me to do?* And being one night in a most profound penitence, she said from the bottom of her heart: "O my Lord! What must I do to please thee? For I have nobody to teach me. Speak to my soul and it will hear thee." At that instant she heard, as if another had spoken within her: *Forsake all earthly things. Separate thyself from the love of the creatures. Deny thyself.*[11]

At other times writers have devised their own, often quite poetic, formulations of the asensory quality of the divine voice. To the author of the book of Kings, God's message came to Elijah as a "still small voice." To Saint Ambrose, in the fourth century, it came "without utterance . . . without the sound of words."[12] To Hildegard of Bingen, a twelfth-century German mystic, the voice of God spoke words that were "not like those which sound from the mouth of man, but like a trembling flame, or like a cloud stirred by the clean air."[13] Thomas à Kempis, a fifteenth-century German monk, wrote in his influential *Imitatio Christi,* "Blessed are those ears that receive the whispers of the divine voice, and listen not to the whisperings of the world. Blessed indeed are those ears that hearken not to the voice which soundeth outwardly, but unto the truth which teacheth inwardly."[14] Finally, in sixteenth-century Spain, Teresa of Ávila, the most articulate and gifted of devotional writers, described what she referred to as the "locution"—in the words of one scholar, "supernatural words that fall upon the inner ear with the authenticity of actual speech." Teresa wrote:

The words are perfectly formed, but they are not heard with the physical ear. Yet they are received much more clearly than if they were so heard; and however hard one resists it is impossible to shut them out. For when, in ordinary life, we do not wish to hear, we can close our ears or attend to something else; and in that way although we may hear we do not understand. But when God speaks to the soul like this, there is no alternative; I have to listen whether I like it or not, and to devote my whole attention to understanding what God wishes me to understand.[15]

Why has the language of divine voice-hearing been so frequently and scrupulously removed from the language of the bodily senses? One answer to this question is that the experiences are reflections of religious doctrine. Mystics are often assumed, incorrectly, to be individualistic in the extreme, revolutionary followers of their own spiritual consciences. But even for those for whom this is remotely true, the religious atmosphere has already been set in place by thinkers of such persuasiveness that their interpretations of Scripture and faith have become impossible to avoid inside or outside of the cloister. As the classicist Gilbert Murray once noted, religious development occurs by a process of agglomeration. New ideas settle upon the old, like sand on a coastal shelf.[16] And one of the fundamental sedimentary layers of Western faith is the conception of God as an exclusively metaphysical force—a being incompatible with the human body.

Some theologians have expressed this idea in terms that leave no room for misunderstanding. Maimonides, the twelfth-century rabbi and philosopher, argues in his *Guide for the Perplexed* that even the biblical prophets did not hear God by way of the physical senses, as they so often purport. Rather, they used the language of the senses to refer to the *idea* of God. How else can man explain his spiritual connection with the deity, Maimonides asks, than to use the language of the senses? The senses are all man knows; they are how he understands and refers to the world. But to think that man could actually receive a physical visitation from heaven runs counter to the divine separateness of God.[17]

Maimonides's viewpoint has more conventionally been expressed in terms of a sensory hierarchy, with the metaphorical, spiritual senses placed at the top of the heap and the literal, bodily senses placed at the bottom. A fifth-century analysis of Genesis by Saint Augustine exemplifies this scheme. Taking the act of reading as his starting point, Saint Augustine divided the sense of vision into three parts: "When we read this one commandment: 'Thou shalt love thy neighbor as thyself,' we experience three kinds of vision. One through the eyes, by which we see the [written] letters; a second through the spirit, by which we think of our neighbor even when he is absent; and third, through an intuition of the mind, by which we see and understand love itself." The psychologists Theodore Sarbin and Joseph Juhasz have termed these three classes of sensory experience the "corporeal," the "imaginative," and the "intellectual," and it is their understanding that the religiously devout tend to value them in ascending order. "The mystical world-view regards these three types of [experience], from corporeal to intellectual, as progressively more real, since they relate to objects progressively less subject to change," Sarbin and Juhasz write. "Thus a basic duty of man is to struggle for ever higher levels of [experience], ever greater detachment from the world, regardless of the content of the experience."[18]

That the Augustinian hierarchy has remained an apt and influential model for divine sensory experience is suggested by Richard K.'s voice-hearing, which fits the scheme both in kind and in valuation. Even today, Richard hears all three classes of voices, and although he has come to accept them all, the only one he cherishes is what he calls his spiritual "gift."

Nevertheless, doctrine alone can't explain why descriptions of divine voice-hearing have so often been metaphorical. After all, theology is written by men and women who have had their own encounters with faith, and in the overwhelming majority of cases those encounters were in the metaphorical mode. Experience, in other words, precedes and dictates doctrine. What is more, doctrine can't explain why hearing, and not some other sense, has been the metaphor of choice for mystics and saints in search of a way to describe a direct perception of God's presence. Why is sound so suitable as a spiritual metaphor?

Two twentieth-century philosophers, both Jesuits, have tried to answer this question. The late Walter Ong, of Saint Louis University, wrote of the ear as if it were the primary organ of the spirit. To Ong, hearing was primal to faith because it is the most intimate and existential of senses. "Sight isolates, sound incorporates," he wrote in *Orality and Literacy*, the book for which he is best known. "Whereas sight situates the observer outside what he views, at a distance, sound pours into the hearer. . . . By contrast with vision, the dissecting sense, sound is thus a unifying sense. . . . The auditory ideal, by contrast, is a harmony, a putting together."[19] It was an argument he had made fifteen years earlier in *The Presence of the Word*:

> *Sound is more real or existential than other sense objects, despite the fact that it is also more evanescent.* Sound itself is related to present actuality rather than to past or future. It must emanate from a source here and now discernibly active, with the result that involvement with sound is involvement with the present, with here-and-now existence and activity. . . . Moreover, since sound is indicative of here-and-now activity, the word as sound establishes here-and-now personal presence. Abraham knew God's presence when he heard his "voice." (We should not assume that the Hebrews necessarily thought of a phys-

ical sound here, only that what happened to Abraham was more like hearing than anything else.) "After these events God put Abraham to a test. He said to him, 'Abraham.' He answered, 'Here I am' " (Gen. 22:1). As establishing personal presence, the word has immediate religious significance, particularly in the Hebrew and Christian tradition, where so much is made of a personal, concerned God.[20]

Jacques Ellul, of the University of Bordeaux, wrote in similar terms about the holiness of sound. In *The Humiliation of the Word*, Ellul decried the visuality of the modern West as having resulted in a "rupture with God" and produced what can be read most profitably as a prayer for the spoken word as an evanescent spiritual force, the object of belief itself: "Thus speech is basically presence. It is something alive. . . . The word is never an object you can turn this way and that, grasp, and preserve for tomorrow or some distant day when you have time to deal with it. . . . The word exists now. It is something immediate and can never be manipulated. Either it exists or it doesn't." Like Maimonides, Ellul reduced divine voice-hearing to a metaphor for God's presence:

It goes without saying that when we read that God speaks, it does not mean that he pronounces words and that he has a vocabulary and follows syntactical rules. This comparison is used of course to help us understand the action and person of God. Only a very obtuse and rankly materialistic person could fail to understand what the Bible says so clearly. He would have to refuse to accept this language for what it is: metaphorical, an analogy, not an anthropomorphism.[21]

For those of us who are not devout, who have no experience with the search for the meaning of God or for a spiritual presence in human life, arguments such as these can be taken either as fodder for skepticism or as the illumination of a foreign sphere of experience. What it cannot be taken as is the final word. Couched in metaphorical terms, divine voice-hearing does not wither away but remains, however removed from the sense of sound, as an experience. Something happens when a believer claims to hear the voice of God.

In 1964, the psychologists Theodore Barber and David Calverley asked seventy-eight secretarial students to close their eyes and listen to a recording of Bing Crosby's "White Christmas," at the time the best-selling single in history. The subjects did as they were asked, but Barber and Calverley never placed the needle on the record. Instead, after thirty seconds of silence, they asked the volunteers to rate the vividness of their experiences. Nearly half stated that they had clearly heard the song in their head; 5 percent stated that they had actually heard the song playing in the room. An "auditory image" could be generated from suggestion alone, Barber and Calverley concluded.[22]

The White Christmas test, as it is known, has been replicated several times and in several different ways, both with psychiatric patients and with "normals," and it is often cited in support of the point that, as the psychologist Richard Bentall has written, "many more people at least have the capacity to hallucinate than a strictly medical model implies should be the case."[23] More specifically, however, it has helped highlight the point that a person's state of mind can play a critical role in the production of hallucinations. The subjects of the experiment were neither schizophrenics nor professed hallucinators, but Barber and Calverley were able to make several of them hear a song simply by telling them that they should expect to hear one. By way of a suggestion, a group of nonhallucinators were temporarily made into hallucinators.

The role of mental state had been noted in the literature of hallucination before Barber and Calverley. Indeed, it has always been the most sensible way to explain why the content of hallucinations varies according to the time and place in which a person lives. For example, visions of the Devil are more often reported in the developing world than in the West. Today, most hallucinations reported by psychiatric patients have technological themes (for example, the CIA planting a radio receiver in a person's fillings), but in the Middle Ages they were invariably religious. People living in tribal cultures are more susceptible to hallucinations of ancestors than people living in industrialized cultures. The superstitious Victorians even saw ghosts more frequently than people of other eras.

But the White Christmas test suggests the importance of a more specific and more personal state of mind than that which is dictated by cultural atmosphere. It suggests that people who hallucinate are more credulous than people who do not. It suggests that the capacity to hallucinate is directly related to the tendency to believe.

The hypothesis that hallucinators are uncommonly credulous was tested more explicitly in 1985 by Murray Alpert, a psychiatrist at New York University. Alpert told three groups of patients—hallucinating schizophrenics, nonhallucinating schizophrenics, and hallucinating alcoholics—that they would hear voices as they listened to white noise. The results of the experiment supported the results of the White Christmas test. Alpert's hallucinating subjects were much more likely than the nonhallucinators to report hearing voices and were even more likely to do so if the instructions Alpert gave them were detailed.[24]

Studies such as these have helped underscore the importance of suggestibility in human experience. They have also played a key part in the search for a universal model of hallucination, something that researchers have been attempting to devise for several decades without much consensus. The psychologists Peter Slade and Richard Bentall, for example, have used the evidence spurred by the White Christmas test in support of an argument that hallucinators suffer from a dysfunction of the ability to distinguish between public and private events, a skill that they refer to as "reality discrimination."[25] But although the lack of this skill is clearly related to the subject of divine voice-hearing, the credulity of hallucinators can lead to a psychological state that is perhaps even more closely related to the phenomenon and more directly evocative of the experience to which it refers: passivity.

The subject of passivity has been raised in relation to hallucinations by the philosopher Daniel Dennett. In his popular book *Consciousness Explained*, Dennett observed that hallucinators often claim to be in some sort of reverie when they hear their voices or see their visions. Indeed, a passive state of receptivity seemed to Dennett to be so endemic to reports of the phenomenon that it had to be critical. "Hallucinators usually just stand and marvel," he wrote. "Typically, they feel no desire to probe, challenge, or query, and take no steps to interact with the apparitions. It is [therefore] likely . . . that this passivity is not an inessential feature of hallucination but a necessary precondition for any moderately detailed and sustained hallucination to occur."[26]

There are a couple of reasons not to take Dennett's conclusion at face value. The lack of objective scrutiny on behalf of hallucinators might, after all, be due to the simple fact that the experience can be terrifying and therefore hardly conducive to a clinical stance. There is also the influence of culture to consider; as contemporary voice-hearers well know, hallucinations are a psychiatric phenomenon meant to be feared, not observed. And yet there is also a great deal of evidence in support of Dennett's observation. Hallucinators usually do "just stand and marvel." My father, for example, was often in a pseudohypnotic state when he heard his voices. During hallucinatory episodes, my mother remembers, he would stare off into the middle distance, "lost to the world." And if this is true of voice-hearers such as my father, who was not religious, for divine voice-hearers it is nearly definitive. From Saint Paul on the road to Damascus to Richard K. in his charismatic church, believers who have claimed to hear the voice of God or his messengers have claimed to do so in a state of psychological surrender, if not outright trance.[27]

Several prominent scholars of religion have drawn the conclusion that passivity is the psychological state that lends the literature of divine voice-hearing its indirect quality. "True auditions," Evelyn Underhill wrote in her classic *Mysticism*, using the traditional term for voices, "are usually heard when the mind is in a state of deep absorption without conscious thought."[28] William James argued similarly in *The Varieties of Religious Experience*: "[W]e cannot, I think, avoid the conclusion that in religion we have a department of human nature with unusually close relations to the transmarginal or subliminal region."[29]

And yet, as both Underhill and James knew and lamented, it is just this state of absorption or passivity or trance—whatever one wants to call it—that has made the saint, the prophet, and the mystic seem to be natural subjects for psychiatry. It was a territorialism that angered Underhill almost as much as what was attempted by the literal-minded on the opposite side. Fighting on the "eternal battle-ground" of religious experience, she saw the dogmatic forces of science and religion foolishly duking it out:

On the one hand we have the strangely named rationalists, who feel that they have settled the matter once and for all by calling attention to the obvious parallels which exist between the bodily symptoms of acute spiritual stress and the bodily symptoms of certain forms of disease. . . . French psychology, in particular, revels in this sort of thing: and would, if it had its way, fill the wards of the Salpêtrière with patients from the Roman Calendar. . . . As against all this, the intransigent votaries of the supernatural seem determined to play into the hands of their foes. They pin themselves, for no apparent reason, to the objective reality and absolute value of visions, voices, and other experiences which would be classed, in any other department of life, as the harmless results of a vivid imagination.[30]

The armies of science and religion are still fighting, of course. But the people about whom they fight remain largely noncombatants, doing their best to attend to the sounds beyond the fray and then straining past those into a world of silent messages, which they deliver to the world in words we can understand.

7

ENIGMATICAL DICTATION

Eloquence is heard; *poetry is* overheard.

—JOHN STUART MILL, "Thoughts on Poetry and Its Varieties"

In 1981, Sarah Arvio, a twenty-six-year-old poetry student in Columbia University's graduate writing program, went to hear James
Merrill speak. Merrill was then one of the most celebrated poets in
the country. He had already published most of the work that would
be collected the following year in *The Changing Light at Sandover,* an epic
trilogy that many consider Merrill's greatest artistic achievement and
some place among the greatest works of twentieth-century literature. Yet even before its full publication, *Sandover* had gained the bulk
of its attention less for its poetic quality than for its unusual genesis.
For more than twenty years, Merrill claimed, he and his lover, the
writer and artist David Jackson, had used a homemade Ouija board
and, as a marker, a teacup to communicate with spirits from beyond
the grave. Merrill had turned these allegedly supernatural dis-
patches—from Jesus, Muhammad, W. H. Auden, Maria Callas, a
first-century Greek Jew named Ephraim, and so on—into the core of
his masterwork, around and through which he wove his own elegant verse.

Arvio had undergone similar experiences. Seven years before, her
twin sister had grasped her hand and directed a pencil across a sheet
of blank paper. After her sister let go, Arvio was amazed to find that,

when she used no effort of her own, the pencil continued to write in her hand, making "letters and sweeps and curls" on the page. Since that time, Arvio had practiced this method of so-called automatic writing, and over the years the markings had become more articulate. Eventually they'd begun to dispense predictions and advice. She'd filled notebook after notebook with these jottings.

After Merrill's reading, Arvio approached him and revealed her own method of receiving spiritual messages. "I do it, too," she said. "I use a pen."

"Oh, I envy you," Merrill responded warmly. "A cup is so cumbersome."

"But all mine talk to me about is love."

"That's as it should be," he said. "You're young. Love is the subject of the young. Later, they'll talk about other things."

He was only half right. Arvio's "visitors," as she has come to call them, still talk primarily about love, but they have branched out in other ways. More than a decade after meeting Merrill, Arvio was out walking in Manhattan, where she lives and works as a translator for the United Nations, when she heard a voice speaking what seemed to be lines of poetry. She stopped, took out a pen and a pad of paper, and began to write down what she heard. The words came quickly, with "swirls and flourishes," and when they had finished, to her surprise, Arvio had almost the full text of a poem. She titled it "Floating."

I said some nonsense or other to them
and they mocked back, "but we're your one design,"
or "you're our one design"—which was it?

The pen slipped and capered on the page,
escorted by ripplings in the atmosphere
like breeze with nothing to blow against.

"We wear no form or figure of our own
—a wisp, a thread, a twig, a shred of smoke—
to tell us from the motions of the air.

We'd love to live in even a bubble,
to wrap around its glossy diaphanous,
reaching and rounding, as slinkily real

as a morning stretch or a dance in a field.
But we know only this air, and memory,
once, or several times, removed and turned,

the pang of a once-had, a maybe-again,
that shifting half-light, our home and habitat,
those hours, soft-toned, windless, that favor passage,

the usual relay of twilights. And,
how often a century? The sun eclipsed,
that 'created' half-light, not dusk or dawn:

us glowing through, our light, our element,
in which we show best, glow best, what we are.
Yesterday some snowflakes slipped through us,

refreshing kisses passing through our heat.
Ah, we wanted to say. If we could have,
we'd have laughed right out from sheer surprise."

And what else? "We've got you to stand for us."
And I have you, I said, to float for me.[1]

It was the first of many poems that would come to Arvio with
great speed and force in the following months. They came to her on

airplanes and on trains, in bathtubs and in restaurants, at home and at work. Sometimes they came out whole, and she had to rush to record them. Other times they came out in fragments, and she had to fill in the remaining lines herself. Sometimes they did not come at all; for two years Arvio received not a single word. But after six years of waiting, listening, recording, and editing, she finally had enough poems to put together her first book. *Visits from the Seventh*, a cycle of forty-nine poems in two "rounds," was published in 2002.

Visits from the Seventh was a remarkable debut. After a long apprenticeship—she was forty-seven when *Visits* was published—Arvio delivered a work that was allusive, playful, idiosyncratic, controlled, and deeply moving. The critics received it well. And as with *Sandover*, in the company of which it has been placed, they were quick to note the unusual manner in which the book was composed. They were fascinated by her ethereal voices, which served double duty as the book's impetus and its central object of inquiry. The poet Mark Strand commented that they "drop in and out like a beautiful quixotic chorus." Edward Hirsch wrote that Arvio "has been channeling voices, splitting herself off and listening to her inner musings, carrying on dialogues with the dead. She has turned herself into a poet of two minds, a spiritual apprentice to those 'abstracted from humanness on the physical plane.'" (The quotation is Arvio's.)

But Arvio's visitors were not so easy to understand as Merrill's glamorous ghosts. For one, they spoke in so many different tones of voice that they were less like a chorus than a cacophony. In the book there are visitors who attempt to comfort the narrator of the poems ("Haven't we sat with you for hour on hour?"); those who admonish her ("But how could you tell him? Never ever / have we allowed—have we intimated— / you should share our visits with anyone"); those who mock her attempts to explain their existence ("The sixth [sense] is sex, silly. The *seventh* is / our sense, the one we sometimes share with you"); even those who try to deceive her ("There are ones out there as false as any / [a 42nd Street of the Heavens]"). The drama in Arvio's book emerges from her attempts to make sense of these disparate and often difficult voices—to separate the useful from the useless, the healthful from the harmful, the illuminating from the obscuring.

Another reason it is difficult to encapsulate Arvio's visitors is that although she herself often refers to them as "voices," they appear to have no clear sensory bearing. It was a point she took pains to make clear to me in a long, carefully worded e-mail written in 2004 from Rome, where she was working on her second book, *Sono*.

I want to explain that I don't "hear" voices. Or rather, I don't have auditory hallucinations. These are voices that separate themselves from the other voices of my thoughts; a sudden, somewhat different voice comes forward, and, recognizing what it is, I begin to write. They aren't voices outside myself; they don't resemble a voice in a room, for instance.

Indeed, her visitors' lack of physical substance makes it difficult for Arvio to say exactly what her visitors do resemble.

I actually don't know how I could know where mine come from, how I have managed to sort the good from the bad, whether I am dabbling in the occult at all. Whether my voices are figments of my imagination, or whether they come from elsewhere. What could tell me? On the other hand, I'm surprised by what I write. I find a kind of web of connections that I can't imagine creating on my own. I tap into a source of knowledge I don't think I have, or perhaps might barely have. Sometimes I think I must be accessing some sort of collective information source, like Jung's collective unconscious. I'm fascinated, enriched, and baffled.

For all the uncertainty that they possess and even have bred, however, Arvio insists that she has learned a specific artistic lesson from her visitors, one that James Merrill seems to have learned as well. "I have learned," she wrote, "never to force my hand, never to apply my will. My best poems are the ones that came to me with no effort."

In the early nineteenth century, toward the end of his life, William Blake was looking through a sketchbook owned by the painter John Constable when he came across a drawing Constable had made of an avenue of fir trees on London's Hampstead Heath. "Why, this is not drawing, but *inspiration!*" Blake exclaimed. "I never knew it before," Constable replied, "I meant it for drawing."[2]

When this brief exchange took place—the only conversation recorded between the two men—the phenomenon to which Blake was referring was at a low historical point, as Constable's bewildered response suggests. The Enlightenment was in its full rationalist bloom, and the mainstream of poetry and the visual arts was dominated by the ideal of reason, dedicated to the careful explication and imitation of nature. Constable's work would influence the more imaginative Romantics who followed, but it was well suited to his times. His paintings, highly detailed scenes of English rural life, reflect a meticulous sensibility. Still, he undoubtedly understood Blake's comment. The word *inspiration* might have been rarely used in the period, but it still carried the meaning Blake intended.

Today, we can't be so certain he would be understood correctly. When Blake died, in 1827, *inspiration* carried only two meanings: the act of drawing air into the lungs, which is its etymological meaning, and a related religious one—the infusion of ideas into the mind by God or gods. As the nineteenth century progressed, however, a third meaning—one more suggestive of a heightening of everyday feeling—began to creep into use and supplant the old. Late in the century one can find the word *inspiration* used in this new way in sermons, poems, and essays. By the early twentieth century the new meaning had overtaken one of its predecessors; Webster's 1913 dictionary places it second behind "the act . . . of breathing." By the turn of the millennium, it had triumphed even over respiration. The fourth edition of the *American Heritage Dictionary*, published in 2000, defines inspiration first as the "stimulation of the mind or emotions to a high level of feeling or activity," as in, "Our teacher was an inspiration to us all."

More than two centuries removed, can we possibly understand what Blake was trying to say? Is the old meaning alive in the way it was for Blake, who attributed to it some of his greatest works: *The Marriage of Heaven and Hell, Milton, Visions of the Daughters of Albion?* Writing in 1888, Friedrich Nietzsche already thought it necessary to spell out the experience to readers who were unaccustomed to hearing about it. "Can anyone at the end of this nineteenth century have any distinct notion of what poets of a more vigorous period meant by inspiration?" he asked in *Ecce Homo.*

> If not, I should like to describe it. Provided one has the slightest remnant of superstition left, one can hardly reject completely the idea that one is the mere incarnation, or mouthpiece, or medium of some almighty power. The notion of revelation describes the condition quite simply; by which I mean that something profoundly convulsive and disturbing suddenly becomes visible and audible with indescribable definiteness and exactness. One hears—one does not seek; one takes—one does not ask who gives: a thought flashes out like lightning, inevitably without hesitation—I never had any choice.[3]

One hundred twenty years later this description would seem to be, on the surface of things, less pertinent to the act of artistic creation than it ever was before. Critics today tend to treat those artists who claim external sources for their work as outliers at best, and at worst, charlatans. A common explanation for Merrill's Ouija board experiments, for example, is that he was creating an artistic role for his less productive lover. And yet if we don't live in a "vigorous period," as Nietzsche called those times in which artistic inspiration was openly declared, or in a time in which artistic creation is experienced in revelatory terms, that doesn't mean the core of the phenomenon—that temporary erasure of the will that Nietzsche described—is irrelevant. When we look beneath the surface, it becomes obvious that artists continue to experience inspiration intuitively as a natural conduit of their art. And those who do so most routinely—and in a manner that can tell us the most about the development and essence of the phenomenon—are poets.

Theodore Roethke once revealed in a lecture how his poem "The Dance" came about. It was 1952, and he was living alone in a large house in Edmonds, Washington. He was forty-four years old and teaching poetry at the University of Washington, in Seattle. For weeks Roethke had been teaching his students the five-beat line and reading exemplars of that form: Walter Raleigh and John Davies. For months, however, he had been unable to write anything of worth himself, and he had come to consider himself a fraud. Then, one evening, Roethke was sitting at home when "The Dance" suddenly came to him. It came quickly and with great strength, and in less than an hour he was done:

> I felt, I knew, that I had hit it. I walked around, and I wept; and I knelt
> down—I always do after I've written what I know is a good piece.
> But at the same time I had, as God is my witness, the actual sense of

a Presence—as if Yeats himself were *in* that room. The experience
was in a way terrifying, for it lasted at least half an hour. That house,
I repeat, was charged with a psychic presence: the very walls seemed
to shimmer. I wept for joy. . . . He, they—the poets dead—were
with me.[4]

This anecdote is an example of what we might call "modern" inspiration. It exhibits two complementary mechanisms. First, there is
a conscious attentiveness to craft, as exemplified by Roethke's weeks-
long studying and teaching of the five-beat line. Second, there is the
unconscious activity of the creative faculty, as exemplified by the subconscious composition and miraculous-seeming arrival of the
poem—which, indeed, carried the same meter as the poems Roethke
had slowly been working into his bones:

Is that dance slowing in the mind of man
That made him think the universe could hum?
The great wheel turns its axle when it can. . . .[5]

Reception and revision: These are the two essential ingredients in
the composition of poetry, and authors have naturally altered the
measurements of the recipe to suit their tastes. Percy Bysshe Shelley
relied almost exclusively on inspiration and could not write without
it. "Poetry is not like reasoning," he argued, "a power to be exerted
according to the determination of the will. A man cannot say, 'I will
compose poetry.' "[6] As a consequence he left behind mostly fragments and fell into despair when inspiration was absent. Rilke spent
years waiting for many of his poems to arrive, which they sometimes did with unaccountable force. Of his *Sonnets to Orpheus*, he
wrote, "They are perhaps the most mysterious, even to me, in their
way of arising and imposing themselves on me, the most enigmati-

cal dictation I have ever sustained and achieved." But he also composed when inspiration was dim and fickle.[7] He wrote to his wife that his *New Poems* was the result of *"work*, the transition from inspiration that comes to that which is summoned and seized."[8] Pushkin combined inspiration and revision into an apparently seamless whole, writing in a heady rush of enthusiasm and afterward, in a like-minded state, blotting out up to three-quarters of what he had set down. A. E. Housman's verse would often "bubble up" from some unseen place, but later it needed to be "taken in hand and completed by the brain, which was apt to be a matter of trouble and anxiety, involving trial and disappointment, and sometimes ending in failure."[9]

If poets have differed greatly in the level of emphasis they placed on inspiration, however (as well, of course, as in the artistic success they have been able to draw from it), they have not differed greatly in the quality of the experience itself. There are a few examples of poems that have come to their authors with physical force, but modern inspiration has almost always been asensory in nature—psychological rather than physical, silent rather than vocal, a metaphorical rather than an actual voice. This is a notable historical development. Poetic inspiration was not always of the mind alone. It was once also of the body and of the ear. This fact represents the most substantial gulf between the composition of ancient poetry and that of modern poetry.

The best example of ancient inspiration is the poet Hesiod's eighth-century BCE *Theogony*, the earliest known genealogy of the Greek gods and one of the canonical texts of classical Greece. The *Theogony* begins, as many poems in ancient times did, with an invocation of the Muses of Olympia. Hesiod was a shepherd, and he writes that the Muses came and spoke to him as he was tending his flock on Mount Helicon. "You shepherds of the wilderness," they said, "poor fools, nothing but bellies,

we know how to say many false things
    that seem like true sayings,
but we also know how to speak the truth
    when we wish to."
       So they spoke, these mistresses of words,
    daughters of great Zeus,
and they broke off and handed me a staff
    of strong-growing
olive shoot, a wonderful thing;
    they breathed a voice into me,
and power to sing the story of things
    of the future, and things past.[10]

As with the gods in the Homeric epics, critics have interpreted the role of the Muses in Hesiod in various ways—as a traditional representation of the arts and sciences, as a symbol of religious piety, even as an early example of literary self-aggrandizement. But unlike with the Homeric gods, who serve an obvious narrative function, few critics have been able to dismiss completely the physical force of the Muses. In the *Iliad*, the gods are characters in the poem. In the *Theogony*, they seem to write the poem itself.

That said, the exact extent to which Hesiod meant his Muses to be taken literally—did they really speak to him?—is a matter of conjecture. Until the mid-nineteenth century, when references to them all but petered out, poets employed the Muses almost as a matter of routine, either as a metaphor for poetic rapture or as formal shorthand for the entire classical tradition. This allegorical usage, which has become an inexorable part of the European literary lexicon, has made it difficult to see the Muses for what they might originally have been—a physical experience of literary inspiration.

The most convincing piece of evidence that the Muses were physically heard can be found in the classicist E. R. Dodds's 1951 land-mark study *The Greeks and the Irrational.* Considering the possibility that Hesiod actually heard the Muses speaking to him, Dodds noted that the poet's experience took place on a remote mountaintop. The phenomenon of hearing voices and seeing things in solitary and ex-treme settings, Dodds observed, is known even in modern times. For example, on an arduous trek across a remote Antarctic island, in 1915, the explorer Ernest Shackleton hallucinated an additional hiker. He described the experience in his famous memoir, *South:*

> I know that during that long and racking march of thirty-six hours over the unnamed mountains and glaciers of South Georgia [Island] it seemed to me often that we were four, not three. I said nothing to my companions on the point, but afterwards Worsley said to me, "Boss, I had a curious feeling on the march that there was another person with us." Crean confessed to the same idea. One feels "the dearth of human words, the roughness of mortal speech" in trying to describe things intangible. . . .[11]

A more recent example of hallucinations occurring in extremities of fatigue and silence appears in *Storms of Silence,* a book by the British adventurer Joe Simpson, who is well known from the movie *Touch-ing the Void.* In a chapter titled "Ghost Stories," Simpson describes voices he heard while ascending Huascarán, Peru's highest mountain:

> For a moment, in the silence after the shouted conversation, I thought the voices had gone but then I heard them again far back on the edge of my hearing. They had plagued me ever since we had left the high camp at the Garganta col at two in the morning. At first I thought I might have left my Walkman on with the volume turned down. On checking, I found it switched off and carefully wrapped in a scarf in the top packet of my sack. I pulled back the balaclava

exposing my ears to the icy wind, thinking that it might be the rub-
bing sounds of the fabric. The voices were still there. . . . When they
surged loudly there was something oddly familiar about them. I
dredged my memory, trying to think what it was. Although muted
and distant, the noise was instantly recognizable as human voices and
laughter. It had the same cadences, the rising and falling sounds of
murmured conversation, and every now and then the high-pitched
shriek of a child's laughter at play. *Child's laughter. That was it!* I could
hear children playing in a schoolyard.[12]

Shortly afterward, Simpson learned that he was at the site of an av-
alanche that had killed more than eighteen thousand people in a
nearby village twenty years before.

These modern examples are easier to grasp than historical evidence that bases Hesiod's inspiration in the peculiar consciousness of
the ancient mind. For instance, the psychologist Julian Jaynes has
shown that the inhabitants of ancient civilizations often heard aloud
the voices of idols and figurines, which they produced in great numbers for religious purposes. One example of this is a passage from an
Assyrian letter dating from the first millennium BCE:

I have taken note of the portents. . . . I had them recited in order before Shamash . . . the [statue] of Akkad brought up visions before me
and cried out: "What pernicious portent have you tolerated in the
royal image?" Again it spoke: . . . it made inquiry concerning Ningal-
Iddina, Shamash-Ibni, and Na'id-Marduk. Concerning the rebellion
in the land it said: "Take the wall cities one after the other, that a
cursed one will not be able to stand before the Gardener."[13]

The Old Testament also contains evidence that the inhabitants of ancient civilizations heard religious statues speaking. In the book of
Ezekiel, the king of Babylon consults with several teraphim, or idols,

in order to learn how he should behave: "For the king of Babylon has halted at the fork where these two roads diverge, to take the omens. He has shaken the arrows, questioned the household gods, inspected the liver."[14]

The Old Testament is also a good place to turn because it contains the accounts of Hesiod's contemporaries the Hebrew prophets, all eighteen of whom claimed to have heard and to have obeyed the voice of Yahweh. Like Hesiod, Amos lived during the eighth century BCE, and like Hesiod, he was a shepherd who heard a voice while tending his flock in the fields. Predictably, he protested and was overcome: "I am not a prophet . . . nor do I belong to a prophetic brotherhood. I am merely a herdsman and dresser of sycamore-figs. But Yahweh took me as I followed the flock, and Yahweh said to me, 'Go and prophesy to my people Israel.' "[15] The opening passage of the Amos book suggests that he received his call to prophesy audibly:

Yahweh roars from Zion,
and makes himself heard from Jerusalem;
the shepherds' pastures mourn,
and the crown of Carmel dries up.[16]

To be sure, even if Amos and the rest of the prophets heard the voice of Yahweh audibly, this doesn't prove that Hesiod heard the voices of the Muses in the same way. It doesn't even prove that he intended for his readers to believe that he did. Yet the sources we have do cohere in a historical picture of a time in which metaphor had not yet infiltrated the marrow of experience—in which the hearing of a voice was still in possession of a physical vitality that was intimately associated with highly valued callings, be they religious or literary. This may not serve as proof that the ancients heard voices, but it does spur the question: What was it that caused that vitality to recede into silence?

AS mentioned earlier, the central theme of Julian Jaynes's controversial book is that over the course of centuries there occurred a profound shift in the neurological structure of the human mind. To Jaynes, the precursor to internalized consciousness as we know it today was a tendency toward unbidden auditory hallucinations caused by a physical split between the hemispheres of the brain. It is a speculative theory, but it is built on firm ground. The record of how man has conceived of the agency of his own experiences altered demonstrably during the time we have been able to observe it.

Poetic inspiration provides us with one of the better examples of the mutability of human consciousness. By comparing Hesiod with Theodore Roethke, or Hesiod with any of the recent poets who have emphasized the work of the unconscious mind in the act of poetic creation—W. B. Yeats, A. E. Housman, Allen Ginsberg—we are able to witness two modes of artistic creation, the first "primitive" and willless, the second "modern" and contingent on the intellect. But the question of what caused this shift from pole to pole cannot be answered without first identifying the quality that altered between them. This preliminary question can be answered in reference to the poets' relationship to language. To Hesiod and the ancients, language was by its nature something to be heard; it had physical immediacy. To Roethke and the moderns, language is something to be thought; it has psychological immediacy. What has occurred between the two modes of creation seems to be the death of the aurality of language.

There are many, of course, who would take exception to the proposition that language is no longer audible at its core. To an extent these dissenters have a point. There are today significant pockets of the culture in which aurality is considered language's defining characteristic. Many of these pockets are religious, as in the case of those branches of Christianity that place a premium on ecstatic spiritualism. Some, however, are poetic. For instance, in 1950 the poet Charles Olson published a manifesto, *Projective Verse*, that called for a poetry based on the breath of the poet rather than on logic or meter. That call has since been answered by many poets. One of these, Peter Davidson, states his intention in the foreword to his collection *Breathing Room*, to attend closely to the sensory basis of poetry:

> The breath is the most intimate aspect of our existence. It connects us to the biosphere. Breath makes our voice operate. It enables oxygen to penetrate our bodies. Breath lends us rhyme and meter, the means by which poetry came into existence. Time may be able to teach us new ways of using our minds, but I very much doubt whether it can teach us anything new about ways of breathing—or even about what happens to our being when we can no longer breathe. Poetry began, I think, as a mnemonic device to enable an illiterate populace to remember prayers, to recite the order of worship, or, in a more secular use, to recount the inventories of warehouses in ancient Babylon. That's why we wrote in rhyme and meter, so that we could remember what we thought we had compiled; hence the connection of words to breath to sense to mind to memory to rhythm to emotion to memory.[17]

What is expressed here is an aspect of poetic creation that hasn't changed in nearly three thousand years. Language can never be separated from the lungs and from the breath. It was first spoken; in its original state, language is audible speech. Yet as Davison admits, inadvertently or not, to place an emphasis on the aurality of language in the modern world smacks of nostalgia. In the middle of an encomium for breath, he lapses into the past tense, as if he is making what he knows to be a conservative plea for a return to a purer time, a time in which body and language were more intimately related.

This sense of nostalgia reflects an important truth about the history of voice-hearing. As shown, the mournfulness that is sometimes expressed by religious thinkers about the loss of the culture's ability to truly hear, whatever values are woven into that act, is misplaced. At the same time, hearing has lost something vital, so that it is often necessary to speak of it as if it were in quotation marks—as something internal rather than external, as "hearing."

This shift from literal to metaphorical auditory experience is often overlooked, and one consequence has been that the reports of voice-hearers have frequently been misinterpreted. William Blake is a case in point. During his lifetime, Blake frequently claimed that his art came from external, divine sources. About his epic poem *Milton*, he wrote to one of his patrons: "I have written this poem from immediate Dictation twelve or sometimes twenty or thirty lines at a time without Premeditation & even against my Will. [The] Time it has taken in writing was thus renderd Non Existent . . . & an immense Poem Exists which seems to be the Labour of a long Life all producd without Labour or Study."[18] And later: "I may praise [the poem] since I dare not pretend to be any other than the Secretary the Authors are in Eternity."[19] To another patron Blake wrote that he preferred the countryside to the city because there the "voices of Celestial inhabitants are more distinctly heard & their forms more distinctly seen."[20]

In exchange for these confessions, Blake was often accused of insanity—which was no light matter considering that several of his contemporaries, such as William Cowper and Christopher Smart, were for a time incarcerated in asylums. One reviewer, commenting on Blake's illustrations, described them as "the offspring of morbid fancy," and of Blake's poetry wrote, "Should he again essay to climb the Parnassian heights, his friends would do well to restrain his wanderings by the strait waistcoat."[21] Others, though less harsh, were no less dismissive. Late in life Blake was walking down a London street when a young girl asked her father who he was. "He is a strange man," her father replied. "He thinks he sees spirits."[22] What these critics missed was that Blake was not speaking literally. He was describing an internal, psychological experience in archaically external terms— and self-consciously so. There is evidence for this in the way Blake describes the experiences of the Hebrew prophets in *The Marriage of Heaven and Hell*:

> The Prophets Isaiah and Ezekiel dined with me, and I asked them how they dared so roundly to assert that God spake to them; and whether they did not think at the time, that they would be misunderstood, & so be the cause of imposition.
>
> Isaiah answer'd. *I saw no God nor heard any, in a finite organical perception; but my senses discover'd the infinite in everything*, and as I was then perswaded & remain confirm'd; that the voice of honest indignation is the voice of God, I cared not for consequences, but wrote.
>
> Then I asked: does a firm perswasion that a thing is so, make it so?
>
> He replied. All Poets believe that it does, & in ages of imagination this firm perswasion removed mountains; but many are not capable of a firm perswasion of anything."[23] [Italics added.]

There is further evidence in the way Blake spoke about his voice-hearing in informal social settings. The biographer Peter Ackroyd reports that Blake "once declared that ghosts appeared only to unimaginative people, which suggests that he believed his visions to be in part shaped by the powers of his own imagination. They were 'mental,' without the physical presence of ghosts; when he described one of them to an inquisitive lady he tapped his forehead to reveal its source. He understood that they came from 'Here, madam.' "[24]

Of course, Blake could have heard voices both internally and externally. As with Richard K., varied auditory experiences are possible and probably more common than we think. But it seems more plausible that Blake's voice-hearing was nothing more than an attempt to describe a tendency toward modern inspiration in easily comprehensible physical terms, and that historical developments had created a sensory atmosphere in which "metaphorical" auditory experiences were the vastly dominant form in which voice-hearing took place.

Poets themselves have made this argument, both explicitly, in Nietzschean laments, and implicitly, in works that have portrayed the downfall of ancient aurality as the impetus for modernity. More often than not they have celebrated that transformation as a victory for the human mind and for the Christian faith. A time-honored theme of Western literature is that the birth of Christ silenced the cacophony of the pagan world forever. Hence, John Milton's "On the Morning of Christ's Nativity":

> The Oracles are dumb;
> No voice or hideous hum
> Runs through the archèd roof in words deceiving.
> Apollo from his shrine
> Can no more divine,
> With hollow shriek the steep of Delphos leaving.
> No nightly trance, or breathèd spell,
> Inspires the pale-eyed Priest from the prophetic cell.[25]

And A. E. Housman's "The Oracles":

'Tis mute, the word they went to hear on high Dodona mountain
  When winds were in the oakenshaws and all the cauldrons tolled,
And mute's the midland navel-stone beside the singing fountain,
  And echoes list to silence now where gods told lies of old.[26]

Aurality did not die such an abrupt death, of course. Paganism and
Christianity coexisted for centuries before the latter's strength grew
dominant, and before it did, even the oracles, those convenient sym-
bols of pagan credulity, continued to speak. Yet these dramatically
partisan imaginings reflect an undeniable and long-standing historical truth about the Christian attitude toward the pagan world,
particularly as it relates to poetic inspiration. Christ made the re-
structuring of the sensory order a theological imperative when he declared, in the Gospel of Luke, that the "old oracles of error are to be
replaced by a new oracle of truth," and Christian poets responded
early on by attempting to dismantle the pagan tradition. The main
way they did this was by expressly rejecting the Muses in favor of
quieter, more soulful, more internalized forms of inspiration. "Hearts
dedicated to Christ are closed to the Muses and Apollo," wrote Saint
Paulinus of Nola in the early fifth century, and poets echoed this
sentiment throughout the Middle Ages and into the Renaissance,
mainly through the act of locating Christian replacements for the
Muses. In the thirteenth century, Dante invoked the Word of God.
In the fourteenth, Boccaccio invoked the Virgin Mary. In the seventeenth, Milton invoked the Holy·Spirit.[27] Finally, in the eighteenth
century, Blake closed the door completely with a lament addressed
"To the Muses":

Whether on Ida's shady brow,
  Or in the chamber of the East,

The chambers of the sun, that now
  From antient melody have ceas'd;

Whether in Heav'n ye wander fair,
  Or the green corners of the earth,
Or the blue regions of the air,
  Where the melodious winds have birth;

Whether on chrystal rocks ye rove,
  Beneath the bosom of the sea
Wand'ring in many a coral grove,
  Fair Nine, forsaking Poetry!

How have you left the antient love
  That bards of old enjoy'd in you!
The languid strings do scarcely move!
  The sound is forc'd, the notes are few![28]

These redefinitions of the terms of poetic inspiration reflected not only what had become religiously permissible and impermissible in a Christianized world, but also what had become psychologically necessary. Sensory experience is as contextual as anything else, and the context of Christianity is the eternal soul. On this new ground an attendance to the audible Muses would not only have been apostasy, it would have been impossible. Physical inspiration would not have fit into the Christian worldview. Hearing could no longer pertain to poetry.

Still we shouldn't overestimate the role of Christianity in silencing the Muses. Even messianic religions have their causes, and the poetic invocation of the silent soul precedes the birth of Christ by so many years that it can only have a different and deeper source. The spiritual invocation first occurs, it seems, in the work of Pindar, who in the fifth century BCE called upon his soul—in Greek, *psyche*—to lead him into a state in which he could compose his odes. It makes an even more prominent appearance in Ovid's *Metamorphoses*, written in the first year of the first Christian millennium. In the opening line Ovid speaks of his soul urging him to write.

Where did this new invocation come from, and what does it mean? The word *soul*, as E. R. Dodds has shown, had been well known to the Greeks for centuries. But Pindar and Ovid use it differently from their predecessors. To someone in Hesiod's day, the soul was treated as little more than a synonym for the body. The two were divisible only in death, when the life force of the soul left the deceased. Pindar speaks of the soul as if it were the divine dwelling within him. It is a separate substance to him, one that has superhuman powers to which he can appeal. The soul, it appears, had become the pagan gods, condensed and internalized.

8

INTERLUDE

fLOATING

*Little by little, hearing became my favorite sense; for just
as it is the voice that reveals the inwardness which is
incommensurable with the outer, so the ear is the instrument
whereby that inwardness is grasped, hearing the sense
by which it is appropriated.*

—SØREN KIERKEGAARD, *Either/Or*

One of the more memorable things my father ever told me
when I was young was that he had taken mescaline. I was fifteen years old at the time, and we were sitting in the living room
watching Stanley Kubrick's 2001: *A Space Odyssey*. I don't know why
he told me. Perhaps he recognized in me a need for proof that one
could make it to adulthood in spite of a tendency toward dissipation.
Perhaps he was indulging a moment of nostalgia. Whatever the case,
as the credits rolled, my father told me that when the movie was first
released, twenty-five years earlier, he had swallowed several hundred milligrams of mescaline and watched it four consecutive times
from the front row of a Manhattan movie theater.

"By the last time," he concluded wistfully, "I was more or less
straight."

To a teenager with $50 of pot hidden in his underwear drawer, this
announcement was welcome news—insurance for the inevitable day

when I would be caught. But I attribute the memory's strength and longevity to the secret that was revealed to me the following year, for since that time it has been impossible not to question the prudence of a man who, though he had since childhood suffered from unwanted voices, would willingly ingest a sizable amount of a potent hallucinogen and spend eight straight hours watching Keir Dullea hurtle through the Day-Glo vortex of the space-time continuum.

When my stash was found, that very year, this was my parents' position as well. Looming over a mess of pipes, bags, and screens laid out like police evidence on the kitchen table, they dismissed my plea of precedent with the claim that my father's experimentation had been self-destructive. Not only was it not an invitation to me, they said, it was a cautionary tale. Using drugs had exacerbated my father's emotional instability and worsened his voices, and it had helped cause his breakdown and hospitalization. If I wasn't careful, I could suffer the same fate.

Their claim was not without scientific merit. Recreational drugs work by affecting the distribution and levels of neurotransmitters in the brain, and they appear to do so in a way that mimics the neurological changes caused by psychiatric illnesses. Recently, researchers in New York announced evidence that marijuana use in adolescence causes defects in the developing brain that are identical to defects found in the brains of those diagnosed with schizophrenia. Through a technique known as diffusion tensor imaging, they examined the brains of four groups: adolescents with schizophrenia who did and did not use marijuana, and adolescents without schizophrenia who did and did not use marijuana. In all but the last, the researchers detected abnormalities in an area of the brain known as the arcuate fasciculus, a central language and auditory pathway that may play a role in producing auditory hallucinations.[1]

Mescaline also produces a neurological portrait similar to that found in those diagnosed with schizophrenia. In 1992, German researchers gave the drug to twelve physically and mentally fit men. About three and a half hours after ingesting half a gram of mescaline powder, the subjects experienced the equivalent of an "acute psychotic state," including cognitive dysfunction, anxiety, and delusions. More notably, the drug produced psychosis-like neurological changes. Patients diagnosed with schizophrenia often show a decrease of functioning in the right hemisphere of the brain. The mescaline subjects showed the same deficiency.[2]

The relationship between drug use and mental illness isn't completely clear, however. The causal route may not be from drugs to pathology but from pathology to drugs. In 1996, another German study examined 232 men and women hospitalized for schizophrenia for the first time. Of those who had used recreational drugs, usually marijuana, only 27 percent did so prior to the onset of their symptoms. The remaining 73 percent began to take drugs either in the same month or at least one month after their symptoms had started. These findings confirm what many psychiatrists have observed in practice: Patients often use drugs as a form of self-medication or as a more acceptable explanation for a frightening and sudden alteration in their mental lives.[3]

Nevertheless, it's fair to say that for people predisposed to mental illness, the use of psychedelic drugs comes with a higher risk. This doesn't mean that it is necessarily ill-advised. In my father's case, in fact, the use of drugs may have been therapeutic. Self-experimentation is inherently willful, and for a person whose days are marred by frequent incursions against the conscious will, using drugs can be considered a form of proactive defense. My father had perceptions that altered themselves without warning, and so, aware or unaware of the risks but one hopes aware of the irony, he chose to alter his perceptions voluntarily. He chose to engage in an act that can be interpreted as a thumbed nose at the hijacked will that most of us have the luxury to avoid confronting.

For a while now, I have been looking for a drug that would let me hear voices. There aren't many choices. Plenty of drugs available to the partygoer of my generation alter perception—LSD, psychedelic mushrooms, ecstasy, heroin. But most act on the sense of sight. There is a neurochemical reason for this, but there is probably also an economic one. Sight is a more marketable sense than hearing. People don't want to hear voices. They want to see things. They want to experience everything, as one textbook on hallucination puts it, from the "distortions of colour, shape and size of objects" to "Walt Disney characters in action."[4]

There is one substance that's known to cause voice-hearing, but it has to be taken in massively prohibitive quantities to achieve the effect. Also, one would have to endure a period of psychotic paranoia along with the voices. A description of just what this would be like was published in 1970 by two psychiatrists at New York University. The researchers somehow gained permission to give large hourly doses of amphetamines to a group of normal volunteers. One subject was given nearly 500 milligrams over the course of a day. (A conventional daily dose of Dexedrine prescribed for narcolepsy is anywhere from 5 to 60 milligrams.) This resulted in an experience that they kindly referred to as "florid paranoid psychosis":

> Before the experiment [the subject] had made a "deal" with an attendant on the ward, to whom he owed several dollars. As he became psychotic, he "heard" a gang coming on the ward to kill him (sent by the attendant). His paranoid feelings included the experimenter who he assumed had "set up" the "trap." He was at times quite hos-

tile. Explanations that his feelings were amphetamine-induced were rejected with sardonic mock agreement, i.e. "Oh, sure, ha! Is that the way it's going to be?" etc. At other times he would become panicky and tearful and beg the experimenter to explain what was "really going on."[5]

My psyche could not possibly endure this. Luckily, it didn't have to. There was an alternative, even a better one. In theory, the most reliable and time-tested way to cause your mind to produce voices is also the subtlest and safest. It was the way of Hesiod and Muhammad and Shackleton. When modern pharmacology failed me, I turned to silence.

But silence posed its own problem, namely, where to find it? In the last hour my apartment has echoed with the noise of a truck belching diesel fumes, a sports car with a spine-rattling bass booster, a motorcycle that set off numerous alarms in its wake, police sirens, a construction crew drilling into stone, a crowd of teenagers on their way to school, and a stroller bearing a colicky infant. A trip to the country wouldn't solve this problem. The sounds from cars, trains, and airplanes echo into the recesses of even the remotest areas of the country, so that even the shrillest and most histrionic of complaints about the modern world's self-pollution now seem to be based in cold logic. There is no place today to escape from sound and its insidious ability to bully the ear into observation.

In a way, however, this problem has created its own solution by fostering a cadre of dissenters dedicated to establishing islands of silence in a sea of noise. Several months ago I was lucky enough to find one in Manhattan in the person of Sam Zeiger, the owner and operator of Blue Light Floatation, an organization run out of his loft apartment on West Twenty-third Street. For $60 an hour Zeiger offers the use of a state-of-the-art flotation chamber in his apartment. The chamber is a large bath sealed off as much as possible from light and sound and filled with water and enough Epsom salts to create complete buoyancy—approximately one thousand pounds.[6]

Zeiger advertises Blue Light as a place for "anybody of any age who wants to release themselves from excess mental and physical stress caused by an overload of day-to-day external stimuli." It is something of a rarity, especially in New York: There is only one other flotation chamber available for public use in the city. This hasn't always been the case. In the 1970s and '80s, sensory deprivation, as it is often called, enjoyed something of a vogue. Its P. T. Barnum was a government neurophysiologist named John C. Lilly. He invented the flotation tank in 1954 as a way to study how the brain reacted when it was cut off from external stimuli, and in 1977, after much self-experimentation, he published a best-selling book on the subject called *The Deep Self*. Consequently, flotation centers began to pop up across North America. The fad was fueled by the 1980 movie *Altered States*, in which (to distill a complicated plot) William Hurt, through a combination of sensory deprivation and a Native American hallucinogen, turns into an ape. In the past two decades, the technique has dwindled in popularity, retreating to New Age bastions such as California and Arizona, and into academia, where it is used to study the therapeutic effects of sensory deprivation on a number of medical and psychiatric conditions. In the research literature, the use of flotation chambers is referred to as REST, for Restricted Environmental Stimulation Technique.

Zeiger is among those who still consider flotation a means of self-exploration. His dedication to the procedure is discernible in his appearance. A bushy-haired man with glasses, a soft unlined face, and a gentle demeanor, he looks in the best possible way like an aging hippie. The decorative scheme of his apartment mirrors this impression. Displayed on the walls are both artwork produced by Zeiger—

portraits carefully done in pencil of shamans and other spiritual figures—and native prints of geometric shapes painted in earth tones. His bookshelves, which occupy one wall of a high-ceilinged living room, contain Henry Miller's *Rosy Crucifixion* trilogy, the novels of J.R.R. Tolkien, and Timothy Leary's *Flashbacks*. Overall, the effect is an endorsement of experimentation over order, the spirit over the intellect.

But then Zeiger is also a businessman who believes deeply in his product, which he maintains with a sense of propriety and hygiene that he made clear to me on my visit. I had taken the subway to Manhattan feeling nervous; the prospect of lying naked and wet in the apartment of a man I didn't know, even one whose facilities *Esquire* had reviewed favorably, was discomfiting. But Zeiger had a disarming professionalism. After a brief introduction, delivered in a calm, almost anesthetizing voice, he laid out the rules that govern what he calls "the tank."

The first and most important rule was that all guests had to take a shower first. This, Zeiger explained, was intended to minimize the amount of bodily oils and bacteria that enter the tank, which is heated to a tropical 94.5 degrees. Zeiger had taken other sanitizing measures. Just before I arrived, he told me, he had "ozinated" the tank, pumping it full of O_3, which is a natural water purifier. "The weather sometimes makes ozination difficult," he said. "With the air conditioner on, the ozone can shoot out of the room very quickly."

Zeiger set up a Japanese screen at the end of the vestibule, which houses both the tank and the bathroom, and, after inviting me to share a cup of herbal tea with him after my float, left me to shower. After doing so, I tiptoed across the hallway to where the tank's entrance stood—a sturdy wood-paneled door of the sort that leads to steam baths and saunas. Inside was a chamber that resembled a small locker room; it had a blue mat on the floor, a pair of pegs for tow-els, and off in the corner what looked like a small private generator—the tank's filtration system. The entranceway to the tank was a thin brown sliding door. I had paid for an hour.

The first problem with floating in a pitch-black tank of body-temperature saltwater for the first time is that the medium is so vis-cous that the slightest movement creates undulations on the surface that rush to the four walls of the tank, ricochet off, and perpetuate themselves endlessly, producing a sort of miniature wave pool on which one floats helplessly like a leaf in a puddle. This tends to ruin the desired effect of total sensory deprivation by causing one to drift away from the open water and to the sides. Zeiger had given me a tip on how to combat this. I was to place my hands on either end of the tank, hold myself motionless until the water's movement sub-sided, and then, very gently and very slowly, let myself go. The method worked well enough, but I was fidgety and a novice, so my concentration was often interrupted by the feel of warm fiberglass on my skin.

The second problem was my own fault. When I had called to make my appointment, Zeiger told me not to have any caffeine be-forehand. Given that his Web site markets the tank as a pathway to "deep inner peace," the reason for this should have been obvious. But I had an addiction to placate. And so, after three cups of strongly brewed black coffee, my mind rushed with thoughts—about the day behind me, about the evening in front of me, and, in possible con-firmation of the claim that sensory deprivation expands the bounds of consciousness, about the hidden or typically ignored subjects on the periphery of my mind. My thoughts were constant.

The hyperactive thought problem was exacerbated by a choice I made five or so minutes in (time was naturally hard to measure) to close my eyes. Open, they had produced the flashing patterns of ghostly light that are caused by sudden entry into a dark room or by pushing against the eyelids. The gradual focusing of these images into discernible shapes, a sort of Rorschach test in motion, was actually quite pleasant—the fluttering lights looked like birds' wings approaching from a distance—but it distracted me from the task at hand. But there was also a drawback to closing my eyes. Without the diversion of the light before my eyes, I had to contend with the diversion of my thoughts, which soon revved themselves into a frenzy. They were of all sorts: philosophic (to what extent was the detachment from the senses possible?), pragmatic (I needed a new keychain), and, oddly, pornographic. Something about the fact of midday nudity and the titillating sensation of weightlessness encouraged an almost clinical sexuality, and I spent long minutes inventing and mentally diagramming new positions for intercourse.

My only tool in prying myself from these thoughts was some training I had received some years before after enrolling in a series of classes in Buddhist meditation. The classes were based on the teachings of a Tibetan monk, a videotaped greeting from whom inaugurated the course. According to the monk, who wore a Rolex watch and suffered from a visibly runny nose, the breath is the body's metronome. It centers and orders the mind. Every time we found our thoughts wandering from our attendance to the breath, we were calmly and without judgment to nudge ourselves back. I left the class after only three sessions, but over the years I'd practiced the little I'd learned and became proficient enough to be able to apply the methods in the flotation tank. Whenever distracting thoughts entered my mind, I reminded myself that my job was to listen for a voice. Over time I achieved a measure of victory. Gradually, I was able to perceive sounds in the tank. I was first able to detect the noises produced by my own body, muffled then increasingly clear. I heard my heart beating, my stomach acids churning, my lungs compressing and expanding, the blood rushing past my ears. Soon even the stray drop of condensation striking the surface of the tank and the sloshing of the thick water weren't able to distract me from attending to these sounds.

Success breeds success. My ability to hear the subtle noises of my body became a push toward the auditory, and as it did, I progressed. Before long, my mind was manufacturing its own sounds. Bells struck, bullets whizzed, horns sounded. These sounds increased in vividness the more that I concentrated, and they consumed more and more of my attention. I was suddenly reminded of a passage I had read in a book by Emil Kraepelin, who originated the concept of schizophrenia. At the beginning of a course of the illness, Kraepelin wrote,

> there are usually simple noises, rustling, buzzing, ringing in the ears, tolling of bells ("death-knell"), knocking, moving of tables, cracking of whips, trumpets, yodel, singing, weeping of children, whistling, blowing, chirping, "shooting and death rattle"; the bed echoes with shots; the "Wild Hunt" makes an uproar; Satan roars under the bed.[7]

As the disease progresses, Kraepelin wrote, these noises are transformed into voices. One of his patients heard an unknown secret language. Another heard children. Another heard gnats. Some heard voices coming from their own bodies: "[T]he spirits scream in the belly, in the feet, and possibly also wander about; a patient heard them speaking in his purse." I both hoped and dreaded, based on Kraepelin's authority, that the sounds in my head would develop into full-blown voices. Hearing my own chirps and buzzes, I expected them to up and announce themselves, like houseguests. But my mind was stubborn. No matter how hard I tried, sound would not morph into sense.

Time passed imperceptibly in the dark as I clenched my eyelids in a ridiculously unnecessary pose of concentration. Only one thing staved off complete frustration: a deeper, more abiding frustration at my own idiocy. By definition, an expedition has a goal. Mine was to hear a voice, to ascend or descend—the answer would come with the achievement—to the experience that had marked my father's life. But the more I tried and failed, the closer I came to the realization that even success would be pointless. My father once said to me that the subject of all art can be boiled down to sex and death, and even sex can be boiled down to death. The epiphany I had as I hovered forty feet above Chelsea was that I chose the wrong goal. I had paid for silence so that I could hear a voice, but what I really wanted was to hear my father's voice.

When you are naked and alone and in the dark, there is nothing to do with epiphany other than accept it. Once I had decided to listen for my father's voice, I concentrated my attention on a platitude he had expounded as a panacea against angst, disappointment, depression, even his own impending death. That platitude, which seems more like wisdom the older I get, was "It's only life. Don't take it too seriously." I made this my mantra. I pulled it to the center of my attention, returning to it again and again as if it were my breath. But I could not seem to set it in my father's voice. I couldn't remember my father's voice. What had it sounded like? Had it been gruff? Gentle? Feminine? Masculine? Had he spoken quickly or slowly? Had he retained an accent, a New York brogue? It had been too long. I had waited too many years. It was too late.

Then, as if to mock my failures, the world returned. The sound of birds chirping softly above a foundation of gentle piano chords came over a speaker embedded in the roof of the tank, alerting me that my time was coming to a close. The music jolted me. I felt for the rubber button at my side that controlled the light, squinted at the image of my shriveled body soaking in a pool of water, and crawled out into the bright, harsh day.

9

PERSONAL DEITY

SOCRATES VERSUS THE STATE

*Socrates was condemned to death by taking a dose of
hemlock not because he betrayed his city to the enemy
or committed temple robbery, but because he swore new
oaths and claimed—surely as a joke as some say—
that something daimonic gave signs to him.*

—FLAVIUS JOSEPHUS

My favorite story from the history of voice-hearing appears
in a work of historical fiction by the ancient Greek writer
Plutarch. The work takes place just prior to the restoration of democracy in the city of Thebes in 379 BCE, approximately 425 years before Plutarch's birth. Three years earlier, Thebes had become a
Spartan puppet state, overseen by a cabal of local oligarchs. The
story's action centers on the preparation by a group of exiled democrats to ambush and slaughter a party of these rulers as they sit and
drink. As the democrats wait for the right moment to attack, they engage in a philosophical debate that comes to focus on Socrates'
daimonion—the admonitory sign that came to him unexpectedly
throughout his life and stopped him from engaging in certain actions.
The conversation is begun by Theocritus, a friend of Socrates', who
describes what happened one day when the philosopher was walking along the streets of Athens:

Socrates happened to be climbing the hill . . . and he was at the same time asking Euthyphro questions and lightheartedly testing him. Suddenly he stopped, went quiet and became withdrawn for quite a time; then he turned around and started to head down the box-makers' street. He recalled those of us friends who had already gone ahead with the information that his personal deity had come to him. So most of the group turned back without him, including myself . . . but some of the young ones carried straight on, with the intention of showing up Socrates' personal deity. . . . As they were going along the statuaries' street, past the lawcourts, they encountered a herd of pigs: the pigs were covered in mud and there were so many of them that they were jostling one another. There was no escape; the pigs bumped into some of them and knocked them to the ground, and the rest of them just got filthy. . . . [C]onsequently, whenever we think of Socrates' personal deity, we chuckle, although at the same time we are impressed by how God never abandoned him or overlooked him under any circumstances.[1]

There are a number of reasons to be attracted to this story. One is the improbability of a philosophical discussion preceding a mass political execution. Another is that it mitigates a reputation too pure for its own good. For centuries Socrates has been character-ized as the prototypical Western thinker. He is our hero of ration-ality, celebrated for his intolerance of pretension, cant, and superstition. "Saint Socrates, pray for us!" Desiderius Erasmus is said to have cried. Less excitably, John Stuart Mill wrote, "Mankind can hardly be too often reminded, that there was once a man named Socrates . . . , acknowledged master of all the eminent thinkers who have since lived."[2]

Plutarch's anecdote scuffs this stainless steel image. In its apoc-ryphal but honest way, it reveals a man who, though he was without doubt a rigorous thinker and a tireless pursuer of semantic precision, happened also to have heeded the instructions of a divine voice, and one that was so protective as to save him from nothing so lofty as a herd of filthy swine.

Socrates shouldn't require this help. His life and work helped drive the Greek Enlightenment, that explosion in rational thought which ran its course in the second half of the fifth century BCE, but scholars have long known that era to have been thoroughly awash in gods, oracles, and cults, and not just in philosophy, arts, and the sciences. They have also long known that Socrates was an active participant in the religious as well as in the philosophical spirit of his time. Indeed, his intellectual renown rests on his faithfulness: The "Socratic method" for which he is known—the manner of proceeding carefully along logical pathways, interrogating reputed experts in their fields, and always standing in a position of professed ignorance—has its origin in a cryptic proclamation of the Delphic oracle of Apollo, which stated that Socrates was the wisest man in all of Athens. Both a believer and a logician, Socrates attempted through his famous tireless questioning to discover what the god might mean.

Yet the religious facet of Socrates' character is typically missing from modern representations of him, or else conspicuously subdued. This is not difficult to understand. Once a man's sanctity has been established, it is nearly impossible to diminish it in any noticeable way, and Socrates has been an object of veneration for centuries. But the sheer immaculateness of his intellectual reputation, its seeming imperviousness to scholarship that has not otherwise hesitated to admit the complexities of the Greek mind, does suggest that his caretakers have been complicit. Since E. R. Dodds published *The Greeks and the Irrational*, it has been impossible to maintain the old view of the Greeks as intellects alone. Socrates, the most notoriously rational of them all, has somehow eluded this reassessment. In this light, the value of the *daimonion* is humanistic. Appropriately examined—neither dismissed as beneath importance or contempt nor pressed too harshly into ideological service—it helps restore Socrates to a nuanced form that he has scarcely known since his death 2,400 years ago.

The extent of our biographical knowledge of Socrates can be fit into a single paragraph. He was born in Athens in or around 470 BCE. He was married to a woman named Xanthippe. He served in the military and fought with honor in the Peloponnesian War against Sparta. He had three sons. He had a profound influence on several prominent Athenians. He was charged by Athens with corrupting the young through religious nonconformism, found guilty, and executed by hemlock in 399. These are the basic facts. Beyond them, historical conviction stretches thin. The limiting element here is what is known as the Socratic problem, which is that Socrates left behind no account of his experiences or his thought. His entire adult life was lived verbally. In his seventy-odd years, he does not appear to have held a job, or even to have left Athens for any purpose other than war. He simply held conversations around the city. The impermanence of his vocation means that a careful distinction is typically made between the "historical" and the "literary" Socrates.

The distinction is in a sense meaningless, for the only way we know Socrates is through literary portraits of him. Socrates was fortunate in this regard. His ubiquitous presence around Athens and his talent for exposing the intellectual and moral pretensions of his interlocutors earned him the admiration of the city's youth. A band of followers sat at his knee (probably literally) and learned to imitate his method of questioning. Among them was the brilliant Plato.

Plato's Socrates begins like Boswell's Johnson and winds up like Roth's Zuckerman. The protagonist of nearly thirty dialogues written over the course of almost fifty years, the Platonic Socrates develops from an apparently biographical replica into an alter consciousness, a dramatic stand-in who can expound the author's ideas more convincingly than the author can himself. He becomes a character, and such a compelling one that the Socrates of the collective imagination is unmistakably Plato's: ironic, suspiciously humble, quick-witted, tireless, and as elusive as a snake. Plato was by no means the only writer of his generation to hit upon the idea of commandeering Socrates into dramatic or philosophical service. After the master's death, Socratic dialogues became a literary fad much in the way that bleak, allusive poetry sprouted up after *The Waste Land*. But Plato's work had the good fortune of being one of only two examples of the genre to survive more or less intact, and the second—the work of his near-exact contemporary Xenophon—is not as voluminous, sophisticated, or engaging. Compared with Plato's Socrates, Xenophon's is unsophisticated and inelegant. He is often dull, sometimes vulgar, and dismayingly weak in philosophical insights.

This isn't to say that Xenophon's Socrates is an imposter. He may, in fact, be more authentic by virtue of his banality. It is to say that the Socratic problem gets its intractability from the great difficulty of reconciling the surviving sources. That is why Albert Schweitzer, in his book *The Quest of the Historical Jesus*, expressed relief that his subject was not that other famous martyr. Jesus, he wrote, was at least depicted by "simple Christians without literary gifts." Socrates comes to us via "literary men who exercised their creative ability upon the portrait."[3] The situation is even worse than that. Looking back at classical Greece from the twenty-first century, we see two visions of Socrates, two men who are often different in both character and the quality of their minds. It can sometimes seem as if they share only a vague familial resemblance, as if they were brothers separated at birth and raised by different families.

And yet, as with brothers, there are resemblances. The *daimonion* is one. Xenophon's everyman and Plato's genius may be dissimilar in spirit, but both authors portray their hero as having been routinely visited by a divine source; both write that the experience was well known in Athens; and both suggest that the *daimonion's* implications for the city's traditions and mores played a significant role in Socrates' indictment, conviction, and execution. This last agreement is key. Socrates' trial is not only the final act of his life, it is its culmination and its beacon to immortality. Just as the impact and importance of Darwin's theory was illuminated by the Scopes trial, the impact and importance of Socrates' mind was illuminated by his own, of which both Plato and Xenophon left accounts. And just as Christianity grew from the drama of Christ's crucifixion, Western philosophy as we know it grew from the drama of Socrates' execution. The injustice of the teacher's death galvanized his students, Plato in particular.

Still, because the sources are so thin, there is no satisfying agreement on what caused Socrates' martyrdom. Many scholars have argued that the primary motive behind Socrates' prosecution was political. Socrates' offense, the argument goes, was to have been an enemy of democracy and an all-around nuisance. It's true that Socrates' trial can't be understood without reference to the political and cultural atmosphere of late-fifth-century BCE Athens, and to Socrates' part in it, which was at best offensive and at worst treacherous. At the time of Socrates' trial, Athens had just endured arguably the most convulsive twenty-five-year period in its history. It had been forced to accept an embarrassing, bitter defeat at the hands of Sparta in the Peloponnesian War, and its democratic system had twice been overturned by oligarchic coups, the second of which, in 404 BCE, ushered in a period of brutal extrajudicial executions, followed by paranoia and discord. Socrates had not played a direct part in these coups, but he was ideologically involved by virtue of his teaching.

The historical record indicates, for example, that Socrates had direct involvement with Critias, a prime mover in the murderous second oligarchy, the so-called Dictatorship of the Thirty, which left more than one thousand slaughtered democrats in its aftermath. In a speech delivered to an Athenian jury court fifty years after Socrates' death, the famous orator Aeschines praised the body for having put Socrates to death "because he was shown to have educated Critias."[4] This comment, which suggests the tenor of the popular Athenian view, echoes an earlier speech made by the orator Polycrates. That speech, titled "Accusation of Socrates," has been lost, but its argument has been preserved by Xenophon, who summarized and denounced it in his *Memorabilia*, a sort of hodgepodge of Socratic apologetics and reminiscences. According to Polycrates, Xenophon wrote, Socrates' pernicious influence lay in the fact that

> he encouraged his associates to make light of constitutional practice by saying that it was foolish to appoint political leaders by lot, and that nobody would employ a candidate chosen by lot as a pilot or carpenter or musician or for any other such post—although if these posts are badly filled, they cause less harm than political appointments; and the accuser said that this sort of talk encouraged the young to despise the established constitution and made them unruly.[5]

Polycrates makes a more expansive philosophical charge than Aeschines, and what he suggests—that Socrates was antidemocratic—is indisputable. In both Xenophon and Plato, Socrates professes a distaste for the direct democracy on which the Athenian state was based and continually dismisses and even mocks the idea that the populace could be a source of wisdom. His elitism was an intellectual assault on the political foundation of the city, and it would have been doubly insulting for the fact that Socrates was not shy about airing his opinions. In Plato's dramatization of Socrates' trial, the so-called *Apology*, Socrates even takes the time to lecture his main accuser, Meletus, on the folly of trusting the masses:

Tell me, my good sir, who improves our young men?

The laws.

That is not what I am asking, but what person who has knowl-edge of the laws to begin with?

These jurymen, Socrates.

How do you mean, Meletus? Are these able to educate the young and improve them?

Certainly.

All of them, or some but not others?

All of them.

Very good, by Hera. You mention a great abundance of bene-factors. But what about the audience? Do they improve the young or not?

They do, too.

What about the members of the Council?

The Council-members, too.

But Meletus, what about the assembly? Do members of the as-sembly corrupt the young, or do they all improve them?

They improve them.

All the Athenians, it seems, make the young into fine good men, except me, and I alone corrupt them. Is that what you mean?

That is most definitely what I mean.

You condemn me to a great misfortune. Tell me: does this also apply with horses do you think? That all men improve them and one individual corrupts them? Or is quite the contrary true, one individ-ual is able to improve them, or very few, namely, the horse-trainers, whereas the majority, if they have horses and use them, corrupt them? Is that not the case, Meletus, both with horses and all other animals? Of course it is, whether you . . . say so or not. It would be a very happy state of affairs if only one person corrupted our youth, while the others improved them.[6]

This is clever, deflating, and quintessentially Socratic. Indeed, while as a drama the *Apology* is among the most emotionally affecting of Plato's works—the knowledge of its tragic outcome makes it so—it is also among the most intellectually lopsided. Meletus is a blustering, self-righteous idiot, ripe for Socratic evisceration. And if we consider the passage not as drama but as journalism, the only conclusion we can draw is that it could not have played well from the dock. The blatancy of Socrates' condescension to his accusers even led Xenophon to venture an explanation, though it is an unsatisfying one. Socrates, he wrote, wanted to lose his case in order to avoid the infirmities of old age. Call it suicide by arrogance.

Does the unpopularity of Socrates' political beliefs and the obnoxiousness with which he broadcast them, prove that they were the ultimate cause of his persecution? It couldn't have helped. According to a census of the characters in Plato's work conducted by the Danish historian Mogens Herman Hansen, nearly half of the men with whom Socrates consorted were "criminals and traitors."[7] Socrates also had a long-standing reputation, deserved or not, as a morally corrosive element. In 423, almost a quarter-century before his trial, he appeared as a character in Aristophanes' comedic play *The Clouds*. The proprietor of a *phrontisterion*, or thinking shop, Aristophanes' Socrates is a corrupt, fast-talking pseudo-intellectual who teaches young men how to prevail in unjust causes. At the end, his shop is burned to the ground, and he is savagely beaten.

But all this suggests only that politics permeated the atmosphere within which Socrates was convicted. It does not suggest that politics was the cause of that conviction. There is good reason to believe that it was not. First, it would have been illegal. Following the downfall of the Dictatorship of the Thirty, a reconciliation agreement was signed into law that granted political amnesty to all but the surviving members of the oligarchy. Socrates' political actions, or at least those that occurred prior to 402, when the law took effect, would have been protected under this amnesty. Second, Socrates does not appear to have engaged in any indictable offense. He did not leave Athens, as many loyal democrats did, but he also did not submit to the authority of the Thirty—friends or not. As he tells the jury in Plato's *Apology* (in one of his reluctant submissions to the convention of self-defense) when ordered by the Thirty to arrest a wealthy trader and deliver him for execution so that the trader's assets could be liquidated by the state, he refused.[8]

There is a third, more substantial reason to discount the political interpretation of Socrates' trial. If Socrates' enemies had wanted to try him for his political transgressions, for an odiousness that included nonparticipation, a notion antithetical to Athenian democracy, they could have. With some cleverness, laws can be circumvented, and there even existed ones with which Socrates' politics could have been ensnared. But they didn't. Socrates was pulled into court not so much on the grounds that he had subverted Athenian politics, but more on the grounds that he had subverted Athenian religion. The historical record makes this clear. The third-century Roman Diogenes Laertius has even recorded the official indictment, which had been preserved in the Athenian archives:

> This indictment is entered on affidavit by Meletus son of Meletus of the deme [district] Pitthus against Socrates son of Sophroniscus of Alopeke. Socrates is guilty of refusing to recognize the gods recognized by the State and introducing other, new divinities. He is also guilty of corrupting the youth. The penalty demanded is death.[9]

For the sake of clarity, the writer and translator Robin Waterfield has schematized this indictment as (1a) not recognizing the official gods of the city, (1b) introducing new gods, and (2) corrupting the young.[10] Put this way, it becomes clear that charge number two follows logically from charge number one and is therefore ancillary to it. One cannot corrupt a young man's mind by doing nothing, after all. Furthermore, Socrates himself confirms the religious impetus of the indictment in Plato's *Euthyphro*, a dialogue set on the street just prior to his trial:

> *Euthyphro:* Tell me, what does [Meletus] say you do to corrupt the young?
> *Socrates:* Strange things, to hear him tell it, for he says that I am a maker of gods, and on the ground that I create new gods while not believing in the old gods, he has indicted me for their sake, as he puts it.[11]

In order to understand the religious charges leveled against Socrates and to determine whether he was in fact guilty of them—for an assessment of legality can proceed even when our sense of justice balks—some background on Athenian religion is necessary. For the modern reader it is a system simple enough to apprehend but nearly impossible to comprehend. Steeped as we are in the effluvia of two thousand years of monotheism, our unifying concept of organized religion is orthodoxy—tenets by which one's level of adherence can be determined. We breathe religious rules and debate beliefs. Athenian polytheism had no organized system of doctrines. It had no book on which religious beliefs or actions were based. It had no organized system of churches. It had no priestly class. The only thing Greek state religion had that resembled a gravitational center was what we would today call a literary canon: the epics of Homer and the poetry of Hesiod. And even these authors, with whom all Athenians were familiar, could not stabilize the restless, volatile gods. The Athenian pantheon was a bewildering, ever-shifting array of characters—of proper Olympian gods, of popular demigods, and of quasi-divine legendary heroes.

At the same time, Greek religion was not a completely anarchic affair. It may not have been centralized, but it was certainly penetrative. For the Greeks, piety was inseparable from daily life, the sacred inseparable from the profane. Mark McPherran, a professor of philosophy at Simon Fraser University, in British Columbia, has summed up the matter well: "Greek religion did not comprise a unified, organized system of beliefs and rituals held at arm's length from the social, political, and commercial aspects of life that we would term 'secular.' Rather, it was a complex tangle of practices and attitudes that pervaded every *polis*-member's life in a variety of ways." It was "seamlessly integrated into everyday life," and like Athenian democracy, it was vitally, indispensably participatory.[12] Piety meant frequent and often communal action through prayer, sacrifice, purification rituals, banquets, and festivals. No one was exempt.

In light of the centerlessness of Greek religion, it is nearly impossible to fathom how Socrates could have been found guilty, or even seriously accused, of not recognizing the gods of Athens. There were no "official gods"—or, rather, there were so many of them that the term *nonrecognition* is meaningless. Without a theological yardstick, Socrates' faith could not be measured. What is more, the surviving evidence suggests that Socrates was diligent about performing the proper rituals and avoiding the improper ones. Both Plato and Xenophon wrote, we might say, as retroactive defense attorneys and should always be read with one eyebrow raised, but in their work Socrates comes across convincingly as a devout Athenian, unhesitating in his adherence to ritualistic tradition. In the *Phaedo*, the touching Platonic dialogue that tells the story of Socrates' last hours, Socrates composes a hymn to Apollo while waiting for his execution, one of only two times he is reported to have written anything down. His dying words are even a request that one of his followers offer a sacrifice to the Greek god of medicine and healing:

The coldness was spreading about as far as his waist when Socrates uncovered his face—for he had covered it up—and said (they were his last words): "Crito, we ought to offer a cock to Asclepius. See to it, and don't forget."[13]

The only way in which it could be argued legitimately that Socrates did not recognize the proper gods of the city is in his almost monotheistic idealization of them. The Greek gods, though worshipped and idolized, were frequently human in their psychology. They fought, made love, committed murder and adultery, forged and broke alliances. But Socrates held the gods to a higher theological standard. To him, divinity meant perfect wisdom, and the popular stories of heavenly strife were nothing but the fantasies of poets.

Socrates' moral elevation of the gods has often been emphasized by those who have intellectual and emotional stock in the Socrates of legend—a martyr for the cause of Reason, slaughtered for his philosophical purity. Gregory Vlastos, the foremost scholar of ancient Greek philosophy in the second half of the twentieth century, had this to say:

> What would be left of . . . the . . . Olympians if they were required to observe the stringent norms of Socratic virtue . . . ? Required to meet these austere standards, the city's gods would have become unrecognizable. Their ethical transformation would be tantamount to the destruction of the old gods, the creation of new gods—which is precisely what Socrates takes to be the sum and substance of the accusation at his trial.[14]

The theme has also been taken up by Christian apologists, who have sometimes sought to remake Socrates not in the image of Jesus, as is traditional, but in the image of John the Baptist—a harbinger of truth in a world of heathens. But the theory that Socrates was killed for his claim of absolute divine morality ultimately teeters for lack of support. There are some intimations that Socrates' contemporaries were troubled by his theology; in the *Euthyphro*, Socrates himself wonders whether he has been indicted because he finds it hard to believe the traditional stories about the gods.[15] But during the trial, no one even hints at the possibility that Socrates' guilt lies in his religious innovations. Meletus even denies him any belief at all, charging Socrates with atheism, an absurd claim that Socrates easily demolishes.[16] Furthermore, Socrates' innovations were not all that fresh. Several prominent intellectuals before him, such as Pindar, Xenophanes, Euripides, and Heraclitus, had openly criticized traditional Greek religion, and none had been persecuted by their cities.[17] Of course, as with his politics, Socrates' well-known theological dissent likely influenced his fate. Once indicted and brought in front of the jury—an intimidating mass of five hundred men—he was on trial for the whole of his life and all his beliefs. But without proof or even convincing evidence that Socrates failed to recognize the gods of Athens, we can conclude that the only charge with legal teeth was introducing new gods. And the only thing that could have given those teeth their bite was Socrates' *daimonion*.

There are a number of reasons to conclude that Socrates' *daimonion* was at the core of the charge that he invented new gods and therefore was at the core of the entire trial. First, though we no longer have the prosecution's verbal arguments against Socrates, those that preceded his "apology," we are told by Plato that Meletus "saw fit to travesty" the *daimonion* in his presentation to the jury.[18] Second, in the *Euthyphro*, the eponymous seer whom Socrates meets at the start of his legal travails, makes it abundantly clear that the *daimonion* is what precipitated the trial: "I see, Socrates; it's because of your saying that you are constantly visited by your supernatural voice. So [Meletus] has indicted you for introducing unorthodox views; and he is coming into court to misrepresent your conduct, because he knows that it is easy to misrepresent this sort of thing to the masses."[19] But the most convincing piece of evidence occurs in Xenophon's brief, poorly written, but invaluable *Apology*, in which Socrates explicitly links his *daimonion* to the charge that he introduced new gods:

> As for my claim that a divine voice comes to me and communicates what I must do, how in claiming this am I introducing new deities? Those who rely on bird-calls and the utterances of men are, I suppose, receiving guidance from voices. Can there be any doubt that thunder has a voice or that it is an omen of the greatest significance? And take the priestess who sits on the tripod at Pytho—doesn't she too use a voice to announce messages from the god? Moreover, that God has knowledge of the future and communicates it in advance to whomever he wishes—this too, as I say, is a universal claim and belief. But whereas others state that it is birds and utterances and chance meetings and oracles which forewarn them, I call it divine, and I think that in using this description I am being both more accurate and more devout than those who ascribe the power of the gods to birds. Furthermore, I have evidence to show that I am not attributing things falsely to God: I have often told friends what God has advised and I have never been found to be wrong.[20]

According to Xenophon, this elicited from the jury a *thorubos*—a clamor of disapproval. Some of the jury members "didn't believe what [Socrates] was saying, while others were jealous that he might have had more from the gods than they." The speech stands out as the most dramatic moment in the text. The tumult only increases when Socrates goes on to recount the famous and ironic Delphic proclamation that he is the wisest man alive.[21]

What was it about Socrates' *daimonion* that so scandalized the jury?

Mark McPherran enumerates three reasons in his book *The Religion of Socrates*, which makes a definitive case for the legal and religious centrality of the experience to Socrates' trial. The first reason pertains to the technically blasphemous relationship that Socrates had with his *daimonion*. The Greek gods were believed to have the ability to make contact with humans. They intervened both for their own sake and for the sake of mortals. But traditional Greek religion also set the gods apart from men by forbidding true relations between the two. Gods and men did not converse. One ordered and the other obeyed. In later antiquity the gulf between mortal and immortal widened further. By Socrates' time, one could establish contact with the gods only at a formal remove, in the manner of the Delphic oracle, with a priestess serving as the medium between Apollo and whoever was asking his advice. Socrates obeyed one half of Greek tradition: He always and without hesitation obeyed his *daimonion*'s commands. But he flouted the other by proclaiming a level of intimacy that would have been profoundly offensive to conventional Greek piety. Socrates' deity, as Plutarch wrote, was "personal." It was private, exclusive. It spoke only to him. It was, therefore, unacceptable. As the historian Robert Garland has written, "The situation may not have been unlike that which prevails in the Roman Catholic Church today, where an alleged vision is treated as a mere delusion unless proof to the contrary can be supplied."[22] We can take this thought even further. The situation was not unlike what has prevailed throughout all of history. Claims of faith based on personal experience have always been suspect precisely because they are not prone to communal scrutiny.

The second reason McPherran gives follows directly from this. Because Socrates' *daimonion* was by definition unverifiable, because it could not be subjected to public standards of wisdom or beneficence or decency, it could, by a short, paranoid stretch of the imagination, be deemed harmful to Athens. This imputation is familiar as well: Private religious experiences are still often feared for their demonic potential. And to the Greek mind the very word *daimonion* left ample room for the implication of a broad array of dark forces. This was especially true in Socrates' day. In addition to the two great scourges of the fifth century BCE—the Persian War, which Athens effectively won, and the Peloponnesian War, which it did not—a plague broke out in the city in 430 that decimated a third of the population, and fundamentalists emerged proclaiming the fury of the gods and the guilt of Athens. Three decades later the mood was still jittery and apocalyptic. The presence of an untested and untestable deity in the midst of Athens, one potentially involved in "black magic," would undoubtedly have stirred the jury to fear for the spiritual and physical health of the city.

It was the third and final implication of Socrates' *daimonion*, however, that ultimately resulted in his conviction and death. Socrates was a stubborn, raffish, chronically unemployed, disputatious pest of a man in a city shimmering with the intolerance of its own decline; his demise was nothing if not overdetermined. But he might have survived had he not ignored one of the city's most cherished civic functions. In accordance with a tradition that had been developed over the course of centuries, Athens had four rigid rules that all new gods were forced to follow in order to gain legal entrance to the city, almost as if they were applying for a visa. First, the god had to contact an individual by means of an epiphany—a voice, for example, or a vision or a sign. Second, the person who received the epiphany had to gain the support of the citizenry and the priests of any rival gods by arguing in public for the new god's goodwill. Third, the individual and the new god's partisans had to petition the Boule, the upper Athenian assembly, to send the matter to the Ekklesia, the lower, popular assembly, where it would be put to a vote. Finally, the new god had to receive the support of an oracle, a move that was considered the divine parallel to the support of the city.[23]

It is obvious that Socrates fulfilled his first obligation. He had heard a voice that, although he did not identify its source, might have suggested to many the arrival of a new deity. And in light of his contract with the Delphic oracle, it could be argued, with a bit of ingenuity, that he fulfilled the last. But the city was utterly absent from Socrates' experience. It never entered the frame of his conception of the *daimonion*. It had ample time to do so. In Plato's *Apology*, Socrates declares that he has been receiving divine visits since "early childhood."[24] If we take this to mean since he was ten years old, that's sixty years that Socrates, from the perspective of Athens, kept his experience to himself. This is no crime when viewed through the lens of modern liberalism, according to which reticence is a right. It is none also when viewed through the lens of modern faith; for many mystics publicity is unholy and privacy the crux of divinity. But according to the Athenian code—a code applied by a band of small-minded, retributive hypocrites, but a code nonetheless—those long years of selective privacy bespoke a capital offense, and the verdict was just. The hemlock flowed legally.

mark mcpherran has observed that during the twentieth century, Socrates was conventionally portrayed as the Bertrand Russell of Athens—a cool atheist wrapped in a toga. In the past twenty years, the tide has shifted somewhat. In academic circles it is increasingly legitimate to speak of Socrates as a man of faith as well as a man of reason. But this development has had a countervailing effect. To many scholars a faithful Socrates is still an embarrassing Socrates, and the mounting emphasis on the irrational has led some to find innovative ways to blot out the stain of superstition from Socrates' image. The most tenacious spot, and therefore the most infuriating, has been the *daimonion*—what Gregory Vlastos called, with palpable annoyance, that "unpredictable little beast."[25]

The only way to understand the claims of those who would cut the *daimonion* out of Socrates' biography is to establish its proper place there. Figuring out what someone's voices are like is hard enough with the living; for a man who has been dead for 2,400 years, it approaches the impossible. Yet there are aspects of the *daimonion* that the evidence establishes more or less firmly and that give us a clearer understanding of the experience. The first of these is sensory. In the twenty-eight Platonic dialogues whose authorship is not generally disputed, the *daimonion* appears eleven times. Nine of these appearances are descriptively vague: Five refer to the experience as a "sign" (*semeion*), and four refer to it as a divine "something" (*to daimonion*). But in the *Apology* and in the *Phaedrus*, a dialogue on love and the art of rhetoric, as well as in Xenophon's *Apology*, it is referred to specifically as a voice (*phone*). Precisely what kind of voice neither Plato nor Xenophon reveals. Was it internal or external? Audible or psychological? Socrates' disciples are incurious on the finer points. But on the matter of modality we can be reasonably certain, based on the mere existence of the description, that the *daimonion* was sensory in quality and that it was verbal.

What it said is more difficult to discern. The most pointed descriptions of the *daimonion* appear in Plato's *Apology*, but that work touches less upon content than structure. Socrates tells the jury, for example, that his *daimonion* "always dissuades me from what I am proposing to do, and never urges me on";[26] that it has often checked him "in the middle of a sentence"; and that it opposes him "even in quite trivial things if I [am] going to take the wrong course."[27] These statements clearly suggest that the *daimonion* was admonitory, but how did it admonish? Did it say "no" or "halt"? Did it offer arguments? Did it suggest alternative courses of action? The only answers we have to these questions are the scattered anecdotal appearances of the *daimonion*, and they are frustratingly elliptical. In the *Phaedrus*, Socrates relates how his voice stopped him from committing impiety. "My friend," he says to the young title character of the dialogue, "just as I was about to cross the river, the familiar divine sign came to me which, whenever it occurs, holds me back from something I am about to do. I thought I heard a voice coming from this very spot, forbidding me to leave until I made atonement for some offense against the gods." Socrates goes on to explain what happened. While delivering a discourse on love at Phaedrus' prompting, he felt a deep uneasiness, but he couldn't or didn't try to understand what the sensation meant until the divine voice forced him to do so. He then realized what his error had been. He had spoken of love as if it were a bad thing, when "love is a god or something divine." It can't be bad.[28]

This is the *daimonion* at its most demonstrative. Elsewhere, it is laconic to the point of silence. In Plato's *Euthydemus*, a complex drama about wisdom and argumentation, Socrates explains to his friend Crito how he came to have an illuminating conversation in the Lyceum (the future site of Aristotle's school) with two men whom he had never met before. "I was sitting by myself in the undressing room just where you saw me and was already thinking of leaving. But when I got up, my customary divine sign put in an appearance. So I sat down again, and in a moment the two of them . . . came in, and some others with them. . . ."[29] The *daimonion* does not tell Socrates why he should sit down. It doesn't predict the future. As far as we are told, it doesn't even tell him *to* sit down. It simply "puts in an appearance," and he understands what he is meant to do.

Little is added to our understanding of the *daimonion* from its remaining appearances. In Xenophon's *Symposium* and Plato's *Theaetetus*, it rejects the return of a prodigal student, as if it were an internal admissions officer. In the *Republic* we learn that few others have had a similar experience. In Xenophon's *Memorabilia* we learn that Socrates and others considered it to be unfailingly correct. In Plato's *Apology* we learn that even the *daimonion*'s absence could be meaningful. Socrates interprets it as proof that his death is for the best:

You too, gentlemen of the jury, must look forward to death with confidence, and fix your minds on this one belief, which is certain: that nothing can harm a good man either in life or after death, and his fortunes are not a matter of indifference to the gods. This present experience of mine has not come about mechanically; I am quite clear that the time has come when it was better for me to die and be released from my distractions. That is why my sign never turned me back. For my own part I bear no grudge at all against those who condemned me and accused me, although it was not with this kind intention that they did so, but because they thought that they were hurting me; and that is culpable of them.[30]

Is there anything definitive that we can pull from this slender profile? Is there any quality that emerges as a constant? Only one: the demand of strict obedience. Not once does Socrates disobey or even question his *daimonion*. From the examples that we have, both the trivial and the grave, the rule that coalesces is that in Socrates' relationship to his deity, dissent was inconceivable. The wisdom of the *daimonion* was absolute, its word final. This is not to say that Socrates' obedience was irrational. On the contrary, it was formed by reason. Socrates began to hear his voice when he was a child, and unless we conclude that he obeyed it reflexively, as even saints rarely do, it must only have been through the slow growth of trust in its reliability that he came to banish thoughts of resistance. Theoretically, life is scientific. Experiences multiply like lab experiments, and based on falsifications and confirmations, beliefs and behaviors are formed. Most of us are lucky enough to find a few shakily reliable theories. Socrates found a law: The *daimonion* was always right. And once that law was established, rationality fell from the equation. In his old age, Socrates did not have to apply his intellect to determine what the *daimonion* wanted. He knew what it wanted. It wanted him to stop whatever he was doing or about to do. Intelligent thought might have been necessary to determine precisely what that transgression was, but obedience was immediate.

The strict devotion of Socrates to his *daimonion* is the hurdle that some modern thinkers have refused to jump. In his book *Socrates: Ironist and Moral Philosopher*, Gregory Vlastos based a lengthy dismissal of the *daimonion*'s importance on a famous passage from the *Crito*, the Platonic dialogue set in Socrates' jail cell just days before his execution. The passage, a self-declaration, is curt, resolute, and defiant: "I am not just now but in fact I've always been the sort of person who's persuaded by nothing but the reason that appears to me to be best when I've considered it."[31] It also has absolutely nothing to do with the *daimonion*. Socrates is merely proclaiming his fidelity to his own intellect over the capricious opinions of "the many." Nonetheless, on the authority of this sentence, Vlastos drew two conclusions about the *daimonion*. First, that on several occasions it is nothing more than a " 'hunch'—a strong intuitive impression" such as we all have at times and find retroactive ways of articulating.[32] Second, that on other occasions it is a legitimate religious experience, but one without meaning. It is a flicker, a mere switch for the intellect. Here Vlastos erected a thick wall between the irrational and the rational:

[All Socrates] could claim to be getting from the *daimonion* at any given time is precisely what he calls the *daimonion* itself—a "divine sign," which allows, indeed requires, *unlimited scope for the deployment of his critical reason* to extract whatever truth it can from these monitions. . . . [T]here can be no conflict between Socrates' unconditional readiness to follow critical reason wherever it may lead and his equally unconditional commitment to obey commands issued to him by his supernatural god through supernatural signs. *These two commitments cannot conflict because only by the use of his own critical reason can Socrates determine the true meaning of any of these signs.*[33]

Both of Vlastos's interpretations wither in the face of the evidence, the first because Socrates shows elsewhere that he is capable of having rational hunches without calling the experience *daimonic*, and the second because at times the *daimonion* indisputably trumps his critical reason. As a negative force it must oppose something, and what it opposes is Socrates' rationally thought-out actions.

Vlastos is not the staunchest of rationalists. He admits that Socrates was a religious man and that to deny him his faith would be a "surgery which kills the patient."[34] Others have not been so circumspect. In a 1985 essay, the philosopher Martha Nussbaum stripped the *daimonion* of all spiritual meaning, essentially recasting it in her own image as a metaphor for the intellect itself, "an ironic way of alluding to the supreme authority of dissuasive reason and elenctic argument."* Her support for this proposition is based less on evidence than ideology. Nussbaum simply values, and wishes Socrates to value, reason above belief: "The *daimonion* is called *daimonion*, a divine thing, because human reason *is* a divine thing, a thing intermediary (as a *daimon* is intermediary) between the animal that we are and the god that we might be. By taking his cue from this *sui generis* sign and not from the authority of tradition, Socrates is telling us that reason, in each of us, *is* the god truly worthy of respect, a presence far more authoritative than Zeus or Aphrodite."[35]

How can we say for certain that Nussbaum is wrong? Once reported, voice-hearing leaves the sanctity of the self and enters the fair territory of interpretation in which a perennial obstacle is the maw of metaphor. Swallowed, the experience transforms into witchcraft, into demonic possession, into schizophrenia, into intellect. It

---

*The word *elenctic*, an adjectival form deriving from the Greek word *elenchus*, refers to the ostensibly salutary form of argument to which Socrates exposed his interlocutors, commonly referred to as "Socratic."

is almost a right. With Socrates there is even a good reason to sanction the process. Irony is the essence of the Socratic method. For the purpose of education, Socrates could turn meaning on its head. But one's sense of order and truth must ultimately revolt against an interpretation that takes Socratic irony to be complete. It would be anarchical, even destructive, to conclude that everything Socrates said was in the service of a truth separate from the words themselves. It would also be anachronistic and antithetical to that basic tenet of human nature which disallows perfection. We may wish for Socrates to follow reason alone, but if we take his words in their proper contexts as our guide, the only conclusion we can draw is that Socrates, for all his peerless abilities to reason, to apply logic to the disorder of thought and action, believed strongly and completely in a phenomenon in which rationality was barely a factor. He followed his voice.

DIGNA VOX

JOAN OF ARC VERSUS THE CHURCH

More than her defiance of the Church's authority, more than her claims to know the future, more than her perhaps heterodox enthusiasm for the host, she was condemned for experiencing the other world as simply and as concretely as she experienced this world every day.

—MARINA WARNER, *Joan of Arc*

On the second floor of the Metropolitan Museum of Art, at the end of a long gallery dotted with Rodin sculptures, Jules Bastien-Lepage's painting *Jeanne d'Arc* hangs on a tall white wall. A magisterial eight feet by nine feet, thickly painted and lush with color, the canvas dominates the gallery as if it had just moved into the area and intended to show off its prosperity. The impression is partly one of comparative size. Its neighbors, paintings by Alfred Stevens and Alexandre Cabanel, are a great deal smaller. Mainly, though, it is one of comparative subject. As anyone who has encountered representations of Joan knows, she tends to dwarf the importance of everything around her. Her charisma is brash. She should be isolated. Johan Huizinga, the distinguished Dutch historian, excluded her from his classic *The Waning of the Middle Ages* because he knew she would throw off the book's balance.

In Bastien-Lepage's portrait, unbalance is the point, but the artist achieves this effect in a way that is difficult at first to articulate. Joan is portrayed in the garden of her childhood home in the village of Domrémy, in the northeast of France. She is wearing peasant clothes: a sackcloth skirt and a blue blouse tied across her belly and chest. Her head is cocked quizzically to the side, her long neck is outstretched, and her left hand reaches to touch the hanging leaves of a tree. In this setting and in this position, the passing viewer could easily mistake her for an ordinary country girl in repose, perhaps daydreaming of a suitor. But if one stands in front of the painting, one's gaze inevitably comes to rest on Joan's eyes, and the true nature of the scene flashes into focus. Her eyes are bright, blue, and wide, and she stares with them into the distance as if she is possessed or in a trance. They are so absorbent, so gaping and terrifying, in fact, that it can take several moments to notice that deep in the background, brushed in with the weeds and the branches, the artist has included the source of Joan's rapture. Three haloed saints, two in flowing robes and one in golden armor, hover ethereally above ground that to this day is considered by many to be sacred—the birthplace of a saint.

It is not considered so by everyone. When Bastien-Lepage's painting had its premiere in Paris, in 1880, Emile Zola castigated the artist for spoiling an accomplished work of naturalism with unfortunate superstition. He approved of Bastien-Lepage's attempt to get at "the real Joan of Arc, a simple peasant in the setting of her small Lorraine garden," but he found the supernatural tableau intrusive:

[The artist] thought he should portray the moment when Joan hears voices to dramatize the painting and put it in a historical setting. The young girl was sitting under an apple tree, working, when she heard the voices; she stood up, her eyes fixed, in ecstasy, she took a few steps, her arm extended, listening. The movement is done well. We can feel the hallucination in it. . . . But M. Bastien-Lepage, probably to make his subject more intelligible, thought to paint in the branches of the tree the vision of the girl, two saints and a knight armored in gold. To me, this is unwelcome; Joan's attitude, her gesture and her hallucinating eyes, were enough to give the whole drama; and this childish fleeting apparition is nothing but a pleonasm, a useless and awkward sign.[1]

The aesthetic point is well taken. Joan's perennial allure stems from the improbable gulf between her origins and her achievements. The outline of the tale can be quickly told. A poor girl from an obscure village, Joan arrived in 1429 at the court of the dauphin Charles of France, a vacillating pretender to the throne of a country literally split in two by the Hundred Years' War with England, its longtime dynastic rival. Armed with little more than an iron will and a professed divine mission—to take France back and crown Charles king—Joan was given an army and a royal sanction, with which she helped turn the tide of the war in France's favor with a series of stunning military victories. Her moment was brief. By 1431 she had been captured by the English, tried by the Inquisition, and burned as a heretic. But those two years were long enough to stamp into history the indelible force of her personality. No accoutrements, heavenly or otherwise, are needed.

Still, Bastien-Lepage's ghostly tableau adds an element to this story that Zola's criticism only serves to highlight. That element is not Joan's voices, which both delivered and accompanied her on her mission, but, rather, the battle over their meaning. Joan's life, the familiar interpretation goes, was the epitome of heroism. Her power was individual and indivisible. From the moment that she stepped out from the pastures of Lorraine and into the brutal arena of history, her life was tragically subject to what the critic Mark Schorer has called, in the context of William Blake's life, the "politics of vision." Her experience of voice-hearing was immediately and forever torn between the poles of insubstantiality and physicality, between the metaphorical and the literal, the personal and the public.

The tension inherent in Joan's voices is not her own. It is an unavoidable consequence of publicity and always has been. Between Socrates and Joan (both of whom referred to their voices as their "counsel"), only the shape of the pool has changed; the shock of immersion has remained the same. But Joan's voices made a comparatively large splash—more outwardly consequential, starker, and more violent. This is attributable partly to the dualist spirituality of her age and its tendency to see demons lurking in the inexplicable. But it also has to do with the perilous language Joan used to describe her experiences, language that ultimately clashed with the mind-set of her alleged superiors. As with Socrates, this clash resulted in a trial, but in this case we have a transcript and not an apology, a record from which there emerges a historical as opposed to a legendary Joan. And that Joan is, at her core and in the best possible way, simple. Facing an army of scholars, she never cloaked her experiences in abstract terms that muddled the line between the sensual and the spiritual. She couldn't. Illiterate and unschooled in everything but the most basic aspects of devotion, there was for Joan only the matter-of-fact. She heard voices; they told her what to do; she obeyed. This obedience is the essence of Joan and the engine of both her success and her demise.

Domrémy, the town in which Joan was born and that has since been renamed in her honor Domrémy-la-Pucelle—Domrémy-the-Maid—sits on the border between Lorraine and Champagne on the banks of the Meuse River, less than a hundred miles from present-day Germany. It is a sleepy town that has not changed much in the past six hundred years, with broad, verdant pastures, cobblestone roads, and medieval architecture. The most conspicuous difference is that much of the village is now given over to Joan's memory. Halfway up Domrémy's main street, a shop sells overpriced spoons with Joan's face on them and postcards of Ingrid Bergman burning in Victor Fleming's *Joan of Arc*. At the top of the hill, a sleek visitors' center has just been completed, "a discreet and silent place," according to its brochure, that "takes the visitor into a new world of images, sounds and light to discover life during the Middle Ages and the many faces of Joan." Halfway between these spots there is Joan's childhood home, preserved as a tourist attraction, and behind it is the fertile garden, now just a patch of grass, where Joan first heard her voices.

Or, rather, *allegedly* first heard her voices. Joan's life has been more carefully researched than almost any other medieval figure, but as she was an anonymous peasant whose public life did not begin until she was seventeen, her early years can only be viewed as if through a shroud. The famous pastoral scene immortalized by Bastien-Lepage comes from the transcripts of Joan's trial. Responding to an early question about her voices, Joan said that "from the age of thirteen, she received revelation from Our Lord by a voice. . . . And the first time she was greatly afraid. And she said that the voice came that time at noon, on a summer's day, a fast day, when she was in her father's garden, and that the voice came on her right side, in the direction of the church. And she said that the voice was hardly ever without a light, which was always in the direction of the voice."[2]

This is not the only extant origin story about Joan's voices, nor is it the first. After her most celebrated military victory—the lifting of the siege of Orléans in May 1429—Perceval de Boulainvilliers, a prominent courtier to Charles VII, wrote to the duke of Milan in praise of Joan's victory and offered a self-consciously literary account of her rise. Boulainvilliers is in agreement with Joan regarding the age at which her voices began, but in his letter the setting has changed to a nearby meadow, where Joan has been competing in a footrace.

While she is resting, a boy—a relative? a friend? mysteriously, the letter claims she couldn't tell—informs Joan that her mother is calling for her to return home. But when she rushes back to the house, her mother denies having sent for her.

> Thinking then that the boy had played a trick on her, she started back to rejoin her companions, when suddenly a luminous cloud appeared before her eyes, and out of the cloud came a voice, saying, "Jeanne, you are destined to lead a different kind of life and to accomplish miraculous things, for you are she who has been chosen by the King of Heaven to restore the Kingdom of France, and to aid and protect King Charles, who has been driven from his domains. You shall put on masculine clothes; you shall bear arms and become the head of the army; all things shall be guided by your counsel." After these words had been spoken, the cloud vanished, and the girl, astounded by such a marvel, at first could not give credence to it, but, in her ignorant innocence, remained perplexed as to whether she should believe it or no.[3]

Between Joan's story and Boulainvilliers' we should favor Joan's. But the comparison reveals two common features. The first is the vagueness of Joan's voices. In the minds of her partisans and in her own mind during the first stages of her trial, Joan's counsel had no identity beyond its divinity. A revelation from "Our Lord," a voice from a cloud—the similarity is the absence of personification, of a mouth from which the voice emerged. The element of solidity would be supplied by Joan's enemies or, more specifically, by the collision of her experience with their ideas.

The second feature that the two stories have in common is the conspicuous gap between Joan's revelation and its unveiling. For four years Joan remained in Domrémy alone with her voices, and then suddenly she burst forth into the world of knights, dukes, and kings.

Why did she wait so long to proclaim her mission? The likely answer is that she had not yet been given it. Shortly after her story of the voice in the garden, Joan told her judges that in the beginning her counsel had merely "taught her how to behave."[4] They had acted as a sort of divine superego; they told her to go to church and to preserve her virginity. It was only later on that these passive moral instructions hardened into the public and the political, and Joan was coaxed into the position of national savior.

To understand the transformation that Joan's voices made, history has to serve as context. Divine voice-hearers often portray their experiences as, and even train them to be, removed from the worldly domain. But this was never true of Joan. Her voices were always intimately connected with her everyday experiences, and the most formative of her experiences were of violence. By the time Joan was ten, the conflict between France and England had devolved into a civil war, with the powerful Duke of Burgundy allied with the enemy and the country divided along the Loire River. And, like towns along the Mason-Dixon line during the American Civil War, Domrémy was a microcosm of the struggle. Not only was it prey to the side effects of warfare—poverty, famine, banditry—but the area in which it lay was neatly split along political lines. Maxey, a nearly identical village across the Meuse, favored the duke; Domrémy favored the dauphin. The children from the towns, Joan reported at her trial, would come home battered and bloody from fighting one another.[5]

The war also compromised the safety of the town. In 1425, Burgundian soldiers, along with some English, drove off Domrémy's cattle and burned the church in which Joan had been baptized. It was the same year that she began to hear her voices. Three years later the threat of additional marauding drove Joan and her family to seek refuge in the nearby town of Neufchâtel. For two weeks they slept in an inn, until it was safe to return. For a girl of Joan's nature, a girl who thrived on clarity and honor, it must have been a disturbing up-heaval. It certainly stoked her anger. At her trial she made her hatred of the enemy absolutely clear. She knew of one Burgundian in Dom-rémy "whose head she would like to see chopped off." (But only, she added piously, "if it had pleased God.")[6] Is it any wonder that it was around this time that Joan's voices began to speak of revenge, of vic-tory over the enemies of France, and of stability? She was told, she said, that she "should go into France." Though she was only "a poor woman, who knew nothing of riding or of making war," she obeyed.[7] By February 1429, with the help of a devout cousin and the captain of the local French garrison, she made it to Chinon, the site of the French court in exile. She hadn't told her family.

That Joan found a sympathetic audience in Charles is one of the abiding mysteries of her story and arguably the most remarkable achievement. The faith and certainty of a child are one thing. That child's ability to persuade a king, a man surrounded by a thick ret-inue of courtiers, each with his own interests and loyalties, to give her an army and a sizable amount of money is quite another. The achievement is partly due to good historical timing. The medieval period was primed for the arrival of a female savior. As the historian Régine Pernoud has written, "We are dealing with an age in which above the doors of the cathedrals stood the image of a Virgin. From the troubadors' songs to the romances of chivalry, the age of feu-dalism had devoted to Woman a veritable cult. . . . [Joan] was ex-pected by her age; men's minds were prepared for that astounding phenomenon."[8] They were even prepared literally: Fifteenth-century France was replete with prophecies about a maiden who would emerge to rescue the country from its troubles. Some seemed even to point specifically to Joan. One prophecy, attributed to the Arthurian wizard Merlin, spoke of a virgin coming from the Bois Chesnu, the oak woods bordering Domrémy, to save France. An-other, from the visionary Marie d'Avignon, directly addressed the troubles of the Hundred Years' War. "She spoke . . . of having had frequent visions concerning the desolation of France. In one of them Marie saw many pieces of armour which were brought before her, which frightened her. For she was afraid that she would be forced to put this armour on. But she was told to fear nothing, and that it was not she who would have to wear this armour, but that a Maid who would come after her would wear it and deliver the kingdom of France from its enemies."[9]

The grip that such prophecies had on the imagination not only of the peasantry but of the royalty cannot be overestimated as a factor in Joan's success. Charles was particularly prone to them. Broke, mired in defeat and uncertainty, and torn apart by intrigue, the dauphin's cause was grim at the time of Joan's arrival. It was also desperately hungry for divine sanction. In the medieval mind, a disputed crown bespoke a heavenly uncertainty. "God's mandate," the novelist and historian Marina Warner has written of this time, "was a sensitive, finely primed pointer, influenced by individual action and wobbling accordingly, now withdrawing, now returning, now withdrawing again."[10] Charles was in need of a magnet to hold the pointer steady on his head. Joan provided it.

But nothing is left to divinity alone. Joan's claim of heavenly sanction was welcome news, but it was released to a world that was brutal and real, and it is there that it would have to make its way.

The story of Joan's first audience with Charles is a vacuum that has been filled with warring fictions. The most popular legend, which appears in George Bernard Shaw's play and in several other versions of Joan's life, has it that she convinced Charles of her divine legitimacy by picking him out from a crowd of courtiers in which he had hidden to test her. Another has it that she convinced him by revealing her knowledge of a prayer he made in private to the effect that if he were not the true blood heir to the throne—which, indeed, he may not have been—he be allowed to leave France and the troubles of the war. This story claims that Joan reinvigorated Charles by reassuring him of his legitimacy. Still another legend has it that Charles was convinced by the arrival of an angel that swooped down and delivered a crown to him, in a sort of Gallic version of the Annunciation, with the dauphin cast in the role of both Virgin Mary and Messiah, and Joan as the Archangel Gabriel.

These legends all seek to dramatize the "miracle" of Joan's arrival at court—the galvanizing effect she had on the French cause and on a leader previously known to be pusillanimous and incompetent. They accomplish this feat, but they typically ignore what came next. Joan reinvigorated Charles with a sense of divine authority, but that authority was not so convincing that he was going to hand over thousands of troops at the request of a teenage girl. Heaven may well have sent Joan, but armor cost money, and before he was going to take on such an expenditure, committing himself to a great political and military risk, he needed assurance that she did not come from the other side—hell, that is, not England. To test Joan's divine mettle, Charles sent her to nearby Poitiers to be examined for three weeks by a council of learned clergymen.

The record of Joan's interrogation at Poitiers has been lost, and the episode is therefore traditionally passed over as only a minor pit stop on the road to her heroism and martyrdom. But it is the crucial first indication of the dichotomy at the heart of Joan's story. All eras subject voice-hearing to a test. For the Greeks the test was political. Socrates' prosecutors asked, Do the voices subvert or corrupt the workings of the city? In our time the test is psychiatric: Are voices healthy or pathological? In Joan's time the question was theological: Do the voices come from God or from the Devil? This was the deep anxiety of the culture in which Joan lived—anxious because the question could never be answered to anyone's satisfaction. The Devil was the master of disguises, and his favorite disguise was that of his heavenly adversary. No matter how pure Joan seemed, no matter how much confidence she could offer those with whom she came in contact, she could, by a simple, terrifying reversal of the divine equation, be the embodiment of evil.

This horrifying ambiguity was deepened by the fact that Joan's interrogators had only earthly tests with which to determine her voices' divinity. Twenty years after her death, for a number of political reasons, the Catholic Church set up a trial in absentia to rehabilitate Joan's image. There, a professor of theology who had been present at Poitiers reported that he had said to her, "God cannot wish us to believe in you unless he sends us a sign to show that we should believe in you." Joan's response was characteristically blunt and practical. "In God's name, I have not come to Poitiers to make signs," she said. "But lead me to Orléans, and I will show you the signs I was sent to make."[11] Orléans, the military gateway to the north of France, had for months been under heavy siege by the English. Joan's orders, given to her by her voices, were to lift the siege and lead Charles to the ancient city of Rheims, deep within enemy territory, to be crowned king. What else but her success would confirm the divinity of her mission? This logic, in fact, expressed the model of Joan's incredible rise. Her voices would lend her an initial divine authority, the right to be heard and taken seriously, and her success would confirm and compound that authority. The heavenly would open the door for the earthly, and the earthly would reveal the wisdom of the heavenly. It was an effective formula, but it was also risky, for it could be sustained only by achievement. If she faltered, so, too, would her legitimacy. From the beginning, then, Joan walked a tightrope, with good on one side and evil on the other. In this light, her gruesome fate seems almost predetermined.

But with the benefit of hindsight, it is easy to see Joan's death on the horizon. In the moment, armed with at least the curiosity of the

Armagnacs, as Charles's party was called, Joan's voices worked to her advantage by transforming her pluck and her good fortune into the seeming grace of God. An incident that illustrates this well occurred a month after her examination at Poitiers, when she joined Charles's troops, led by Count Jean de Dunois, on the march to Orléans. Joan's voices had told her, and she had told Dunois, that the Armagnac army should attack from the north. Dunois, a seasoned soldier, dismissed Joan's advice and approached from the south. This was a miscalculation since, when they reached the Loire River, they were prevented from crossing by a strong wind. Joan, realizing she had been ignored, turned on Dunois: "You thought you had deceived me but it is you who have deceived yourselves, for I am bringing you better help than you ever got from any soldier or any city. It is the help of the King of Heaven." At that exact moment the wind changed direction and the army was able to cross. Dunois, stunned, was won over to Joan's cause and thereafter believed her to be an instrument of heaven.[12]

Such belief was not universal. In the testimony that we have regarding this period, Joan comes off as cocky, impertinent, volatile, and possessed with a belief in herself that far outweighs her abilities. This type of character could hardly have appealed to experienced captains of war, with their superior knowledge of troop formations, artillery positions, and enemy tactics. Nor should they have all bowed to her authority: Joan's military acumen was not particularly impressive. But her presence was irrefutably electrifying, and she rallied the troops as only a hero can. At the time of Joan's arrival in Orléans, English forces had held a series of fortifications around the city for six months. Within a week the enemy was cleared away and the city saved. Again, Joan had little technical hand in the victory— command of the troops at this point in her career was left to the experts—but her apparent holiness, and her bravery (she received an arrow shot to the shoulder that caused her to fall off her horse), was its spiritual fulcrum, and the victory in return confirmed her holiness. The swiftness of the Armagnac success at Orléans was proof that Joan was the emissary of God's will. Her prophecy, delivered to her in Domrémy and announced at Chinon, was fulfilled at Orléans. Heaven's mandate was now clear: God favored the French.

At the trial for Joan's rehabilitation, Jean D'Aulon, the affectionate and loyal squire whom Charles had assigned to her, told of an episode that occurred just prior to the first significant battle at Orléans. The pair was resting quietly in Joan's tent, waiting for the news of action, when suddenly she sprang out of bed. "In God's name," she exclaimed, "my Counsel has told me that I must attack the English." Not waiting for D'Aulon's help in suiting up, she rushed from the tent, commandeered a page's horse, and hurried to the site of a skirmish in progress at a nearby fort where she had won her first victory.[13]

According to D'Aulon, Joan was often this impulsive. In his testimony, she is constantly leaping on her horse and calling for her standard and sword. For a while this active method was successful. From early May to mid-June 1429, Joan either helped take or was given credit for taking a series of Anglo-Burgundian strongholds surrounding Orléans, forcing the enemy to abandon its campaign in the Loire Valley. She then set out with equal vigor to fulfill the second of her voices' dictates: the crowning of Charles VII at the Cathedral of Notre Dame in Rheims. From June to August, Joan led the dauphin on a long march through enemy countryside, precipitating the return to Armagnac allegiance of a series of cities along the way, and then back again.

It was a remarkable spate of achievements. It was also short-lived, not least of all because Joan's behavior was untenable. Following the coronation, she intended to fulfill a third prophecy that her voices had proclaimed: the liberation of Paris, the capital, from which Charles had been expelled by the Burgundians in 1418. The will was still there, but the political sponsorship wasn't. Tapped for resources and increasingly put upon by a firebrand whose arrogance undermined his ability to negotiate with the enemy, Charles stymied Joan's plans by agreeing to a two-week truce. The decision deeply frustrated Joan, but she had a more authoritative edict than Charles's to follow, and she mustered an army to storm the city. For the first time she failed. Wounded by an arrow through her thigh and thwarted by the tepid fighting of her officers, Joan was ordered by Charles to retreat. More than a military debacle, it was a blow to her image, the source of her power. The voices had never before been proven wrong; now their very provenance was called into question. Compounding the problem was Joan's decision to attack Paris on the feast of the Nativity of the Blessed Virgin Mary, a decision that many deemed impious. The failure seemed almost predetermined.

It isn't necessary to dwell on the depressing events that followed. Joan's success, from Orléans to Paris, lasted less than five months. Her decline would last more than eight. Reading of the events during that period is like watching the dissipation of a great artist in time-lapse photography. Even more dispiriting is the knowledge that Joan might not have fallen so far and so hard had she not been left to her own impetuous devices. Following the defeat at Paris, Joan laid siege to a number of cities, but in all cases she did so as a free lance, without adequate resources or advice. The result was a tragedy that she later claimed her voices had foreseen, but she does not appear to have foreseen the tragedy's scope. On May 23, 1430, while attacking Burgundian forces outside the northern city of Compiègne, Joan was outmaneuvered, pulled from her horse by an archer, and taken hostage. Charles, no longer desiring her presence, declined to secure a ransom, and Joan was bartered between competing interests until she was finally given over to the Inquisition for a full ecclesiastical trial. In little more than a year, she had gone from peasant to hero to prisoner. She would never be free again.

. . .

when joan was pulled to the ground, yanked by a gold and scarlet cloak that she vainly wore into battle, she made a spiritual as well as a physical descent. Religious politics have always been the same. God's sanction is reserved for winners. In the record of Joan's fall, one can almost see the grace change hands. "It has pleased our Blessed Creator to allow and grant us a great grace—*The Maid* has been captured!" the Duke of Burgundy, Joan's great enemy, wrote to the inhabitants of Saint-Quentin shortly after she was taken. He continued gleefully: "Now the error and foolish belief of those who approved and favored this woman will be recognized. We write you this news in the hope that it will give you joy, comfort, and satisfaction, and that you will thank and praise our Creator Who sees and knows all things."[14]

The implication is clear: Joan had lost the endorsement of heaven. Also clear, at least in hindsight, is the action that must follow. Joan had been imbued with legitimacy at Charles's court as the direct result of her voices. They were the key that had unlocked the gate to her new life, and within that life they had been her most powerful weapon—the instrument of severe Anglo-Burgundian embarrassment. Joan's enemies could not reverse their humiliation, but they could reverse her divinity. This is the task they set out to accomplish when, six months after Compiègne, they handed Joan over to Pierre Cauchon, the bishop of Beauvais, to orchestrate her inquisitorial trial.

Joan's trial, which took place in the city of Rouen, not far from the English Channel, in the winter and spring of 1431, is both the centerpiece and endgame of Joan's life. It is also the most classically dramatic and thus a favorite of the many artists and writers who have been attracted to Joan, either as an exemplar of the human spirit or as the embodiment of sainthood. But we do not need a work of art to inflate the drama of Joan's trial or to bring her back to life. The transcripts are enough. In them, Joan's answers to her judge's questions seem to have been recorded faithfully and accurately, and the result is a character infinitely more heroic, because infinitely more human, than the images that have been thrown up by her partisans or her worshippers. In the record, she comes across as defiant, clever, willful, loyal, frightened, petulant, and confused—in short, a nineteen-year-old girl of irreducible complexity.

And of preternatural strength. Joan's trial is not a passion play, but it is undoubtedly an ordeal. During the three months of her trial, Joan was besieged by questions from high-level theologians and lawyers hostile to her ideals and driven by the single goal of her elimination. Unable to read and in any case without recourse to the records of the proceedings, she had to rely on her wit and her memory to keep track. She was the only witness and, in accordance with inquisitorial tradition, had no aid in her defense. When not under interrogation, she was chained to a post in a small locked cell. Her guards were English soldiers who taunted and threatened to rape her. She was not allowed to receive the sacraments, to attend Mass, or to offer her confession. She was never formally tortured—her judges deemed her too stubborn to benefit from the rack—but her treatment was without question torturous.

In light of these conditions, Joan's performance was nothing short of glorious. At times she flatly refused to respond to her judges' inquiries ("Next question!" is a frequent refrain); at others she admonished them ("I warn you not to judge me wrongfully," she told Cauchon, "for you would so put yourself in great danger"); at others she was even playful (in retaliation for an error in citing evidence, she threatened to pull one judge's ears). What she never allowed to enter into the proceedings was condescension. But glory can't save a life; it is what is offered to someone in lieu of being saved. And for Joan, salvation was impossible. In her judges she faced men whose minds were qualitatively different from her own. Trained in the strict scholastic manner of Thomas Aquinas, Joan's judges knew only the dichotomous mode of the Church, in which body and soul are in strict opposition and truth can be attained through careful philosophical reasoning. Joan, by contrast, had an intuitive mind. She found truth in bare experience, no matter how vague or undefined. She knew nothing of philosophy. Faced with her judges' questions, then, she could answer well enough, but she could never understand the intentions behind them or the conclusions they were moving toward. She was on a course she could neither comprehend nor exit.

This clash of consciousness was the engine of the most important line of questioning at Joan's trial. Her judges explored many concerns during those three months—Joan's cross-dressing, her childhood, her interactions with Charles, her military exploits—but they were consumed with her voices. They probed them from every angle: When did Joan first hear the voices? What figures did they represent? Did she see them as well as hear them? Did they tell her to try to escape? Were they present at her arrival in Chinon? Did they foresee her injuries? Did she ever touch them? Smell them? Embrace them? Were they clothed? Bald? Luminescent? What did they sound like? Their desire was always for greater specificity. By coaxing Joan's voices into the world of physical reality, they could prove she had erred. Unless they said otherwise, the holy was ineffable.

Joan's answers to this insistent questioning varied throughout the trial from disobedience to candidness. Taken in sequence, however, they reveal the slow effect of her interrogators' thinking and language on her own. As we have seen, one feature of the early descriptions of Joan's voices is their indistinctness. Joan referred to them quite simply as her "counsel," and she identified their source, equally as simply, as God. During the early stages of her trial, she did not waver much from this stance. Joan first spoke about her voices at her second public session, during which she told of her revelation in the garden in Domrémy, and though she said it was "the voice of an angel" that approached her, this appears to have been more a reverent metaphor than a stab at literal truth. She was more convincing when she used the phrase *digna vox*—worthy voice—and refused to proceed.

Under the constant, wearing pressure of the interrogation, however, her refusals were not bound to last long, and, indeed, Joan's voices soon underwent a swift materialization. At her third public session, two days later, she seems to have sensed the traps being set for her. Questioned by the theologian Jean Beaupère, Cauchon's deputy and the most hostile of Joan's judges, as to whether she saw something along with the voices, Joan answered testily that "it is a beautiful voice, righteous and worthy; otherwise, I am not bound to answer you." Asked whether the voices had eyes and could see, she threw up a shield of folk wisdom: "There is a saying among little children that people are often hanged for telling the truth." But then, at her fourth public session three days later, her voices made a sudden transformation. Questioned by Beaupère as to whether she had heard the voice while in her cell and whether it was "the voice of an angel, or of a saint, or directly from God," her singular inspiration split in two: "She answered that the voices were those of Saint Catherine and of Saint Margaret. And their heads are crowned with beautiful crowns, most richly and preciously." Several questions on, these figures spawned a third, and for the first time the triumvirate of Bastien-Lepage's canvas springs into view:

> She said she also said that she received counsel from Saint Michael.
> Questioned which came first,
> She said it was Saint Michael.
> Asked if it were long ago,
> She answered: I do not speak of Saint Michael's voice, but of the great comfort [he brought me].

Asked which was the first voice that came to her when she was thirteen,

She said it was Saint Michael whom she saw before her eyes, and he was not alone, but was accompanied by angels from heaven.[15]

She would never be able to take it back. But then it is unlikely that she would have wanted to. Joan's acquiescence to the literality of her judges was unconscious. Like many prisoners, she integrated the mind-set of her captors into her own so that when she began to proclaim the identities of her voices, she did so in all honesty, and probably with relief. She also did so according to her own experiences and in accordance with her character. The saints in whose mouths Joan placed her voices might have materialized as the result of prodding, but they were perfect choices for an adventurous, patriotic virgin intoxicated by heroism and brought low by vengeful enemies. Michael, for instance, whose official canonical status is that of an archangel, was intimately connected with the Armagnac cause. When the abbey of Saint Denis fell to the English in 1419, the dauphin Charles ordered that Michael's likeness replace Denis's on the standards of his soldiers. Mont-Saint-Michel, the Benedictine monastery on the coast of Normandy, became the last bastion of French loyalty in the north; throughout the Hundred Years' War, pilgrims would sneak through English blockades to visit it. Marina Warner writes that Michael was the "emblem of French resistance," the saint whose name was the battle cry in heaven against evil and whose traditional role was to save the souls of the faithful from the hands of the enemy.[16]

Catherine made sense on a more personal level. The patron saint, ironically, of Maxey, the village whose children Domrémy's used to fight, Catherine had been through an ordeal similar to Joan's. According to tradition (there is no evidence that she actually lived), Catherine was a high-born virgin in early-fourth-century Alexandria who protested against Emperor Maxentius's persecution of Christians. Brought before him, she defeated the arguments of fifty learned philosophers, all of whom were then beheaded. When Maxentius, impressed, proposed marriage, she refused in order to preserve herself for Christ. She was tortured and thrown in jail for her impudence. An attempt to break her on a spiked wheel ended in failure when the wheel broke apart, and she was finally beheaded. Catherine, Warner writes, "stood chiefly for independent thinking, courage, autonomy, and culture. She was the saint chosen by young unmarried women in France."[17]

Margaret of Antioch, like Catherine a figure of legend, was also revered for upholding her virginity against the advances of a pagan. Tending her flock one day during the reign of the Roman Empire, Margaret was admired by a magistrate wandering by. She refused his advances and was brought to trial for her defiance. In the words of the *Catholic Encyclopedia*, "Threatened with death unless she renounced the Christian faith, the holy virgin refused to adore the gods of the empire and an attempt was made to burn her, but the flames . . . left her unhurt. She was then bound hand and foot and thrown into a cauldron of boiling water, but at her prayer her bonds were broken and she stood up uninjured."[18] Margaret, too, was beheaded. Like Catherine, with whom she was sometimes represented in the iconography of the Middle Ages, she was often portrayed armed—an important point for the warrior Joan.[19]

Joan's choice of saints bespoke a genius for symbolism that has always been a significant factor in her fame. A prodigy of self-representation, she allied herself with images with which she will always be associated because they fit so well with her cause. In life, however, that alliance was her undoing. It led her into a trap of duality the existence of which she could only intuit but that her judges had dedicated their lives to uphold. Joan had been free to worship angels and saints, but to sense them, to hear their voices, was to contaminate holy spirit with sinful flesh. The inhabitants of heaven could not be substantial unless they were demonic simulacra, and Joan could not have heard them unless she had become a daughter of Satan.

Could Joan have avoided falling into this theological trap? Unlike Teresa of Ávila, who successfully evaded the Inquisition her entire life, Joan was not equipped with the education necessary to make academic distinctions between the bodily and spiritual senses. She also lacked the knowledge that there was a danger inherent in not making such a distinction. But her main handicap was that her experiences were unwaveringly empirical. At no time did Joan experience the voices as part of her, integrated spiritually in a manner that her judges might, in theory, have accepted. In her simple manner, she spoke of them always as being separate from her. They were holy and she was human, but they spoke aloud. This was not the "still, small voice" of Elijah. These were audible voices. In prison she complained that she couldn't understand what Catherine was telling her because of the noise of the guards.

Joan's judges exploited the particularity of her experiences and her naiveté with terrible efficiency. Experienced scholars and prosecutors, they prodded her with questions so that her spiritual defeat was inevitable. Joan's naming of Michael, Catherine, and Margaret occurred on the fourth day of interrogation. Twelve more days followed before her formal indictment—both in public, among dozens of witnesses, and in her cell, among only a few—and during all the interrogations, the judges homed in on the human senses. What did Michael look like? What did Catherine smell like? What did Margaret feel like? A pattern forms: Joan, exhausted and ever more bewildered, lashes out, stalls, and seeks to limit her responses to proclaiming the great joy that the divine visitations give her. Her judges press firmly on. Finally, on the very last day of her questioning—March 17, 1430—a fatal exchange takes place:

> Asked if she had ever kissed or embraced Saint Catherine or Saint Margaret,
> She said she had embraced them both.
> Asked whether they smelt pleasant,
> She replied: Assuredly they did so.
> Asked whether in embracing them she felt warmth or anything else,
> She said she could not embrace them without feeling and touching them.
> Asked what part she embraced, whether the upper or lower,
> She answered: It is more fitting to embrace them above rather than below.[20]

Joan was aware of many of the popular beliefs regarding the presence of evil on earth; they circulated in the countryside. She knew of mandrakes and fairies, and she knew that witches were thought to be able to fly. But she did not seem to have recognized the more deeply ingrained superstition to which this line of questioning referred. As subtly as the questions were phrased, she did not know that her judges probably had in mind the witches' Sabbath, in which spiritually tainted women consorted with the physical manifestations of demons—kissing them, worshipping them, having sex with them. She did not know that her straightforward answers, however artfully coerced, were being examined through a lens of fear, that her voices were being pulled into a ghoulish drama that had been written into the history of Europe over the course of several centuries.

Later, after they had cornered her into guilt and codified her trespasses in a series of articles of condemnation—submitted both on their own behalf and on behalf of the University of Paris, the leading ecclesiastical authority in France at the time—Joan's judges tried to educate her as to the grave spiritual implications of her experiences. They carefully read to her the charges, which referred to her as "an idolater, and invoker of demons, a wanderer from the Faith." They implored her again and again to submit to the Church Militant, the administrant of Christ's faith on earth. They delivered sermons. They bribed her with promises. But Joan would not submit. In the end, she could not have. Even when she was offered the precise knowledge of her sins as seen through the eyes of the Church, the conflict was intractable and not much different from the conflict that had come between her and Charles. To her judges, they alone were the arbiters of truth. To Joan, the voices were sacrosanct. They represented God, a higher authority than the men who sat in judgment of her.

Joan came to understand the nature of her dilemma and expressed it well. "I believe in the Church on earth," she told an archdeacon who tried to mend her ways, "but for my deeds and words, as I have previously said, I refer the whole matter to God, Who caused me to do what I have done."[21] Her celebrated pluck was also replaced by a brave resignation to her fate: "And if I were to be condemned and saw the fire lit and the wood prepared and the executioner who was to burn me ready to cast me into the fire, still in the fire would I not say anything other than I have said."[22] But abstract fire is different from real fire, and in the proximity of the latter, Joan did bend. On May 24, she was led onto a platform in the cemetery of Saint-Ouen to be publicly excommunicated, in direct view of the executioner and the tools he would use to build the stake and fire. There she collapsed in tears, prayed for guidance, and signed a formal abjuration.

I JEANNE, CALLED THE PUCELLE, A MISERABLE SINNER, AFTER I RECOGNIZED THE SNARE OF ERROR IN WHICH I WAS HELD; AND NOW THAT I HAVE, BY

GOD'S GRACE, RETURNED TO OUR MOTHER HOLY CHURCH; IN ORDER
THAT IT MAY BE APPARENT THAT NOT FEIGNEDLY BUT WITH GOOD HEART
AND WILL I HAVE RETURNED TO HER; I DO CONFESS THAT I HAVE
GREIVOUSLY SINNED, IN FALSELY PRETENDING THAT I HAVE HAD REVELA-
TIONS FROM GOD AND HIS ANGELS, SAINT CATHERINE AND SAINT MAR-
GARET, ETC.[23]

She was then formally sentenced, warned that she should forever
"leave her revelations and other stupidities," and given female dress.
A barber was brought in to shave her head.

Joan's lapse lasted four days. Sometime after her abjuration, she
put her male clothing back on. In the eyes of the Church, it was a
sign that she had relapsed into sin. Visited in her prison cell by a
group of judges on May 28, she insisted that she had revoked her earlier answers only "through fear of the fire." She was then asked if she
had heard the voices of Catherine and Margaret again. She said yes.
In the margin of the record, the clerk transcribing the exchange
wrote "Responsio mortifera"—the fatal reply.[24] The next day, the Church
gave Joan over to the secular arm to be executed. The stake was
erected on May 30 in the marketplace at Rouen. The official record
notes that many observers wept and that many "murmured greatly
against the English." Afterward, Joan's ashes were gathered and
thrown into the Seine.

on a quiet spot above the Meuse River, shouldered into the
northern border of the Bois Chesnu, the Basilica of Saint Joan stands
each night drenched in floodlight. Built outside Domrémy beginning in 1881 and consecrated in 1926—six years after Joan was can-
onized by Pope Benedict XV—the cathedral, with its grand stone
spire and sprawling grounds, dominates the view from the valley,
symbolizing Joan's full, posthumous acceptance by the Catholic

Church. And outside the cathedral, dominating the view in the courtyard, there stands a sculpture that symbolizes the Church's full acceptance of the very iconography it used to destroy Joan. Produced by André Allar in the late nineteenth century, the sculpture portrays Joan in white marble as a young peasant girl, kneeling and lifting her head to the figures of her three saints, cast in illustrious bronze. Michael, bedecked in glorious armor and crowned with a sunlike halo, raises a finger toward heaven; Catherine, standing above a wheel, the symbol of her martyrdom, bears a long sword in her hands; and Margaret, in flowing robes, proffers a helmet for Joan to wear on her divine mission.

Allar's sculpture, which stands protected behind a chain rope, bears all the marks of officialdom, but its interpretation of Joan's inspiration is hardly exclusive. Since the early seventeenth century, artists, historians, and politicians have been bending Joan's voices to fit their own purposes and hopes. A tour of French statuary alone shows the wide room for variation: An elegant marble work by François Rude, produced in the 1850s and now at the Louvre, portrays Joan as Bastien-Lepage outfitted her, in long skirt and peasant blouse; her head is tilted to the side, and she cups a hand to her ear to listen to her counsel, who are not represented. The image is of psychological rapture. A statue by Antonin Mercié, erected on a bridge in Domrémy in 1902 and intended as a secular contrast to Allar's work, has Joan lifting a sword with the help of an imposing woman with pearl-embroidered hair. The woman is the personification of France, and Joan's inspiration is the call of national heroism. Even the militantly nationalist sculptures of Maxime Réal del Sarte, which portray Joan as the protective Mother of France, shepherding the suffering through the Great War, takes a conspicuous position on Joan's voices—they ignore them completely, as if they corrupted the true, patriotic resonance of her story.

In twentieth-century representations, the banishment of Joan's

voices, whether coy, clever, or complete, has far outweighed their religious personification. The dominant impulse of modern artists has
been to rationalize Joan's inspiration—to pull them from the grasp
of the Church and the State and at last hand them over to Science.
The novelist Anatole France, who published a two-volume biography of Joan in 1908, was a pioneer of this method. In his account,
Joan's voices were the result of a hysterical religious fervor fomented
by medieval priests eager to manufacture a savior for France. A fierce
rationalist, Anatole France could not deny the importance of the
voices altogether, but he could drain them of the supernatural. They
were, he concluded, *"ces troubles . . . hallucinations perpetuelles"*—a disorder of perpetual hallucinations.[25]

George Bernard Shaw, whose 1923 play *Saint Joan* is widely cred-
ited with winning him the Nobel Prize, did not go so far as to diagnose Joan ("Visionaries are neither impostors nor lunatics," he insisted
in his celebrated preface to the work) but, like Anatole France, he did
seek a more comfortably rationalistic approach to the mystery of
her experiences. The conclusion Shaw drew posited a sort of demo-
tion of the voices (which, in the end, he conflated into her visions)
from experiences of personal religious import to imaginative out-
bursts of the rational faculty. Joan, he wrote outmodedly, was a
"Galtonic visualizer," a reference to Francis Galton, the nineteenth-
century polymath and pioneer of eugenics. "She saw imaginary saints
just as some other people see imaginary diagrams and landscapes
with numbers dotted about them, and are thereby able to perform
feats of memory and arithmetic impossible to non-visualizers."[26] In
the play itself, this position leads Shaw to contort Joan's belief into
unrecognizable shapes. In Rheims, following Charles's coronation,
she tells the resentful archbishop that he should trust in her voices
"even if they are only the echoes of my own commonsense."[27]

Since Shaw, Joan's voices have received a generally fairer showing—which is to say, one more in line with her own words—no

doubt because there has occurred a backlash against the hyper-rationalism of the late nineteenth and early twentieth centuries. But there remains a palpable undercurrent of embarrassment about Joan's voices. In a recent biography, the novelist Mary Gordon disclaimed, "As historical character, model, or exemplum, Joan would be far more palatable to the post-Enlightenment appetite if she hadn't claimed to hear voices."[28]

This begs a vital question: Does it matter that Joan's voices are somewhat unpalatable? It does, of course, if we want Joan's desires and values to match our own. Being able to stomach her inspiration is then of the utmost importance, for if we can't, we will have to season it or cut away the spoiled parts or spit it out. To some extent we all treat Joan this way. She is a hero, and heroes are receptacles for our love or our hatred. But she is also a historical figure with a solidity and a reality all her own. In this sense, what we think of her voices is of no concern. It was certainly of no concern to Joan. Against odds that can scarcely be measured, she was not impervious. She faltered and she groveled, and in the end her most closely held belief altered according to the beliefs of others. Yet what never changed, not even for a moment, was the internal meaning of her voices, the simplicity of their effect: They gave her joy. When they were present, she was ecstatic; when they were gone, she was bereft. That is why Joan listened to her voices, why she followed them, and why, the one time she abandoned them, she had to return, though it meant certain death. She would rather die with her voices than live without them.

MORBID OFFSPRING

DANIEL PAUL SCHREBER
VERSUS PSYCHIATRY

*In my opinion science would go very wrong to designate
as "hallucinations" all such phenomena that lack objective
reality, and to throw them into the lumber room of
things that do not exist.*

—DANIEL PAUL SCHREBER

Daniel Paul Schreber, a newly appointed judge on the Supreme Appeals Court of the Kingdom of Saxony, in Dresden, began to go mad in the summer of 1893. He had experienced difficulties with his mental health once before, nine years earlier, and had been treated successfully at the psychiatric hospital at Leipzig University, run by the famed brain anatomist Paul Flechsig. Now, anxious about the prominent position he would soon take up, he began to have dreams that his illness had returned. They proved to be prophetic. Schreber began his job in the fall, and he worked so hard and with so little rest that he was soon at the point of collapse. He stopped sleeping. He heard strange crackling noises coming from the walls of his bedroom. In six weeks he had grown so desperate and suicidal that he was forced to leave his job and rush back to Leipzig for emergency treatment.

Flechsig had treated Schreber during his first illness with sedatives and bed rest, but nothing he could do now seemed to alleviate Schre-

ber's insomnia. Sleeping drugs were ineffective, and the asylum offered little solace for an ever-worsening condition. In just a few weeks
Schreber grew so depressed that his doctor found himself unable to
help. Then, after a winter of more failed treatments, Schreber's condition took a turn toward the psychotic. He began to have persecutory fantasies and delusions. He believed that he was a "seer of
spirits"; that the soul of Flechsig was plotting to commit "soul murder" against him; that he was being transformed into a woman so that
his body could be sexually abused; that he was surrounded by ghostly
replicas of human beings; that the world would soon end. He also
began to hear innumerable voices that tormented him day and
night— of Flechsig, of his mother and father, of his wife, of various
"departed souls," of the Pope, of "240 Benedictine Monks," of the
members of the "Students' Corps Saxonia in Leipzig," of the sun. By
the spring of 1894, Schreber was so far gone that arrangements were
made for him to be transferred to Sonnenstein, a state asylum for the
severely mentally ill. He would spend the next eight and a half years
there. His voices referred to it as the "Devil's Castle."

Schreber's first year at Sonnenstein had both a religious and a torturous flavor. Even before his transfer he had begun to develop his
own metaphysics, with peculiar ideas about God and reincarnation.
These theories now grew more elaborate. At the same time, his suffering grew to unbearable heights. His voices made his waking life
hell. They contradicted his every move; they compelled him to curse
himself aloud; they claimed to be recording his life for posterity;
they mocked him; they led him to bellow and bang his fists against
the wall in a futile attempt to drown them out. Worst of all, they convinced Schreber that he was the last surviving man in the world, so
that he was compelled to suffer in silence.

Schreber's doctors at Sonnenstein did little to help him, but toward the end of 1895, his illness began to manufacture its own so-

lution. Earlier, Schreber had considered himself the victim of a cosmic plot. Now he came to believe that he was the universe's redeemer. His fate, he declared, was to grow female sexual organs, become impregnated by God, and restore the world to its lost state of bliss by giving birth to a new race of men. The fantasy brought him comfort, and he spent hours in women's clothing, preening in front of a mirror. He also began to apply what psychiatrists call "reality testing" to his voices' messages. In 1896, Schreber came to realize that he was not alone on the planet, and with this realization he experienced a renewed interest in life. He started to take copious notes on his illness and to seek a greater say in his future. In late 1894, as the result of a financial dispute with his wife, Schreber had been declared legally incompetent. In 1899, he filed a legal petition with the county court to have this status overturned and to gain the right to go home.

His plea failed. The director of Sonnenstein, the psychiatrist Guido Weber, argued that although Schreber had regained his formidable intellectual skills, his beliefs were still delusional and he was still psychotic. The defeat set off a three-year legal battle between doctor and patient. In 1900, Schreber appealed the court's ruling, and to win his psychiatrist's support and better acquaint him with his experiences, he produced a lengthy manuscript that he had stitched together from his notes and that he hoped one day to publish. This gambit failed as well. To Weber, Schreber's book was further proof that he was irredeemably insane, and the intermediate court upheld the incarceration.

Undaunted, Schreber appealed a second time, now to the very court that he had briefly served on more than seven years before. Again, Weber challenged, but this time tepidly, and the court ruled in Schreber's favor. Five months later, in December 1902, Schreber left the asylum. The following year his book was published to acclaim in the medical press. In German, the title was *Denkwürdigkeiten eines Nervenkranken*—The Great Thoughts of a Nervous Patient. But it is better known as *Memoirs of My Nervous Illness.*[1]

THE ABOVE is a description not of the life of Daniel Paul Schreber but of "The Schreber Case," which refers to his experiences and behavior from the years 1893 to 1903. The phrase comes from Sigmund Freud, who in 1911 published a celebrated paper on Schreber titled "Psychoanalytic Remarks on an Autobiographically Described Case of Paranoia (Dementia Paranoides)." Freud had not treated Schreber, nor had he met him. His paper is based solely on Schreber's book. But the acuity of Freud's interpretation has helped raise Schreber into the ranks of psychiatric celebrity, and his book into the ranks of the classics. *Memoirs of My Nervous Illness* has been called the most written-about document in psychiatry's history.

Freud first heard of Schreber from his protégé Carl Jung, whose doctoral dissertation had been published by the same house as the *Memoirs* and who had written a book in which he had discussed the case. Schreber fascinated the two men. They were amused by the neologisms Schreber's voices were constantly inventing, such as "fleetingly-improvised men," and they were staggered by his grasp of complex diagnostic issues. "The wonderful Schreber . . . ought to have been made a professor of psychiatry and director of a mental hospital," Freud wrote to Jung in 1910.[2] The praise was only slightly in jest. At the time, psychoanalysis was facing dire threats, both from within and without, and Schreber's conception of the world, with its strange terminology and obsession with unseen processes, was a convenient and comforting metaphor.[3] What was more, it provided ballast for Freud's revolutionary theory of sexuality. As he writes almost gleefully in his paper: "Schreber expresses himself on countless occasions in the manner of a follower of our prejudice. He always speaks of 'nervosity' and erotic lapses in the same breath, as if the two were inseparable."[4]

The congruence between sex and mental illness is indeed glaring in the *Memoirs*. In the early phase of Schreber's illness, while he is anxiously waiting to take up his judgeship, he is struck by the idea that "it really must be rather pleasant to be a woman succumbing to intercourse."[5] He pinpoints as the onset of the acute phase a night in Flechsig's clinic in which he is wracked by half a dozen spontaneous orgasms. During the first half of his time at Flechsig's, he is tormented by the feeling that his penis has been removed and that he is going to be raped. During the second half, he takes pleasure in sensations of feminine "voluptuousness." These revelations were all welcome material for Freud, who concluded, not surprisingly, that Schreber had homosexual desires (specifically, that he wanted to be sodomized by Flechsig), which "provoked an intensive resistance on the part of Schreber's personality, and the defensive struggle, which might perhaps as easily have been pursued in other forms, elected for reasons unknown to us that of a delusion of persecution."[6]

Freud's interpretation of Schreber's case is outmoded—Schreber expressed not homosexual but transsexual desires—and is not generally well thought of today. The psychiatric critic Thomas Szasz, for example, has criticized Freud for devoting page after page to the erotic tenor of Schreber's illness but "not a word to the problem posed by his imprisonment or his right to freedom."[7] A host of other writers have shifted the focus from Schreber's sexuality to his potentially hostile feelings toward his father, a prominent physician. The elder Schreber, Moritz, published some thirty books on child-rearing, espousing a philosophy of total obedience and advocating the use of such posture-improving inventions as the *Geradehalter*, a system of bars and straps applied to force children into a rigid sitting position.[8] Still other writers have traced Schreber's madness to the social atmosphere of fin-de-siècle Germany. The novelist Elias Canetti even equated Schreber's paranoia with Hitler's, using lengthy quotes from the *Memoirs* to explain the rise of Nazism.[9]

Still, every interpreter of Schreber who has followed Freud owes a great debt to the innovative fact of his analysis. Before Freud, in the late nineteenth century, hallucinations and delusions were considered static phenomena. They were pathological, nothing more. After Freud, they became analyzable. The psychoanalyst Zvi Lothane, the author of *In Defense of Schreber,* a monumental and definitive history of the case, has pointed out that Freud did for psychosis what he had earlier done for the dream—by linking it with thought, emotion, and desire, he imbued it with meaning. Freud, Lothane writes, "restored to hallucinations the dignity of a personal redeeming epiphany."[10]

But Freud's elevation of the status of hallucinations and delusions was largely abstract. Even more than sex, the subject of the *Memoirs* is voice-hearing. Schreber dedicates dozens of pages and several chapters to minute, hairsplitting explications of what he alternately calls "nerve-language," "inner voices," and "rays." His voices, as his constant companions and his abiding torment, naturally become his greatest subject. Yet Freud largely ignored them, consigning them to Schreber's case history—the descriptive, preliminary chapter of his paper. The omission is both glaring and strange, for Freud himself had experienced voice-hearing. As he wrote in an early book on aphasia:

I remember having twice been in danger of my life, and each time the awareness of the danger occurred to me quite suddenly. On both occasions I felt "this was the end," and while otherwise my inner language proceeded with only indistinct sound images and slight lip movements, in these situations of danger I heard the words as if somebody was shouting them into my ear, and at the same time I saw them as if they were printed on a piece of paper floating in the air.[11]

The omission was also influential. Freud's paper holds canonical status in the literature on Schreber. Like the Bible, it can be disputed or dismissed, but it can never be fully ignored. Indeed, a great deal of the Schreber literature is essentially commentary on Freud, as if it were adorning and interpreting a theological text. Whatever the merits of this endeavor, it has led some authors to adopt Freud's analytical framework uncritically. Interpreters of Schreber following Freud have treated the subject of voice-hearing not as an experience and mystery in its own right, but as the mere vehicle for a man's traumas, anxieties, and passions. Its meaning is thought to lie in what may be extracted from it, such as the lasting trauma of being the subject of an authoritarian father's experiments.

There is unquestionable value in this stance. Immanuel Kant, of whom Schreber was a dedicated follower, famously commented, "The lunatic is a dreamer in the waking state." Few people look to the act of dreaming for meaning. They look to the action that takes place within the dream and to the reality to which that action might refer. With Schreber, however, we can't accept this valuation lightly, for it is not our dream that we are examining. It is Schreber's—and the lead we must follow is his.

schreber's book is, on first and even second reading, extremely difficult to follow. In theory, the *Memoirs* has a structure. It begins with an overview of Schreber's religious views, proceeds to a narrative of his experiences as an asylum inmate, and concludes with discussions of sundry topics of personal and metaphysical interest to Schreber—

"the soul's state of Blessedness," "cries of help," "soul-language." In practice, however, the book is discursive and muddled. Locked in an institution with few salutary distractions, Schreber follows his mind where it leads him, and it often leads him astray. The result is a sort of second-rate modernist literary experiment.

Nevertheless, a chronological line of facts regarding Schreber's voices can be traced through the rubble. For example, we learn that the event that marked the beginning of Schreber's illness—the crackling noises that he heard coming from the walls of his bedroom and that, he writes, he thought at first were mice—grew into speech four months later, after the disturbingly orgasmic night in Flechsig's asylum. We also learn that the voices took a parabolic course through Schreber's illness. They began with Flechsig's voice, proliferated until they became "nonsensical twaddle" in his head, and ultimately quieted down. By the time Schreber had actively begun to fight for his release from Sonnenstein, six years into his incarceration, his voices had come to sound like "sand trickling from an hour glass."

Yet the linear narrative of Schreber's voices tells us very little about what they meant to him and what they felt like, and nothing at all about how he lived with them on a day-to-day basis. To understand these things we have to look at Schreber's voices not chronologically but descriptively. What nouns does he use to explain them? What verbs? What adjectives? Unfortunately, these questions have complex answers. Freud has observed of Schreber's theology that it is "so peculiar, so full of contradictory determinants, that it is only with a dose of good faith that we can hold on to the expectation of finding 'method' in this 'madness.' "[12] The statement applies to Schreber's phenomenology as well. Besieged by twaddle, his descriptions grow confused.

The problem doesn't at first appear to be great. Like Jesus Christ, to whom he compares himself, Schreber states explicitly that he does not intend his words to be taken literally: "To make myself at least somewhat comprehensible I shall have to speak much in images and similes, which may at times perhaps be only *approximately* correct; for the only way a human being can make supernatural matters . . . understandable to a certain degree is by comparing them with known facts of human experience."[13] Throughout the *Memoirs*, Schreber appears to treat voice-hearing as one of these "supernatural matters" and the physical sense of hearing as a "known fact of human experience" by reference to which voice-hearing can be understood. He makes this point quite clearly in the book's fifth chapter, in which he seeks to strip common physical sound from his experiences:

> In my opinion [voice-hearing] is best understood when one thinks of the processes by which a person tries to imprint certain words in his memory in a definite order, as for instance a child learning a poem by heart which he is going to recite at school, or a priest a sermon he is going to deliver in Church. The words are *repeated silently* (as in a *silent prayer* to which the congregation is called from the pulpit), that is to say a human being causes his nerves to vibrate in the way which corresponds to the use of the words concerned, but the real organs of speech (lips, tongue, teeth, etc.) are either not set in motion at all or only coincidentally.[14]

The passage is a model of mystical description. As Teresa of Ávila described her divine "locutions" more than three hundred years before, they were like speech without sound: "The words are perfectly formed, but are not heard with the physical ear." And yet, Schreber's description also contains a word that sets him apart from the body-averse mystics. That word is *nerves*, and it is the dominant concept in the *Memoirs*. To Schreber, everything unseen is conceived of in terms of nerves. The soul is contained within the nerves of the body. Each "nerve of intellect" contains within it the total "mental individuality" of a human being. God is made of nerves in infinite supply. God communicates with man by way of "nerve-contact." Voice-hearing is consistently described with the term *nerve-language*.

Schreber's adoption of the language of neurology makes obvious sense. In their groping after clarity, describers of the ineffable always latch on to the vocabulary of the times, and late-nineteenth-century Germany was the heyday of neurology—the time and place in which the idea that the mind was based in the brain found its most convincing proponents. As an intellectual and a patient, Schreber was well attuned to this atmosphere: He had read the psychiatrist Emil Kraepelin's textbooks, on which the current *Diagnostic and Statistical Manual* is based, and his first doctor, Flechsig, was an internationally renowned neuropsychiatrist. But Schreber used the language of these men in a way and to an extent that has come to seem like parody, and that was certainly, if unintentionally, subversive. By marshaling medical terminology for a metaphysical purpose, Schreber issued a gentle reprimand, a reminder that although the concepts might change, the truth does not.

Schreber's neuro-mystical rhetoric also provided him with a perfect match for the feel of his voice-hearing, which was both forceful and insubstantial. For regular people, Schreber writes, the mind is set in motion by one's own will. But for him it is set into motion by the will of others or by the will of God. Schreber describes invisible rays like cosmic telephone wires entering his head and producing speech. This compulsive, verbal thinking is the harrowing essence of his experience:

We are used to thinking all impressions we receive from the outer world are mediated through the five senses. . . . However, in the case of a human being who like myself has entered into contact with rays and whose head is in consequence so to speak illuminated by rays, this is not at all [true]. I receive light and sound sensations which are projected direct on to my *inner* nervous system by the rays; for their reception the external organs of seeing and hearing are not necessary. I see such events even with eyes closed and where sound is concerned would hear them as in the case of the "voices," even if it were possible to seal my ears hermetically against all other sounds.[15]

Again, Schreber, who is diligent throughout the *Memoirs* about putting the word *voices* in quotation marks, echoes Teresa: "For when, in ordinary life, we do not wish to hear, we can close our ears or attend to something else; and in that way although we may hear we do not understand. But when God speaks to the soul like this, there is no alternative; I have to listen whether I like it or not, and to devote my whole attention to understanding what God wishes me to understand."[16] What has been lost, dramatically lost, is the sweetness of the experience, the *dulcedo Dei* of religious rapture.

The mystical connection fails to apply in another way—or, rather, it doesn't always apply. There are moments in the *Memoirs* in which the quotation marks dissolve and Schreber's voices emerge as literal fact. This is suggested obliquely at times by reference to space and volume. Schreber hears Ariman, one half of his idea of God, resound "in a mighty bass as if directly in front of my bedroom windows."[17] He hears the sun talking in a "low whisper." At other times the physicality of Schreber's voices is explicit. "In contra-distinction to . . . inner voices," he writes, "I hear outer voices particularly spoken by birds, which come to me from outside, from the birds' throats."[18] To further complicate matters, Schreber also has experiences halfway between sense and thought. The sound of bees buzzing and trains rattling mix with the voices in his head and "seem" to speak aloud.

What are we to make of this mess? It is a stew in which language, thought, and perception are hopelessly mixed—which, no doubt, is why so many writers have focused on the cause of the disorder. To attend to the disorder itself could make one as mad as Schreber. Better to dig down to the solid bottom of the pot. The problem with this approach is that it avoids the difficult work of understanding the reality of Schreber's daily life. Schreber's madness may well say something about the rise of German totalitarianism, but the primary subject of the *Memoirs* is the unseen assault on a man's consciousness. Day to day, Schreber lived in the middle of a complex flux of experiences the only common feature of which was that they nullified his will. Any interpretation that does not attend to the sensation of this nullification does not attend to Schreber's actual experiences.

A second problem with interpretations of Schreber that attempt to get at the root of his madness is that they inevitably treat his experiences as what Schreber dismissively calls "the morbid offspring of my fantasy." Since Freud, they consider his voices to be laden with meaning, but they posit that meaning as having risen from the subconscious depths of his mind, without his awareness. This may indeed be true so far as metaphors for madness go, but for Schreber it could not be further from the truth. For the better part of a decade, he waged strenuous battle against his voices. They were the bane of his waking life. At the end of that time, however, the battle Schreber chose to wage was for the right to consider his voices as having extrinsic value, as the carriers of an insight regarding the true nature of God. His survival, he felt, depended on that right. *"I have never had a single moment in which I did not hear voices,"* Schreber wrote.[19] They had taken everything from him: his career, his home life, his freedom, his dignity. But somehow he had learned to convert them into his own brand of sanity. He would not be robbed of that hard victory.

. . .

In 1994, in the *New York Review of Books*, the author Rosemary Dinnage wrote, "If Freud had not been intrigued by the *Memoirs*, Schreber's story might have been forgotten as others were, no doubt, from
the madhouses of the eighteenth and nineteenth centuries."[20] This is
the conventional, well-founded wisdom about Schreber: A madman
wrote a book, and a genius rescued it from obscurity. Dinnage concluded by saying, however, that the reason people after Freud went
on reading and writing about the *Memoirs*, and will go on doing so,
is not the rather disappointing psychoanalytic theory that launched
Schreber's fame but the remarkable, almost impossible dichotomy of
the author's mind. Schreber's allure lies in his uncanny ability to jux-
tapose statements of florid insanity with statements of crystalline
logic. Schizophrenia, the diagnosis that clinicians typically apply to
Schreber, is a misnomer: Splitting is not a feature of the schizophrenic mind. But there do appear to be two men living side by side
in Schreber—a credulous madman ("Therefore 'scorpions' were re-
peatedly put into my head, tiny crab- or spider-like structures which
were to carry out some work of destruction in my head"[21]), and a
scrupulous attorney ("If one compares the conclusions reached above
with the regulations of the Directive of 1893, one must not expect
to find in the various regulations an express confirmation of these
conclusions which have been drawn from general principles"[22]).

Toward the end of his stay at Sonnenstein, Schreber was able to
draw more and more on the second of these characters. His ability
to reason returned to him, and he reawakened to some of the intellectual pursuits that had occupied him prior to his hospitalization.
From the years 1894 to late 1896, his hospital chart reveals a man in
almost constant torment: "Does not do a thing, does not read a
thing." "Claims his body is completely changed, the lung has all but

disappeared, everything he sees around [him] is only a semblance." "From time to time stands totally still in one spot and stares at the sun and grimaces in the most bizarre way." "Thunders on the piano and bellows . . . at times really obscene words." Then, gradually, life returns: "More talkative and approachable, reads more." "Reads a lot, plays a great deal and well both piano and chess." "Amiable upon approach, even though quite reserved and aloof, well oriented about current events, reads a lot and discusses legal issues."[23]

Schreber's interest in reading was both therapeutic and practical. Reading, especially poetry, helped distract him from his voices. But it also armed him for the fight for freedom he was gearing up for and in which he must have sensed he was the underdog. He had had ample time to assess his own mind and values. He wanted now to know the mind and values of his adversary. Toward that end, Schreber obtained and read two editions of Emil Kraepelin's landmark textbook on psychiatry, published in 1896 and 1899.

He could not have chosen a more authoritative source. More than anyone else, Kraepelin can lay claim to the title Father of Modern Psychiatry, and his textbook to the status of founding document. Released in nine successive editions from 1883 to 1926, the textbook was Kraepelin's vehicle for a series of ideas that revolutionized psychiatry. His most remarkable idea—that the identification and prognosis of mental illness can be based on a patient's symptoms—is now the basis of clinical practice and so no longer seems quite so fresh. But in the 1890s it held the psychiatric world rapt, and Kraepelin was hailed as a prophet for the profession.[24]

Schreber turned to Kraepelin with a specific question: How did psychiatry define voice-hearing? The answer he got, of course, was that it defined voice-hearing as a hallucination—the perception of an external event that does not in reality exist. Schreber vehemently opposed this position. He did not deny that voices might require a "morbidly excited nervous system" to form or that many of the patients whom he read about in Kraepelin had mistakenly ascribed reality to the products of their imagination. But he rejected the generalized application of psychiatric terminology, which, he observed, would negate all claims of supernatural influence. Schreber, labeled as a religious paranoiac, issued an urgent plea on behalf of faith. "If psychiatry is not flatly to deny everything supernatural and thus tumble with both feet into the camp of naked materialism," he wrote, "it will have to recognize the possibility that occasionally the phenomena under discussion may be connected with real happenings, which simply cannot be brushed aside with the catchword 'hallucinations.' " As evidence, he cited not only himself but the Roman emperor Constantine, whose vision of a cross in the fourth century led to the global spread of Christianity; the Crusaders at the eleventh-century siege of Antioch, who saw visions of Christ; and Joan of Arc.[25]

Schreber's rejoinder echoes the logic of other religious-minded dissenters to the rise of medical psychiatry, such as the Catholic physician Brierre de Boismont, who was particularly concerned about the implications of the concept of hallucination for Western faith. Schreber's arguments even presage those made by his exact contemporary William James. In *The Varieties of Religious Experience*, a series of lectures he delivered just as Schreber was preparing his appeal to the Dresden supreme court, James sought to shift the basis of interpretation of voices and visions from pathology to personal value. He even argued, along with Schreber, that mental instability might be a necessary precondition for revelation—if it in fact existed. "If there were such a thing as inspiration from a higher realm," James said, "it might well be that the neurotic temperament would furnish the chief condition of the requisite receptivity."[26]

The difference between Schreber and men like Brierre and James is, of course, that Schreber's protest was delivered not from within the psychiatric profession or academia, but from within a locked psychiatric asylum. And the audience to which it was directed was not an august society of clinicians or a sympathetic crowd of philosophy students, but a handful of legal and medical authorities to whom he had little access but who nevertheless had the ability to keep him locked up until he was dead. It was that dire: Schreber was nearly sixty years old and in poor health. What is worse, he was on the weak side of an intractable conflict. His fate was to be decided by a standoff between two unyielding worldviews—the one rational, the other religious. "The only difference of opinion," he wrote in his writ of appeal, "is whether the subjective sensation of hearing voices is caused *only* by pathological functioning of my own nerves, or whether some external cause acts on them, in other words whether the sound of voices is, so to speak, a trick on the part of my own nerves, or whether some being outside my body speaks into me in the form of voices." He laid out the problem for the judges as starkly as he could: *"In essence it is one assertion versus another."*[27]

There was a very specific "another." In the first year of the new century, as Schreber's condition improved and he was increasingly able to control his fits, he was permitted to eat his meals at the table of Sonnenstein's director, Guido Weber. Weber had found Schreber intellectually sharp, "well-behaved and amiable," and he had observed Schreber's ability to make short trips into town and to the home of his wife without creating disturbances. But he refused to put any stake in these improvements. Asked to make a recommendation to the court after Schreber's first attempt at freedom failed, Weber painted a bleak and uncharitable portrait of a patient whose legal wrangling he clearly found enervating. In Weber's estimation, Schreber was hopeless. After years of stormy hallucinations and delusions, "a sediment" of ideas had become "deposited and fixed" in his mind. This passage out of the acute and into the chronic stage of illness had allowed Schreber to lift himself up to a level at which he could reason and function again. But it had forced him to lift himself onto pathological ground. Schreber, Weber wrote to the court, "did not . . . realize and recognize the actual products of his altered perceptions and the combinations built up on them as pathological, nor could he rise above the subjectiveness of his views and reach a more objective judgment of events." It was a paradox. Without sanity in his past, Schreber could not have sanity in his future. Even more perversely, Weber lamented the fact that Schreber was not still in the throes of psychotic torment: "[A]s long as the acute signs of illness lasted one could hope for a favorable outcome of the illness, whereas now when one sees the fixed result of such a process, this hope must be abandoned."[28]

Of all the notable facts about Schreber's case, the most remarkable is that he wasn't driven to despair by the resistance of his captor. By Schreber's own admission, at this time he was still too preoccupied with residual voices to be able to sustain intellectual activity for very long. But the long legal document that he delivered to the Dresden court in July 1901 shows signs of neither temper nor strain. It lays out with quiet, patient precision his right, one might say his human right, to sustain, follow, and endorse whatever system of belief he finds fit. Schreber realized quite clearly that his bind was inquisitorial. Like Joan, he was being told that he must deny himself in order to gain redemption. He rejected the validity of these terms. He rejected them legally, of course, with a logic that exhibits his superior training and mind. But he also rejected them morally. He had paid dearly, he told the court, in order to gain "great and unshakable" knowledge of the nature of God and the universe. He had transformed pain into faith. It no longer mattered what substance he had transformed or if traces of it were still apparent in his "pathological shell." What mattered was his "true spiritual life," and that he considered it true.

Weber's response to Schreber's appeal rehashes many of his old arguments about the pathology of Schreber's beliefs. But by this time the doctor had grown weary of his thankless task, however much he remained obsessed with the paradox: "However objective the medical expert attempts to be in his statements, he will never be able to make the mentally ill patient share his opinion in the objectivity of [his] findings, unless the patient himself were able to judge his condition correctly, whereby he would in fact show that he was *not* ill."[29] In any event, Weber's opinion no longer held much weight. In the panel of judges on the Dresden appeals court, Schreber had found his first and arguably his best readers. Their decision, passed down in July 1902, can be read as much as a confirmation of the rights of saints as a confirmation of Schreber's right to self-determination:

> Dr. Weber stands with his feet firmly planted in rationalism, which denies out of hand the possibility of supernatural happenings. . . . In opposition to him the plaintiff champions fundamentally the contrary point of view: the *certainty of his knowledge of God* and the absolute conviction that he is dealing with God and divine miracles *tower for him above all human science. . . .* Whatever one may think of his belief in miracles, no one is entitled to see in it a mental defect which makes plaintiff require State care. One does not usually and without further reason declare the adherents of spiritualism mentally ill and put them under a guardian, although their way of looking at things supernaturally is also neither shared nor comprehended by the vast majority of their fellow men.[30]

The decision can also be read a third way: as a confirmation of the rights of individuals to endure or accept unusual experiences openly without being deemed of lesser quality than those who do not. It can be read as a proclamation against stigma. Regarding Schreber's *Memoirs*, the judges were of the firm opinion that it was the "product of a morbid imagination." Schreber was clearly deranged. But, they concluded, "this could not possibly lower the patient in respect of his fellow men, particularly as no one can miss the seriousness of purpose and striving after truth which fill every chapter." And so they let him go. "As Dr. Schreber remarks correctly," they noted, "the worst that could happen to him would be that one consider him mad, and this one does in any case."[31]

POSTLUDE

HEARING VOICES

He that hath ears to hear, let him hear.

—MATTHEW 11:15

In the spring of 2003, a friend in England forwarded an article to me about voice-hearing that had appeared in the London *Observer* and that I had missed when it appeared in the American press. The article told a peculiar tale of spiritual visitation:

> Many of the 7,000-member Skver sect of Hasidim in New Square, 30 miles north of Manhattan, believe God has revealed himself in fish form.
>
> According to two fish-cutters at the New Square Fish Market, the carp was about to be slaughtered and made into the Jewish special-ity gefilte fish when it began shouting apocalyptic warnings. Many believe the carp was channelling the troubled soul of a recently-deceased community elder; others say it was the voice of God.
>
> The only witnesses were Zalmen Rosen, a 57-year-old Hasid with 11 children, and his colleague, Luis Nivelo. They say that at 4 pm on 28 January they were about to club the carp on the head when it began yelling.
>
> Nivelo, a Gentile who does not understand Hebrew, was so shocked that he fell over. He ran into the front of the store scream-

ing: "It's the Devil! The Devil is here!" The shop owner rushed to investigate and heard the warnings and commands.

"It said the words 'Tzaruch shemirah' and 'Hasof bah,'" Rosen told the *New York Times*, "which essentially means that everyone needs to account for themselves because the end is near."

The carp commanded Rosen to pray and study the teachings of Judaism, he said. But when he tried to kill it, he injured himself, and it was finally butchered by Nivelo and sold.[1]

When I first read these paragraphs, I was tempted to interpret them as a capsule history of voice-hearing—an allegory for what happened when the phenomenon met modern rationality. A voice arrives with an urgent spiritual message to tell, and before it can be fully heard, it is brutally slaughtered, carved up, and sold. The story seemed to be saying: There is no longer a place for this kind of thing in the world. Even in as traditional a community as Hasidic Judaism, when the voice of God speaks, it is swiftly silenced.

Then I read on, and researched further. As the fish tale circulated— in newspapers, by word of mouth, over the Internet, and from synagogue pulpits—people began to argue about what it meant. Many were skeptical, of course. Nivelo's wife called him crazy; his daughter laughed at him. Many Jews assumed that the talking carp was a prank—the festival of Purim, traditionally a time for practical jokes, was only weeks away. But others were credulous. Rosen received phone calls from all over the world. People wanted to know: Had he received a divine message? If so, what did it mean? He spent hours talking to his rabbi, who came to believe that Rosen had witnessed something holy. So did others in his town and beyond. A local lawyer told the *New York Times*, "If people say God talks to them, we recommend a psychiatrist, but this is different. This is one of those historical times when God reveals himself for a reason. It has sent spiritual shock waves throughout the Jewish community worldwide and will be talked about throughout the ages."[2]

Perhaps. Stranger things have become lastingly famous. But the striking fact to anyone raised in a spirit of skepticism is that it was talked about now. The significance of the event—holiday prank? prophetic warning? *folie à deux?*—became a matter of open, vigorous debate.

This sort of free dialogue would have seemed odd to someone like my father, for whom silence was the inevitable consequence of voice-hearing. Like many people who have unusual experiences, he maintained a stoicism about them that was driven by fear—not only of madness, which can easily destroy a life, but of being called mad, which can as well. To him, as to many others today, privacy was the natural defense against what the world might do.

The tendency to turn inward in response to outward interpretations was exactly what many observers in the late nineteenth and early twentieth centuries, when physiological theories of the mind and its illnesses were at one of their peaks of influence, worried might begin to proliferate. A hundred years ago, the intellectual atmosphere seemed to be growing stifling and reductionist. Unusual human experiences would soon no longer be welcome. "We are surely all familiar in a general way with [the] method of discrediting states of mind for which we have an antipathy," William James wrote in *The Varieties of Religious Experience*.

We all use it to some degree in criticising persons whose states of mind we regard as overstrained. But when other people criticise our more exalted soul-flights by calling them "nothing but" expressions of our organic disposition, we feel outraged and hurt, for we know that, whatever be our organism's peculiarities, our mental states have their substantive value as revelations of the living truth, and we wish that all this medical materialism could be made to hold its tongue.[3]

For a few reasons, James's lament lost some of its force over the course of the past century. In 1952, forty-two years after he died, the first effective antipsychotic medication, chlorpromazine, better known as Thorazine, was introduced onto the market. This simple, efficient tool, which has since spawned many, more effective others, was directed explicitly at those flights that the soul might not find all that exalting. It is hard not to wonder what the illustrious voice-hearers of the past would have thought of this development. It is safe to assume that Joan of Arc and William Blake would have tossed them aside. But what about the reluctant prophet Moses? Would he have dismissed Yahweh's demands as his dopamine system playing tricks on him? Would the tormented Jeremiah ("Cursed be the day / On which I was born! . . . / Because He did not kill me in the womb") have hurried to the drugstore to fill his prescription?

It is not just practical developments that have dampened the old fears of modernity. Today, more than 80 percent of Americans believe that the Bible is the divinely inspired word of God,[4] more than a third believe that God speaks to them directly, and more than 10 percent believe that God still speaks audibly.[5] Increasingly, these beliefs take very public forms. In January 2004, the televangelist Pat Robertson announced that God had told him that George W. Bush was going to win the presidential election by a landslide.[6] That the Lord's polling data proved to be off hardly matters—the president himself had already been reported to have claimed divine communication. In June 2003, according to the Israeli newspaper *Haaretz*, Bush told the Palestinian leader Mahmoud Abbas, "God told me to strike at al Qaida and I struck them, and then he instructed me to strike at Saddam, which I did, and now I am determined to solve the problem in the Middle East."[7]

Modernity's impact on voice-hearing has been limited in depth as well as in breadth. For example, in their clinical work, psychiatrists very often face an experience that they are certain is pathological and requires medical treatment, but the patient simply doesn't agree. The technical term for this is "lack of insight into psychosis," and it is sometimes cited as evidence of an underlying cognitive malfunction.[8] But what this view fails to take into account is the reflexive work of meaning-making that occurs when an individual begins to have unusual experiences and the inevitable resistance of these often hard-won meanings to external influence. People hang on to their own interpretations. Outside of psychiatric care, this resistance is naturally even stronger. The influence that the Dutch psychiatrist Marius Romme, whose work instigated the Hearing Voices Network, has had on academic research is in no small part attributable to his discovery that voice-hearers profess a range of interpretations of and attitudes about their experiences. It came as a surprise to many that there existed people who heard voices who were not ill and who did not consider themselves to be ill.

And yet, if the "medical materialism" that James described has not proved to be quite so thoroughgoing or destructive as was once feared—if it has lost many of its battles and met with its fair share of blockages—it has not been completely ineffectual. The force of experience is resilient. A voice speaks and it creates a listener. Throughout history no amount of dismissal or contempt or fear or even concern has been able to stifle that simple act of hearing, and nothing ever will. But the fact that there exist those who, like my father, remain muffled by their own apprehensions suggests that our own hearing has grown somewhat occluded, and that we have shirked a duty. That duty is more modest than it at first seems. It is not to deliver the voice's message or to believe in the existence of ghosts or spirits or Muses or demons, or even to believe that voices are of any worth whatsoever. It is simply to acknowledge that for those who hear them, voices will always be, by virtue of their presence, "real," and when those hearers speak, to listen, no matter what they say.

·NOTES·

Note: References are given in short form here; for full references, please see the bibliography.

1. PRELUDE: THE PATHOLOGICAL ASSUMPTION

1. Michele Kurtz, "McDermott Is Called Insane."
2. Kim Mueser and Susan Gingerich, *The Complete Family Guide to Schizophrenia*, p. 22.
3. The literature pertaining to the association between auditory hallucinations and violence is not altogether clear, but on the whole it seems to support these contentions. See Ana Fresán et al., "Violent Behavior in Schizophrenic Patients"; Paul Rogers et al., "Content of Command Hallucinations Predicts Self-Harm but Not Violence in a Medium Secure Unit"; and especially Dale McNeil, Jane Eisner, and Renée Binder, "The Relationship Between Command Hallucinations and Violence."
4. Erica Goode, "Experts See Mind's Voices in New Light."
5. J. M. Harkavy-Friedman et al., "Suicide Attempts in Schizophrenia."
6. See chapter eight of Benjamin Sadock and Virginia Sadock, *Kaplan & Sadock's Comprehensive Textbook of Psychiatry*. For a more comprehensive account of the many disorders in which auditory hallucinations can occur, see Peter Slade and Richard Bentall, *Sensory Deception*.
7. Cited in Marius Romme and Sandra Escher, eds., *Accepting Voices*, pp. 165–71.
8. Phil Davison, "James Cameron."
9. Bronagh Stewart and D. M. Brennan, "Auditory Hallucinations After Right Temporal Gyri Resection."
10. See Jennifer Boyd Ritsher et al., "Hearing Voices"; Slade and Bentall, *Sensory Deception*; and Ghazi Asaad and Bruce Shapiro, "Hallucinations."
11. W. D. Rees, "The Hallucinations of Widowhood." See also Christopher Baethge, "Grief Hallucinations."

12. Henry Sidgwick et al., "Report on the Census of Hallucinations."

13. A. Y. Tien, "Distributions of Hallucinations in the Population."

14. Thomas Posey and Mary Losch, "Auditory Hallucinations of Hearing Voices in 375 Normal Subjects."

15. Aldous Huxley, "Visionary Experience."

16. German Berrios, *The History of Mental Symptoms*, p. 35.

17. E. Fuller Torrey, *Surviving Schizophrenia*, pp. 213–14. Also personal correspondence with Kim Mueser.

18. Tanya Luhrmann, *Of Two Minds*, p. 20.

2. THE HOUSE OF MIRRORS

1. Benjamin Rush, *Medical Inquiries and Observations, upon the Diseases of the Mind*, pp. 306–9. This book can be found online at http://deila.dickinson.edu/their ownwords/title/0034.htm.

2. Most of this account of speech and hearing is drawn from the first chapter of Brian Moore's *An Introduction to the Psychology of Hearing*, and from a very useful Web site, www.voice-center.com, which has unfortunately changed significantly since I used it.

3. Pawel Jastreboff and Jonathan Hazell, "A Neurophysiological Approach to Tinnitus." See also Alan Lockwood, Richard Salvi, and Robert Burkard, "Tinnitus."

4. Moore, *An Introduction to the Psychology of Hearing*, p. 17.

5. William Gass, *On Being Blue*, pp. 18–19.

6. Quoted in Ivan Leudar and Philip Thomas, *Voices of Reason, Voices of Insanity*, p. 19. Their source is P. H. de Lacy, ed., *Plutarch's Moralia*, vol. 7. London: William Heinemann, 1959.

7. Heinrich Krämer and Jakob Sprenger, *Malleus Maleficarum*, Part II, Chapter 4; translation by Montague Summers. See www.malleusmaleficarum.org.

8. Chris Frith, Richard Perry, and Erik Lumer, "The Neural Correlates of Conscious Experience."

9. Gerald Edelman, *Bright Air, Brilliant Fire*, pp. 16–19.

10. G. Lynn Stephens and George Graham, *When Self-Consciousness Breaks*, p. 21.

11. L. N. Gould, "Auditory Hallucinations and Subvocal Speech."

12. P. Green and M. Preston, "Reinforcement of Vocal Correlates of Auditory Hallucinations by Auditory Feedback."

13. E.M.R. Critchley et al., "Hallucinatory Experiences in Prelingually Profoundly Deaf Schizophrenics."

14. Tom Wolfe, "Sorry, but Your Soul Just Died."

15. Anthony Weiss and Stephan Heckers, "Neuroimaging of Hallucinations." For "everything goes on in the brain," see Richard Hunter and Ida Macalpine, *Three Hundred Years of Psychiatry*, p. 734.
16. For a summary of the brain areas involved in verbal hallucinations, see Weiss and Heckers; see also Sukhwinder Shergill et al., "Mapping Auditory Hallucinations in Schizophrenia Using Functional Magnetic Resonance Imaging."
17. Atul Gawande, *Complications*, pp. 115–20.
18. Silas Weir Mitchell, "The Case of George Dedlow."
19. Ernest Hartmann, quoted in Peter Slade and Richard Bentall, *Sensory Deception*, p. 143.

3. NOBLE AUTOMATONS

1. *The Iliad of Homer*, p. 64.
2. Julian Jaynes, *The Origin of Consciousness in the Breakdown of the Bicameral Mind*, pp. 73–75.
3. Mike Holderness, "In Two Minds About Consciousness."
4. Quoted in Todd Feinberg, *Altered Egos*, p. 94.
5. Benson Hai and Ib Odderson, "Involuntary Masturbation as a Manifestation of Stroke-Related Alien Hand Syndrome."
6. Daniel Smith, "The Surgery of Last Resort."
7. William James, *Psychology*, p. 84. Unless noted otherwise, italics in quoted material are in the original.
8. Ralph Hoffman, "Verbal Hallucinations and Language Production Processes in Schizophrenia."
9. The study is J. A. Bargh, M. Chen, and L. Burrows, "Automaticity of Social Behavior: Direct Effects of Trait Construct and Stereotype Activation on Action," *Journal of Personality and Social Psychology* 71:230–44 (1996). See Daniel Wegner, *The Illusion of Conscious Will*, p. 128, for a description.
10. Wegner, p. 14.
11. Ibid., p. 64. In the original, this sentence is in italics.
12. See Wegner, pp. 52–55, for a good description of Libet's experiment.

4. INTERLUDE: LISTENING

1. Peter Slade and Richard Bentall, *Sensory Deception*, pp. 170–202. For a more recent overview, see Sukhwinder Shergill, Robin Murray, and Philip McGuire, "Auditory Hallucinations: A Review of Psychological Treatments."

2. Philip Roth, *The Facts*, p. 128.
3. The National Empowerment Center, www.power2u.org. NEC's is not the only voice-hearing simulation program in existence. Janssen Pharmaceutica has developed a virtual-reality program for the same purpose.
4. Quoted in Christopher Frith, *The Cognitive Neurospsychology of Schizophrenia*, p. 95.
5. Ken Steele and Claire Berman, *The Day the Voices Stopped*, pp. 1–11.
6. Walter Freeman, "Happiness Doesn't Come in Bottles."

5. THE TYRANNY OF MEANING

1. D. L. Rosenhan, "On Being Sane in Insane Places."
2. R. L. Spitzer, "Pseudoscience in Science, Logic in Remission, and Psychiatric Diagnosis: Critique of Rosenhan's 'On Being Sane in Insane Places.' "
3. Robert Spitzer, Scott Lilienfeld, and Michael Miller, "Rosenhan Revisited: The Scientific Credibility of Lauren Slater's Pseudopatient Diagnosis Study."
4. Kim Mueser and Susan McGurk, "Schizophrenia."
5. National Institute of Mental Health, "When Someone Has Schizophrenia," www.nimh.nih.gov/publicat/schizsoms.cfm.
6. For the evolution of the concept of schizophrenia, see Richard Bentall, *Madness Explained*, pp. 14–35.
7. Ibid., p. 34.
8. Adityanjee, Yekeen A. Aderibigbe, D. Theodoridis, and W. Victor R. Vieweg, "Dementia Praecox to Schizophrenia: The First 100 Years."
9. E. Fuller Torrey, *Surviving Schizophrenia*, p. 62.
10. Ivan Leudar and Tony David, "Is Hearing Voices a Sign of Mental Illness?"
11. T. R. Sarbin and J. B. Juhasz, "The Historical Background of the Concept of Hallucination."
12. Roy Porter, *Madness: A Brief History*, p. 134. For this period, see also Edward Shorter, *A History of Psychiatry*, pp. 8–13.
13. Tony James, *Dream, Creativity, and Madness in Nineteenth-Century France*, pp. 69–70.
14. Richard Hunter and Ida Macalpine, *Three Hundred Years of Psychiatry*, pp. 17–19.
15. Jean-Etienne-Dominique Esquirol, *Mental Maladies*, p. 110.
16. James, p. 70.
17. Esquirol, p. 111.
18. Ibid., p. 109.
19. James, p. 86.
20. Ibid., pp. 90–91.
21. Ibid., p. 92.

22. Ibid., p. 94.

23. Ibid., p. 96.

24. For Esquirol's definition, see James, p. 70. For *DSM*'s definition, see Richard Bentall, *Madness Explained*, p. 350.

25. Marius Romme and Sandra Escher, eds., *Accepting Voices*, pp. 11–27.

26. Raymond Cochrane, "Accepting Voices."

27. Max Birchwood and Paul Chadwick, "The Omnipotence of Voices."

28. Anthony Morrison, Sarah Northard, Samantha Bowe, and Adrian Wells, "Interpretations of Voices in Patients with Hallucinations and Non-Patient Controls."

29. Bentall, p. 511.

30. Adam James, "Speaking Out."

31. Ivan Leudar and Philip Thomas, *Voices of Reason, Voices of Insanity*, p. 131.

32. Peter Bullimore, "Major Tranquillisers Versus Talking Treatments."

33. Romme's speech can be found at www.psychminded.co.uk/critical/marius.htm.

34. Douglas Turkington, David Kingdon, and Peter J. Weiden, "Cognitive Behavior Therapy for Schizophrenia."

35. Quoted in Leudar and Thomas, p. 56. Bleuler made this statement in his influential 1911 book, *Dementia Praecox or the Group of Schizophrenias.*

36. Ian Stevenson, "Do We Need a New Word to Supplement 'Hallucination'?"

6. THE SOFT-SPOKEN GOD

1. Both Richard K. and the hospital at which he is treated have requested anonymity.

2. The name Full-Movement Council, Richard told me, comes from the work of the rock band Yes, particularly their song "The Ancient Giants Under the Sun."

3. See William James, *The Varieties of Religious Experience*, p. 15.

4. This account of Muhammad's revelation is drawn from Karen Armstrong, *Muhammad*, pp. 72–90. The quotation that begins "Never once did I receive," which appears in the work of the fifteenth-century scholar Jalal ad-din as-Suyuti, can be found on p. 89.

5. M.A.J. Romme and A.D.M.A.C Escher, "Hearing Voices."

6. Nicholas Wolterstorff, *Divine Discourse;* see p. 273 for quotation.

7. Michel de Certeau, *The Practice of Everyday Life*, quoted in Leigh Eric Schmidt, *Hearing Things*, pp. 28–29.

8. Philip Jenkins, *The Next Christendom*, p. 8.

9. Tanya Luhrmann, "Metakinesis."

10. John Bunyan, *Grace Abounding to the Chief of Sinners*, pp. 11, 26, 44, 49, and 53.

11. Quoted in William James, p. 294.

12. Quoted in Evelyn Underhill, *Mysticism*, p. 274.

13. Hildegard of Bingen, *Selected Writings*, p. xx.

14. Quoted in Schmidt, p. 53.

15. *The Life of Saint Teresa of Ávila by Herself*, p. 174; for "supernatural words," see p. 13.

16. See E. R. Dodds, *The Greeks and the Irrational*, p. 179.

17. Moses Maimonides, *The Guide for the Perplexed*, p. 60.

18. T. R. Sarbin and J. B. Juhasz, "The Historical Background of the Concept of Hallucination."

19. Walter Ong, *Orality and Literacy*, quoted in Schmidt, p. 31.

20. Ong, *The Presence of the Word*, pp. 111–13.

21. Jacques Ellul, *The Humiliation of the Word*, pp. 15, 48–49.

22. See Peter Slade and Richard Bentall, *Sensory Deception*, p. 74.

23. Ibid., p. 76.

24. Ibid., p. 98, for a description of this study.

25. Ibid., pp. 206–28.

26. Daniel Dennett, *Consciousness Explained*, p. 9.

27. To mention suggestibility and trance in the same breath raises some difficult issues. For example, it was precisely for the purpose of showing that hallucinations solicited by command were *not* caused by hypnotic trance states that Theodore Barber and David Calverley performed their White Christmas test.

28. Underhill, p. 275.

29. James, p. 433.

30. Underhill, pp. 266–67.

7. ENIGMATICAL DICTATION

1. Sarah Arvio, *Visits from the Seventh*, pp. 3–4.

2. Quoted in Peter Ackroyd, *Blake*, p. 335.

3. Friedrich Nietzsche, *Ecce Homo*, p. 756.

4. From Ralph J. Mills, Jr., ed., *On the Poet and His Craft* (University of Washington Press, 1966); quoted in Lewis Hyde, *The Gift*, p. 144.

5. Theodore Roethke, *The Collected Poems of Theodore Roethke*, p. 101.

6. Quoted in C. M. Bowra, *Inspiration and Poetry*, p. 2.

7. From a letter to Xaver von Moos, written from the Château de Muzot, near Sierre in the Swiss Valais, on April 20, 1923.

8. Quoted in Rainer Maria Rilke, *Selected Poems*, p. 15.

9. A. E. Housman, *The Name and Nature of Poetry*, p. 49.

10. *Hesiod*, p. 124.

11. Ernest Shackleton, *South*, p. 197. The quotation beginning "the death of human words" is drawn from John Keats's poem *Endymion*.

12. Joe Simpson, *Storms of Silence*, pp. 244–46.

13. Quoted in Julian Jaynes, *The Origin of Consciousness in the Breakdown of the Bicameral Mind*, p. 174.

14. Ezekiel 21:26. The phenomenon has also persisted into historical times. The sixteenth-century Peruvian Incas, the eighteenth-century Surinamese Saramakas, and the twentieth-century Ugandan Ik all professed to follow the spoken commands of inanimate objects.

15. Amos 7:14–15.

16. Amos 1:2.

17. Peter Davison, *Breathing Room*, p. ix.

18. William Blake, *The Complete Poetry and Prose of William Blake*, pp. 728–29.

19. Ibid., p. 730.

20. Ibid., p. 710.

21. Ackroyd, p. 269.

22. Ibid., p. 338.

23. Blake, pp. 38–39.

24. Ackroyd, p. 185.

25. John Milton, *Selected Poems*, p. 10.

26. A. E. Housman, *The Collected Poems of A. E. Housman*, p. 127.

27. The literary history of the Muses is traced by Ernst Robert Curtius in *European Literature and the Latin Middle Ages*, pp. 228–46.

28. Blake, p. 417.

8. INTERLUDE: FLOATING

1. "Brain Scans Suggest Marijuana-Schizophrenia Link," www.medpagetoday.com/2005MeetingCoverage/2005RSNAMeeting/tb/2239.

2. Leo Hermle et al., "Mescaline-induced Psychopathological, Neuropsychological, and Neurometabolic Effects in Normal Subjects."

3. Martin Hambrecht and Heinz Häfner, "Substance Abuse and the Onset of Schizophrenia."

4. Peter Slade and Richard Bentall, *Sensory Deception*, p. 16.

5. B. M. Angrist and S. Gershon, "The Phenomenology of Experimentally Induced Amphetamine Psychosis: Preliminary Observations"; quoted in Slade and Bentall, p. 158.

6. Blue Light Floatation, www.bluelightfloatation.com.
7. Emil Kraepelin, *Dementia Praecox and Paraphrenia*, p. 7.

9. PERSONAL DEITY: SOCRATES VERSUS THE STATE

1. Plutarch, "On Socrates' Personal Deity."
2. Both of these quotations can be found in Jaroslav Pelikan, *Whose Bible Is It?*, pp. 16–17.
3. Albert Schweitzer, *The Quest of the Historical Jesus*, p. 6.
4. Thomas Brickhouse and Nicholas Smith, *The Philosophy of Socrates*, p. 196.
5. Xenophon, *Conversations of Socrates*, p. 74.
6. Brickhouse and Smith, pp. 190–91.
7. Ibid., p. 196.
8. Plato, *The Last Days of Socrates*, p. 65.
9. W.K.C. Guthrie, *Socrates*, p. 62.
10. Xenophon, p. 33.
11. Brickhouse and Smith, p. 245.
12. Mark McPherran, *The Religion of Socrates*, p. 20.
13. Plato, p. 183.
14. Quoted in Brickhouse and Smith, p. 237.
15. Plato, p. 25.
16. Ibid., pp. 56–59.
17. McPherran, pp. 142–43.
18. Plato, p. 64.
19. Ibid., p. 20.
20. Xenophon, pp. 43–44. Robin Waterfield, the editor of this volume, includes the following note to explain the use of the capitalized term "God" in the passage: "Despite their usual polytheism, the Greeks often spoke of 'God' in the singular as well, as if all the many gods were aspects of one God, or the divine, which is sometimes identified with Zeus."
21. Ibid., p. 44.
22. Robert Garland, *Introducing New Gods*, p. 18.
23. See Garland, pp. 14–22, and McPherran, pp. 131–33.
24. Plato, p. 64.
25. Quoted in Thomas Brickhouse and Nicholas Smith, "Socrates' Gods and the Daimonion," p. 85.
26. Plato, p. 64.
27. Ibid., p. 74.
28. Brickhouse and Smith, *The Philosophy of Socrates*, pp. 248–49.
29. Ibid., p. 248.

30. Plato, p. 76.
31. Thomas Brickhouse and Nicholas Smith, "Socrates' *Daimonion* and Rationality," in Pierre Destrée and Nicholas Smith, eds., *Socrates' Divine Sign*, p. 43.
32. Gregory Vlastos, *Socrates: Ironist and Moral Philosopher*, p. 283.
33. Ibid., pp. 170–71.
34. Ibid., p. 158.
35. Martha Nussbaum, "Commentary on Edmunds," p. 234.

10. *DIGNA VOX:* JOAN OF ARC VERSUS THE CHURCH

1. This passage may be found, in French, at www.cahiers-naturalistes.com/pages/Bastien.html. The translation is by Noam Kerner.
2. *The Trial of Joan of Arc*, p. 67.
3. Vita Sackville-West, *Saint Joan of Arc*, p. 55.
4. *The Trial*, p. 67.
5. Ibid., p. 74.
6. Ibid.
7. Ibid., p. 67.
8. *The Retrial of Joan of Arc*, p. 5.
9. Ibid., p. 88.
10. Marina Warner, *Joan of Arc*, p. 59.
11. *The Retrial*, p. 87.
12. Ibid., p. 105.
13. Ibid., p. 128.
14. *The First Biography of Joan of Arc*, pp. 99–100.
15. *The Trial*, p. 78.
16. Warner, p. 132.
17. Ibid., p. 134.
18. See "Saint Margaret" at www.newadvent.org/cathen.
19. Warner, pp. 135–36.
20. *The Trial*, p. 127.
21. Ibid., p. 148.
22. Ibid., p. 162.
23. Ibid., p. 164.
24. For the exchange, see *The Trial*, pp. 169–70. For *"Responsio mortifera,"* see Warner, p. 141.
25. Cited in Johan Huizinga, "Bernard Shaw's Saint."
26. George Bernard Shaw, *Saint Joan*, p. 18.
27. Ibid., Act I, Scene v.
28. Mary Gordon, *Joan of Arc*, p. 19.

11. MORBID OFFSPRING:
DANIEL PAUL SCHREBER VERSUS PSYCHIATRY

1. For this translation, see Zvi Lothane, *In Defense of Schreber*, pp. 1–2.
2. C. Barry Chabot, *Freud on Schreber*, p. 34.
3. See, for instance, Eric Santner, *My Own Private Germany*, pp. 24–25.
4. Sigmund Freud, p. 21.
5. Daniel Paul Schreber, *Memoirs of My Nervous Illness*, p. 46.
6. Freud, p. 37.
7. Quoted in Lothane, p. 355. Lothane points out that of all Schreber's interpreters, only Szasz makes this criticism.
8. See William Niederland, *The Schreber Case*, pp. 53–54, 77.
9. See Lothane, p. 353. The book in which Canetti makes this argument is *Crowds and Power*.
10. Lothane, p. 340.
11. Quoted by Rosemary Dinnage in her introduction to the *Memoirs*, p. xxi.
12. Freud, p. 13.
13. Schreber, p. 16.
14. Ibid., p. 54.
15. Ibid., pp. 120–21, n. 61.
16. *The Life of Saint Teresa of Ávila by Herself*, p. 174.
17. Schreber, p. 131.
18. Ibid., p. 200. Voices spoken by birds are strangely common among those suffering from mental illnesses. During one of her bouts with manic depression, Virginia Woolf heard the birds outside her bedroom window speaking Greek.
19. Ibid., p. 271. See also p. 302: "I can only see a real purpose in my life if I succeed in putting forward the truth of my so-called delusions, so that other people will be convinced and mankind gain truer insight into the nature of God."
20. Rosemary Dinnage, "Grand Delusion."
21. Schreber, p. 96.
22. Ibid., p. 320.
23. Lothane, pp. 473–75.
24. On Kraepelin's influence, see Edward Shorter, *A History of Psychiatry*, pp. 100–109; see also Richard Bentall, *Madness Explained*, pp. 9–18. Incidentally, in the beginning of his career Kraepelin worked briefly as an assistant to Paul Flechsig, Schreber's first doctor. The two men hated each other. Flechsig fired Kraepelin after only three months.
25. Schreber, pp. 82–84.
26. William James, *The Varieties of Religious Experience*, p. 31.
27. Schreber, p. 361.

28. Ibid., pp. 341–42.
29. Ibid., p. 389.
30. Ibid., p. 411.
31. Ibid., pp. 438–39.

12. POSTLUDE: HEARING VOICES

1. Edward Helmore, "It's the End of the World According to Carp."
2. Corey Kilgannon, "Miracle? Dream? Prank? Fish Talks, Town Buzzes."
3. William James, *The Varieties of Religious Experience*, pp. 19–20.
4. Alan Wolfe, *One Nation After All*, p. 329.
5. George Gallup, Jr., "Religion in America."
6. Associated Press, "Robertson: God Says It's Bush in a 'Blowout' in November."
7. Arnon Regular, " 'Road Map Is a Life Saver for Us,' PM Abbas Tells Hamas."
8. Martin Weiler, Mark Fleisher, and Delores McArthur-Campbell, "Insight and Symptom Change in Schizophrenia and Other Disorders."

·BIBLIOGRAPHY·

Ackroyd, Peter. *Blake*. New York: Ballantine Books, 1995.

Adityanjee, Yekeen A. Aderibigbe, D. Theodoridis, and W. Victor R. Vieweg. "Dementia Praecox to Schizophrenia: The First 100 Years." *Psychiatry and Clinical Neurosciences* 53:437–48 (1999).

Aristophanes. *Clouds*. Trans. William Arrowsmith. In *Four Plays*. New York: Meridian, 1994.

Armstrong, Karen. *Muhammad: A Biography of the Prophet*. New York: HarperCollins, 1992.

Arvio, Sarah. *Visits from the Seventh*. New York: Knopf, 2003.

Asaad, Ghazi, and Bruce Shapiro. "Hallucinations: Theoretical and Clinical Overview." *American Journal of Psychiatry* 143:1088–97 (1986).

Associated Press. "Robertson: God Says It's Bush in a 'Blowout' in November." January 2, 2004.

Attwater, Donald, with Catherine Rachel John. *The Penguin Dictionary of Saints*, 3rd ed. London: Penguin, 1995.

Augustine. *Confessions*. Trans. R. S. Pine-Coffin. London: Penguin, 1961.

Baethge, Christopher. "Grief Hallucinations: True or Pseudo? Serious or Not?" *Psychopathology* 35:296–302 (2002).

Bennett, B. M. "Vision and Audition in Biblical Prophecy." *Parapsychology Review* 9:1–12 (1978).

Bentall, Richard P. *Madness Explained: Psychosis and Human Nature*. London: Allen Lane, 2003.

Berrios, German E. "Disorders of Perception." In *The History of Mental Symptoms: Descriptive Psychopathology Since the Nineteenth Century*. Cambridge: Cambridge University Press, 1996.

Birchwood, Max, and Paul Chadwick. "The Omnipotence of Voices: A Cognitive Approach to Auditory Hallucinations." *British Journal of Psychiatry* 164:190–201 (1994).

Blake, William. *The Complete Poetry and Prose of William Blake*. Ed. David V. Erdman. New York: Anchor, 1988.

Bourguignon, E. "Hallucination and Trance: An Anthropologist's Perspective." In W. Keup, ed., *Origin and Mechanisms of Hallucinations*. New York: Plenum Press, 1970.

Bowra, C. M. *Inspiration and Poetry*. Freeport, N.Y.: Books for Libraries Press, 1970.

Boyle, Mary. *Schizophrenia: A Scientific Delusion?* 2nd ed. London: Routledge, 2002.

Brickhouse, Thomas C., and Nicholas D. Smith. *The Philosophy of Socrates*. Boulder, Colo.: Westview Press, 2000.

———. "Socrates' Gods and the *Daimonion*." In Nicholas D. Smith and Paul B. Woodruff, eds., *Reason and Religion in Socratic Philosophy*. Oxford: Oxford University Press, 2000.

Bullimore, Peter. "Major Tranquillisers Versus Talking Treatments." *Voices Magazine*, Spring 2003.

Bunyan, John. *Grace Abounding to the Chief of Sinners*. Ed. W. R. Owens. London: Penguin, 1987.

Burkert, Walter. *Greek Religion: Archaic and Classical*. Trans. John Raffan. Oxford: Basil Blackwell, 1985.

Carter, Dorothy M., et al. "Patients' Strategies for Coping with Auditory Hallucinations." *Journal of Nervous and Mental Disease* 184 (3):159–64 (1996).

Chabot, C. Barry. *Freud on Schreber: Psychoanalytic Theory and the Critical Act*. Amherst: University of Massachusetts Press, 1982.

Cochrane, Raymond. "Accepting Voices." *BMJ (British Medical Journal)* 308: 1649 (1994).

Critchley, E.M.R., et al. "Hallucinatory Experiences in Prelingually Profoundly Deaf Schizophrenics." *British Journal of Psychiatry* 138:30–32 (1981).

Curtius, Ernst Robert. *European Literature and the Latin Middle Ages*. Trans. Willard R. Trask. New York: Pantheon, 1953.

Davison, Peter. *Breathing Room*. New York: Knopf, 2000.

Davison, Phil. "James Cameron." *Guardian*, July 27, 2006.

Dennett, Daniel C. *Consciousness Explained*. Boston: Back Bay Books, 1991.

Destrée, Pierre, and Nicholas D. Smith, eds. *Socrates' Divine Sign: Religion, Practice, and Value in Socratic Philosophy*. Kelowna, British Columbia: Academic Printing and Publishing, 2005.

Dinnage, Rosemary. "Grand Delusion." Review of Zvi Lothane, *In Defense of Schreber: Soul Murder and Psychiatry*. *New York Review of Books*, March 3, 1994.

Dodds, E. R. *The Greeks and the Irrational*. Berkeley: University of California Press, 1951.

Edelman, Gerald M. *Bright Air, Brilliant Fire: On the Matter of the Mind*. New York: Basic Books, 1992.

Ellul, Jacques. *The Humiliation of the Word*. Trans. Joyce Main Hanks. Grand Rapids, Mich.: Eerdmans, 1985.

Esquirol, Jean-Etienne-Dominique. *Mental Maladies: A Treatise on Insanity*. Facsimile of English ed. of 1845. Trans. E. K. Hunt. New York: Hafner, 1965.

Feinberg, Todd E. *Altered Egos: How the Brain Creates the Self*. Oxford: Oxford University Press, 2001.

The First Biography of Joan of Arc. With a chronicle record of a contemporary account. Trans. Daniel Rankin and Claire Quintal, with annotations. Pittsburgh: University of Pittsburgh Press, 1964.

Foucault, Michel. *Madness and Civilization: A History of Insanity in the Age of Reason*. Trans. Richard Howard. New York: Vintage, 1965.

Freeman, Walter J. "Happiness Doesn't Come in Bottles." *Journal of Consciousness Studies* 4:67–71 (1997).

Fresán, Ana, et al. "Violent Behavior in Schizophrenic Patients: Relationship with Clinical Symptoms." *Aggressive Behavior* 31:511–20 (2005).

Freud, Sigmund. *The Schreber Case*. Trans. Andrew Webber. London: Penguin, 2002.

Frith, Christopher D. *The Cognitive Neuropsychology of Schizophrenia*. Hove, England: Psychology Press, 1992.

Frith, Chris, Richard Perry, and Erik Lumer. "The Neural Correlates of Conscious Experience: An Experimental Framework." *Trends in Cognitive Sciences* 3:105–44 (1999).

Gallup, George, Jr. "Religion in America." *The Public Perspective* 6 (6), (1995).

Garland, Robert. *Introducing New Gods: The Politics of Athenian Religion*. Ithaca, N.Y.: Cornell University Press, 1992.

Gass, William. *On Being Blue: A Philosophical Inquiry*. Boston: David R. Godine, 1976.

Gawande, Atul. *Complications: A Surgeon's Notes on an Imperfect Science*. New York: Metropolitan Books, 2002.

Goode, Erica. "Experts See Mind's Voices in New Light." *New York Times*, May 6, 2003.

Gordon, Mary. *Joan of Arc*. New York: Viking, 2000.

Gould, L. N. "Auditory Hallucinations and Subvocal Speech: Objective Study in the Case of Schizophrenia." *Journal of Nervous and Mental Disease* 109: 418–27 (1949).

Green, P., and M. Preston. "Reinforcement of Vocal Correlates of Auditory Hallucinations by Auditory Feedback." *British Journal of Psychiatry* 139:204–8 (1981).

Guthrie, W.K.C. *Socrates*. Cambridge: Cambridge University Press, 1971.

Hai, Benson, G. Ong, and Ib R. Odderson. "Involuntary Masturbation as a Manifestation of Stroke-Related Alien Hand Syndrome." *American Journal of Physical Medicine and Rehabilitation* 79 (4):395–98 (2000).

Hambrecht, Martin, and Heinz Häfner. "Substance Abuse and the Onset of Schizophrenia." *Biological Psychiatry* 40 (11):1155–63 (1996).

Harkavy-Freidman, J. M., et al. "Suicide Attempts in Schizophrenia: The Role of

Command Auditory Hallucinations for Suicide." *Journal of Clinical Psychiatry* 64 (8):871–74 (2003).

Helmore, Edward. "It's the End of the World According to Carp." *Observer*, March 16, 2003.

Hermle, Leo, et al., "Mescaline-induced Psychopathological, Neuropsychological, and Neurometabolic Effects in Normal Subjects: Experimental Psychosis as a Tool for Psychiatric Research." *Biological Psychiatry* 32 (11): 976–91 (1992).

Heschel, Abraham Joshua. *The Prophets*. New York: Perennial Classics, 1962.

Hesiod. Trans. Richmond Lattimore. Ann Arbor: University of Michigan Press, 1991.

Hildegard of Bingen. *Selected Writings*. London: Penguin, 2001.

Hoffman, Ralph E. "Verbal Hallucinations and Language Production Processes in Schizophrenia." *Behavioral and Brain Sciences* 9:503–48 (1986).

Holderness, Mike. "In Two Minds About Consciousness." *New Scientist*, July 17, 1993.

Housman, A. E. *The Collected Poems of A. E. Housman*. New York: Henry Holt, 1965.

———. *The Name and Nature of Poetry*. New York: Macmillan, 1933.

Huizinga, Johan. "Bernard Shaw's Saint." In *Men and Ideas*. New York: Harper & Row, 1970.

Hunter, Richard, and Ida Macalpine, eds. *Three Hundred Years of Psychiatry, 1535–1860: A History Presented in Selected English Texts*. London: Oxford University Press, 1963.

Huxley, Aldous. "Visionary Experience." In John White, ed., *The Highest State of Consciousness*. Garden City, N.Y.: Anchor, 1972.

Hyde, Lewis. *The Gift: Imagination and the Erotic Life of Property*. New York: Vintage, 1979.

The Iliad of Homer. Trans. Richmond Lattimore. Chicago: University of Chicago Press, 1951.

Jacobs, Louis, ed. *Jewish Mystical Testimonies*. New York: Schocken Books, 1976.

James, Adam. "Speaking Out." www.psychminded.co.uk. January 11, 2002.

James, Tony. *Dream, Creativity, and Madness in Nineteenth-Century France*. Oxford: Clarendon Press, 1995.

James, William. *Psychology: The Briefer Course*. Notre Dame, Ind.: University of Notre Dame Press, 1985.

———. *The Varieties of Religious Experience*. In *Writings: 1902–1910*. New York: Library of America, 1987.

Jastreboff, Pawel J., and Jonathan W. P. Hazell. "A Neurophysiological Approach to Tinnitus: Clinical Implications." *British Journal of Audiology* 27:7–17 (1993).

Jaynes, Julian. *The Origin of Consciousness in the Breakdown of the Bicameral Mind*. Boston: Houghton Mifflin, 1976.

Jenkins, Philip. *The Next Christendom: The Coming of Global Christianity*. New York: Oxford University Press, 2002.

Kilgannon, Corey. "Miracle? Dream? Prank? Fish Talks, Town Buzzes." *New York Times*, March 15, 2003.

Kraepelin, Emil. *Dementia Praecox and Paraphrenia*. Facsimile of 1919 ed. Trans. R. Mary Barclay. Ed. George M. Robertson. Huntington, N.Y.: R. E. Krieger, 1971.

Kurtz, Michele. "McDermott Is Called Insane." *Boston Globe*, April 11, 2002.

Lennox, Belinda R., et al. "The Functional Anatomy of Auditory Hallucinations in Schizophrenia." *Psychiatry Research* 100:13–20 (2000).

Leudar, Ivan, and Tony David. "Is Hearing Voices a Sign of Mental Illness?" *The Psychologist* 14 (5):256–59 (2001).

Leudar, Ivan, and Philip Thomas. *Voices of Reason, Voices of Insanity: Studies of Verbal Hallucinations*. London: Routledge, 2000.

The Life of Saint Teresa of Ávila by Herself. Trans. J. M. Cohen. London: Penguin, 1957.

Lockwood, Alan H., Richard J. Salvi, and Robert F. Burkard. "Tinnitus." *New England Journal of Medicine* 347 (12):904–10 (2002).

Lothane, Zvi. *In Defense of Schreber: Soul Murder and Psychiatry*. Hillsdale, N.J.: Analytic Press, 1992.

Luhrmann, Tanya M. *Of Two Minds: An Anthropologist Looks at American Psychiatry*. New York: Vintage, 2000.

———. "Metakinesis: How God Becomes Intimate in Contemporary U.S. Christianity." *American Anthropologist* 106 (3):518–28 (2004).

McNeil, Dale E., Jane P. Eisner, and Renée L. Binder. "The Relationship Between Command Hallucinations and Violence." *Psychiatric Services* 51 (10): 1288–92 (2000).

McPherran, Mark L. *The Religion of Socrates*. University Park, Pa.: Pennsylvania State University Press, 1996.

Maimonides, Moses. *The Guide for the Perplexed*. Trans. M. Friedländer. New York: Dover, 1956.

Medwick, Cathleen. *Teresa of Avila: The Progress of a Soul*. New York: Knopf, 1999.

Milton, John. *Selected Poems*. Toronto: Dover, 1993.

Mitchell, Silas Weir. "The Case of George Dedlow." *Atlantic Monthly*, July 1866.

Moore, Brian C. J. *An Introduction to the Psychology of Hearing*. London: Academic Press, 1997.

Morrison, Anthony P., Sarah Northard, Samantha E. Bowe, and Adrian Wells. "Interpretations of Voices in Patients with Hallucinations and Non-Patient Controls: A Comparison and Predictors of Distress in Patients." *Behaviour Research and Therapy* 42 (11):1315–23 (2004).

Mueser, Kim T., and Susan R. McGurk. "Schizophrenia." *Lancet* 363: 2063–72 (2004).

Mueser, Kim, T., and Susan Gingerich. *The Complete Family Guide to Schizophrenia*. New York: Guilford Press, 2006.

The New Jerusalem Bible. New York: Doubleday, 1985.

Niederland, William G. *The Schreber Case: Psychoanalytic Profile of a Paranoid Personality.* New York: Quadrangle, 1974.

Nietzsche, Friedrich. *Ecce Homo.* Trans. Walter Kaufmann. In *Basic Writings of Nietzsche.* New York: Modern Library, 2000.

Nussbaum, Martha C. "Commentary on Edmunds." *Proceedings of the Boston Area Colloquium in Ancient Philosophy* 2:231–40 (1986).

Ong, Walter J. *The Presence of the Word: Some Prolegomena for Cultural and Religious History.* New York: Simon & Schuster, 1967.

Parker, Robert. "The Trial of Socrates: And a Religious Crisis?" In *Athenian Religion: A History.* Oxford: Clarendon Press, 1996.

Pelikan, Jaroslav. *Whose Bible Is It?: A History of the Scriptures Through the Ages.* New York: Penguin, 2005.

Plato. *The Last Days of Socrates.* Trans. Hugh Tredennick. London: Penguin, 1954.

———. *Republic.* Trans. Robin Waterfield. Oxford: Oxford University Press, 1993.

Plutarch. "On Socrates' Personal Deity." In *Essays.* Trans. Robin Waterfield. London: Penguin, 1992.

Porter, Roy. *Madness: A Brief History.* Oxford: Oxford University Press, 2002.

———. *A Social History of Madness: The World Through the Eyes of the Insane.* New York: Weidenfeld & Nicolson, 1987.

Posey, Thomas B., and Mary R. Losch. "Auditory Hallucinations of Hearing Voices in 375 Normal Subjects." *Imagination, Cognition and Personality* 2:99–113 (1983).

Preuss, Julius. "Mental Disorders in the Bible and Talmud." Trans. Fred Rosner. *Israel Annals of Psychiatry and Related Disciplines* 13:221–38 (1975).

Rees, W. D. "The Hallucinations of Widowhood." *British Medical Journal* 210:37–41 (1971).

Regular, Arnon. " 'Road Map Is a Life Saver for Us,' PM Abbas Tells Hamas." *Haaretz,* June 25, 2003.

The Retrial of Joan of Arc: The Evidence at the Trial for Her Rehabilitation. Ed. Régine Pernoud. Trans. J. M. Cohen. London: Metheun, 1955.

Rilke, Rainer Maria. *Selected Poems.* Trans. J. B. Leishman. London: Penguin, 1964.

Ritsher, Jennifer Boyd, et al. "Hearing Voices: Explanations and Implications." *Psychiatric Rehabilitation Journal* 27 (3):219–27 (2004).

Roethke, Theodore. *The Collected Poems of Theodore Roethke.* New York: Anchor Books, 1975.

Rogers, Paul, et al. "Content of Command Hallucinations Predicts Self-Harm but Not Violence in a Medium Secure Unit." *Journal of Forensic Psychiatry* 13 (2):251–62 (2002).

Romme, M.A.J., et al. "Coping with Hearing Voices: An Emancipatory Approach." *British Journal of Psychiatry* 161:99–103 (1992).

Romme, M.A.J., and A.D.M.A.C. Escher. "Hearing Voices." *Schizophrenia Bulletin* 15 (2):209–16 (1989).

Romme, Marius, and Sandra Escher, eds. *Accepting Voices*. London: Mind Publications, 1993.

Rosenhan, D. L. "On Being Sane in Insane Places." *Science* 179:250–58 (1973).

Roth, Philip. *The Facts: A Novelist's Autobiography*. New York: Vintage, 1988.

Rush, Benjamin. *Medical Inquiries and Observations, upon the Diseases of the Mind*. Philadelphia: Kimber & Richardson, 1812.

Sackville-West, Vita. *Saint Joan of Arc*. New York: Grove Press, 2001.

Sadock, Benjamin J., and Virginia A. Sadock. *Kaplan & Sadock's Comprehensive Textbook of Psychiatry*, 8th ed. Philadelphia: Lippincott Williams & Wilkins, 2005.

Santner, Eric L. *My Own Private Germany: Daniel Paul Schreber's Secret History of Modernity*. Princeton: Princeton University Press, 1996.

Sarbin, T. R., and J. B. Juhasz. "The Historical Background of the Concept of Hallucination." *Journal of the History of the Behavioural Sciences* 5:339–58 (1967).

Schmidt, Leigh Eric. *Hearing Things: Religion, Illusion, and the American Enlightenment*. Cambridge, Mass.: Harvard University Press, 2000.

Schreber, Daniel Paul. *Memoirs of My Nervous Illness*. Trans./eds. Ida Macalpine and Richard A. Hunter. New York: New York Review Books, 2000.

Schweitzer, Albert. *The Quest of the Historical Jesus: A Critical Study of Its Progress from Reimarus to Wrede*. Baltimore: Johns Hopkins University Press, 1998.

Shackleton, Ernest. *South*. New York: Carroll & Graf, 1998.

Shaw, George Bernard. *Saint Joan*. New York: Penguin, 2001.

Shergill, Sukhwinder S., Robin M. Murray, and Philip K. McGuire. "Auditory Hallucinations: A Review of Psychological Treatments." *Schizophrenia Research* 32:137–50 (1998).

Shergill, Sukhwinder S., et al. "Mapping Auditory Hallucinations in Schizophrenia Using Functional Magnetic Resonance Imaging." *Archives of General Psychiatry* 57:1033–38 (2000).

Shorter, Edward. *A History of Psychiatry: From the Era of the Asylum to the Age of Prozac*. New York: Wiley, 1997.

Sidgwick, Henry, et al. "Report on the Census of Hallucinations." *Proceedings of the Society for Psychical Research* 26:259–394 (1897).

Siegel, Ronald K. *Fire in the Brain: Clinical Tales of Hallucination*. New York: Dutton, 1992.

Simpson, Joe. *Storms of Silence*. Seattle: Mountaineers, 1996.

Slade, Peter D., and Richard P. Bentall. *Sensory Deception: A Scientific Analysis of Hallucination*. Baltimore: Johns Hopkins University Press, 1988.

Smith, Daniel. "The Surgery of Last Resort." *Granta* 85 (2004).

Smith, Nathan, M.D., Ph.D. *The Smith Family Chronicles*. Self-published.

Spitzer, R. L. "Pseudoscience in Science, Logic in Remission, and Psychiatric Diagnosis: Critique of Rosenhan's 'On Being Sane in Insane Places.'" *Journal of Abnormal Psychology* 84 (5):442–52 (1975).

Spitzer, Robert L., Scott O. Lilienfeld, and Michael B. Miller. "Rosenhan Revisited: The Scientific Credibility of Lauren Slater's Pseudopatient Diagnosis Study." *Journal of Nervous and Mental Disease* 193 (11):734–39 (2005).

Steele, Ken, and Claire Berman. *The Day the Voices Stopped: A Memoir of Madness and Hope.* New York: Basic Books, 2001.

Stephens, G. Lynn, and George Graham. *When Self-Consciousness Breaks: Alien Voices and Inserted Thoughts.* Cambridge, Mass.: MIT Press, 2000.

Stevenson, Ian. "Do We Need a New Word to Supplement 'Hallucination'?" *American Journal of Psychiatry* 140:1609–11 (1983).

Stewart, Bronagh, and D. M. Brennan. "Auditory Hallucinations After Right Temporal Gyri Resection." *Journal of Neuropsychiatry and Clinical Neurosciences* 17 (2):243–45 (2005).

Stone, I. F. *The Trial of Socrates.* New York: Anchor Books, 1988.

Strauss, J. S. "Hallucinations and Delusions as Points on a Continua Function." *Archives of General Psychiatry* 21:581–86 (1969).

Suedfeld, Peter, and Roderick A. Borrie. "Health and Therapeutic Applications of Chamber and Floatation Restricted Environmental Stimulation Therapies (REST)." *Psychology and Health* 14:545–66 (1999).

Suedfeld, Peter, and Stanley Cohen. "Perceptual Isolation, Sensory Deprivation, and REST: Moving Introductory Psychology Texts Out of the 1950s." *Canadian Psychology* 30 (1):17–29 (1989).

Tien, A. Y. "Distributions of Hallucinations in the Population." *Social Psychiatry and Psychiatric Epidemiology* 26:287–92 (1991).

Torrey, E. Fuller. *Surviving Schizophrenia: A Manual for Families, Consumers, and Providers,* 4th ed. New York: Quill, 2001.

The Trial of Joan of Arc. Being the verbatim report of the proceedings from the Orléans Manuscript. Trans. W. S. Scott. London: Folio Society, 1956.

Turkington, Douglas, David Kingdon, and Peter J. Weiden. "Cognitive Behavior Therapy for Schizophrenia." *American Journal of Psychiatry* 163:365–73 (2006).

Underhill, Evelyn. *Mysticism.* New York: Dutton, 1961.

Vlastos, Gregory. *Socrates: Ironist and Moral Philosopher.* Ithaca, N.Y.: Cornell University Press, 1991.

Walsh, Elizabeth, Alec Buchanan, and Thomas Fahy. "Violence and Schizophrenia: Examining the Evidence." *British Journal of Psychiatry* 180:490–95 (2002).

Warner, Marina. *Joan of Arc: The Image of Female Heroism.* Berkeley: University of California Press, 1981.

Wegner, Daniel M. *The Illusion of Conscious Will.* Cambridge, Mass.: MIT Press, 2002.

Weiler, Martin A., Mark H. Fleisher, and Delores McArthur-Campbell. "Insight and Symptom Change in Schizophrenia and Other Disorders." *Schizophrenia Research* 45:29–36 (2000).

Weiss, Anthony P., and Stephan Heckers. "Neuroimaging of Hallucinations: A Review of the Literature." *Psychiatry Research Neuroimaging* 92:61–74 (1999).

Weissman, Judith. *Of Two Minds: Poets Who Hear Voices.* Hanover, N.H.: Wesleyan University Press, 1993.

Wolfe, Alan. *One Nation After All.* New York: Viking, 1998.

Wolfe, Tom. "Sorry, but Your Soul Just Died." *Forbes ASAP,* December 2, 1996.

Wolterstorff, Nicholas. *Divine Discourse: Philosophical Reflections on the Claim That God Speaks.* Cambridge: Cambridge University Press, 1995.

Xenophon. *Conversations of Socrates.* Trans. Hugh Tredennick and Robin Waterfield. London: Penguin, 1990.

· ACKNOWLEDGMENTS ·

This book began its life as an attempt to understand the voices that my father suffered from. Over the course of several years, as I immersed myself in the subject, it grew into something different and, I hope, greater. Whatever good has resulted from that growth—whatever is original or useful in this book—could not have been achieved without the support of numerous people who lent their time, knowledge,and encouragement. Those who deserve particular thanks include Richard Bentall, Julie Downs, Raymond Faber, Christopher Frith, Ralph Hoffman, Louise Johns, Zvi Lothane, Kim Mueser, Philip Thomas, and Marina Warner. Jacqui Dillon, Richard K., and Sarah Arvio were kind and brave to share their personal stories with me and to allow me to share them with others; Leigh Eric Schmidt's historical work and guidance were invaluable resources; Mark McPherran generously devoted countless hours to leading me through the finer points of Athenian culture; Kate Bolick fielded many phone calls and offered keen editorial help; and David Smith provided unwavering moral support.

The preliminary work for this book was conducted at the MacDowell Colony, and I am forever grateful to the men and women there for sheltering me, feeding me, and keeping me in firewood. There is no more idyllic place, and there are no kinder people, than at MacDowell.

This book could not have been written without the help of six wonderful people. From the start, Melanie Jackson was an enthusiastic and astute advocate, and Ann Godoff was a patient, generous, and brilliant editor. I consider myself very fortunate to have them as guides. Abigail Judge, of the clinical psychology program at the University of North Carolina, was a dependable friend and insightful reader throughout the process of writing; she always made herself available to educate me on clinical matters, no matter how much I demanded. Scott H. Smith, formerly of New York, heard more complaints and read more drafts than anyone ever should. Any mistakes that appear in this book are his fault. Marilyn Smith, my mother and most reliable source, needed little persuasion to allow me to reveal the family secret that begins this book. For that, and much more, I owe her many thanks.

Finally, Joanna Cohen lived alongside this book for many months. I remain happily, passionately, and, come to think of it, financially in her debt. I hope to hear her voice as long as I live.